Lecture Notes in Computer Science 2058

Edited by G. Goos, J. Hartmanis and J. van Leeuwen

T0230315

Springer
Berlin
Heidelberg
New York
Barcelona
Hong Kong
London
Milan
Paris
Singapore
Tokyo

Stephen Brewster   Roderick Murray-Smith (Eds.)

Haptic Human-Computer Interaction

First International Workshop
Glasgow, UK, August 31 – September 1, 2000
Proceedings

 Springer

Series Editors

Gerhard Goos, Karlsruhe University, Germany
Juris Hartmanis, Cornell University, NY, USA
Jan van Leeuwen, Utrecht University, The Netherlands

Volume Editors

Stephen Brewster
Roderick Murray-Smith
Glasgow University, Department of Computing Science
17 Lilybank Gardens, Glasgow G12 8RZ, Scotland, UK
E-mail: {stephen,rod}@dcs.gla.ac.uk

Cataloging-in-Publication Data applied for

Die Deutsche Bibliothek - CIP-Einheitsaufnahme

Haptic human computer interaction : first international workshop, Glasgow,
UK, August 31 - September 1, 2000 ; proceedings / Stephen Brewster ;
Roderick Murray-Smith (ed.). - Berlin ; Heidelberg ; New York ; Barcelona ;
Hong Kong ; London ; Milan ; Paris ; Singapore ; Tokyo : Springer, 2001
    (Lecture notes in computer science ; Vol. 2058)
    ISBN 3-540-42356-7

CR Subject Classification (1998): H.5.2, H.5.3, H.5, I.4, I.2, I.6, K.4.2, K.8.0

ISSN 0302-9743
ISBN 3-540-42356-7 Springer-Verlag Berlin Heidelberg New York

Springer-Verlag Berlin Heidelberg New York
a member of BertelsmannSpringer Science+Business Media GmbH

http://www.springer.de

© Springer-Verlag Berlin Heidelberg 2001
Printed in Germany

Typesetting: Camera-ready by author, data conversion by Christian Grosche, Hamburg
Printed on acid-free paper   SPIN: 10781577   06/3142   5 4 3 2 1 0

Preface

Haptic Devices

Haptic devices allow users to feel their interfaces and interactions. This has the potential to radically change the way we use computers. Haptic interaction is interaction related to the sense of touch. This could be based on force-feedback or tactile devices. We can take advantage of our powerful sense of touch as an alternative mechanism to send and receive information in computer interfaces. Haptic technology is now maturing and coming out of research laboratories and into real products and applications. We can therefore begin to focus on its application and general principles for its use rather than just the hardware and technology itself. Important questions are: what are haptics good for? What kind of information can be successfully presented via touch? Do haptics actually improve efficiency, effectiveness, and satisfaction? Arbitrary combinations of information presented to different senses have been shown to be ineffective so how should sight, hearing, and touch be combined in truly multimodal interfaces? We do not want to end up with haptic interfaces that are in fact harder to use than standard ones. Haptics may become just a gimmick for computer games, rather than the key improvement in interaction technology we believe it should be. We felt that it was therefore time to concentrate on *haptic human computer interaction.*

There are other conferences that discuss haptic hardware, but so far there has been little discussion of how haptics can be effectively used to improve the usability of human-computer interactions. There is currently no unified place to present research on general haptic human-computer interaction and so one aim of the workshop was to provide an information resource for those interested in the topic. Because this was the first workshop in the area and we wanted to ensure that we covered a wide range of the ongoing research, we planned to accept work on any aspect of haptic HCI. As it happened we had a very healthy turnout of 35 submissions and after a reviewing process, where each submission was reviewed by two reviewers, this resulted in 17 papers and 5 posters. The workshop took place at the University of Glasgow, UK from the 31st August to 1st September, 2000. We had over 75 attendees from Europe, the USA, and Japan.

Workshop Content

The workshop began with a keynote presentation from Bob Stone of MUSE Virtual Presence giving an overview of the history of haptics. This proved to be an excellent start assuring that all of the attendees (who were from a wide variety of diffent backgrounds such as psychologists, computer scientists, textile designers, sculptors, toy manufacturers, mechanical engineers, and games designers) got a good foundation and knew how we reached the current state of development in haptics research. The rest of the workshop focused on five main themes:

1. Haptic interfaces for blind people,
2. Collaborative haptics,
3. Psychological issues and measurement,
4. Applications of haptics
5. Haptics in virtual environments.

Haptic Interfaces for Blind People

The first paper on this theme is by Challis and Edwards. They propose a series of principles for designing tactile displays that they developed from the results of experiments on Braille music notation. Three of their key principles are: consistent mappings should be kept between the visual and haptic representations; the tactile representation should focus on static data; and height should be used as a filtering mechanism. Penn *et al.* describe a series of investigations into the perception of text, object size, and angularity by blind and sighted users. One interesting aspect of their paper is the comparison of results of similar experiments on different haptic devices (a PHANToM and an Impulse Engine 3000). As the area of haptics is still in its infancy there is little work comparing different devices and the effects that this might have. Van Scoy *et al.* and Yu *et al.* both address the problem of presenting line graphs to visually impaired users. Van Scoy *et al.* focus on the presentation of haptic models of mathematical functions, Yu *et al.* report an experiment on the comparison of two different line modeling techniques to see which was the most effective at making graphs usable. Continuing the topic of education, Wise *et al.* present the results of an investigation into the benefits of haptic feedback in allowing blind students access to college and high-school physics curricula.

Collaborative Haptics

There are three papers in the collaborative haptics section. The first is by Oakley *et al.* who are looking at how haptic effects can be used to help users of collaborative editors synchronize their work and gain awareness of others. Users of collaborative editors work in a restricted environment and there are many problems with awareness. Other researchers have looked at audio or graphical solutions to the problems but no one has really yet considered the possibilities of haptics. Sallnäs looks at a similar problem – collaborative manipulation of objects in a three-dimensional desktop virtual environment. Her results show that when the two users have haptic feedback, collaborative manipulation of objects becomes more successful. The final paper in this section is by Hikiji and Hashimoto. Their paper discusses the design of a system that allows the collaboration of a human with a robot that could provide haptic feedback. The robot could grasp a user's hand and lead (or be led) through a path, avoiding obstacles.

Psychological Issues and Measurement

In the psychological issues and measurement section Jansson and Ivås present two studies: one on practice effects using the PHANToM and the other on exploration modes. Results of the practice effects experiment show very significant improvements in exploration times and accuracy over time. This is important for the design of future experiments. An appropriate amount of training is needed if results are to be robust and reliable. Results of the exploration modes suggest that certain grasps can be more beneficial than others when using the PHANToM. Pollick *et al.* investigate two-fingered grasp of objects to understand the contact forces users apply. Their results can be used for facilitating grasps of objects in virtual environments. There are two papers on texture, and in particular, roughness perception. The first from Wall and Harwin, combines haptics and graphics to investigate the interactions between the two. The second, from McGee *et al.* is about the combination of haptics and audio. The aim here is to investigate congruent and incongruent multimodal cues that might create different illusions of roughness.

Keuning-Van Oirschot and Houtsma discuss the design of a cursor trajectory analysis system for use in future haptic desktop computer interfaces. Other research has shown that individual targets with haptic effects added can improve performance. However, if you have to move over one of these targets on the way to something else (as would happen in a real interface with multiple potential targets) then the haptic effects could obstruct and disrupt your interaction. This paper presents setps towards a trajectory analysis system that could predict the target at which the user is aiming and so only haptify that and none of the others passed on the way to it.

Bougilia *et al.* use a new $3m^3$ workspace haptic device called the scaleable-SPIDAR (described in a later chapter) in an investigation of whether haptics can improve depth perception in VEs. Users can have problems with depth perception in such environments, even when using stereoscopic visual displays, as cues in other senses are often missing. Bouguila *et al.* report an experiment where haptics recombined with a stereoscopic display to allow the manipulation of virtual objects. Kirkpatrick and Douglas provide benchmarks for evaluating the usability of haptic environments for shape perception tasks, with conclusions for future haptic environments.

Applications of Haptic Technology

Crossan *et al.* are investigating the use of haptic technology to aid the teaching of difficult palpation techniques to veterinary students. Medical simulators have used haptics for some time but this has mostly been in the area of minimally invasive surgery training. This paper looks at how haptics can teach skills where the veterinarian's (or doctor's) hands are on the patient, which brings up a new set of haptic challenges. Finally we present two studies on the use of haptics in aircraft cockpits. Van Veen and van Erp show that pilots are heavily visually loaded and under high G-loads visual perception can become severely degraded. Is tactile perception affected in the same way? If it is degraded then it will not be a useful alternative to visual feedback. Van Veen and van Erp present an experiment that shows that tactile perception on the torso is resistant to high G-loads. Van Erp presents an experiment to investigate the use of haptics for navigation in virtual environments. He describes an array of tactile stimulators that might run across the torso and provide directional information.

Haptics in Virtual Environments

Bouguila *et al.* present a new 3m³ workspace haptic device called the scaleable-SPIDAR. The paper describes the design of the SPIDAR and an experiment to test its effectiveness. Stevens and Jerrams-Smith describe the use of haptics in projection-augmented displays. In their display haptics are coincident with information projected on an actual physical model. They propose the concept of 'object presence' – do users feel that an object actually exists in the display? Their hypothesis is that a combined haptic and visual display should increase object presence. One area in which haptics are beginning to take off is in computer games. In the *Lumetila* project Leikas *et al.* have developed a game that uses the player's whole body and body movements for control.

Dillon *et al.* are focusing their work on the use of haptics to present the 'feel' of virtual fabrics for the textiles industry. It is important for clients to be able to sample potential materials over the Internet and haptics can help with this. Dillon *et al.* investigate how factors integral to the fabric selection process, such as weight, thickness, shearness, drape, and stretch, could be presented using a haptic device.

Conclusions

One reason that we decided to run the workshop was that haptic research at Glasgow was new and we wanted to make some contacts with others interested in the same area so that we could discuss ideas. We had no idea how many people would be interested in coming along. In the end we had over 75 attendees from many different countries and with a wide range of backgrounds. We had not anticipated anything like this degree of interest. It seems like haptics is a growing area of importance within the HCI community, but as yet it has had little impact on the mainstream HCI conferences.

One issue that came out of the workshop was that much of the research presented focused around the PHANToM device from SensAble Technologies (the other main commercial device represented was the Wingman force-feedback mouse from Logitech). The PHANToM is very effective for many kinds of interactions, but is not so good for others. Its cost also prohibits its wide use for research and its take-up by ordinary users in ordinary day-to-day situations. The field should try to broaden the use of technology, as we do not want to become restricted in our research to doing only the kinds of things that the PHANToM device supports. Wall and Harwin's work is a step in this direction as they are developing extra end-effectors for the PHANToM to allow it to give more cutaneous feedback. We believe that one thing the field would benefit greatly from is a wider range of devices that can give haptic feedback at a lower cost. This provides a useful link from this workshop to others devoted more to the development of haptic hardware. We need to make sure that our requirements for devices are fed back to the hardware developers so that the next generation of haptic technology will be able to do the things that users need at prices they will be able to afford.

The workshop showed that lots of interesting work is going on using haptics in human-computer interaction. However, the area is still in its infancy in terms both of the hardware and software available and in what we use haptics for. Some key areas for further research that came out of the workshop are: we need more analysis of human haptic abilities and limitations in an HCI context; we must identify the fundamental issues in haptic HCI design; we need an understanding of what kinds of information can be successfully presented in touch and to understand the links between our sense of touch and the other senses as interfaces will inevitably use other media in addition to touch. Answers to the questions in these areas will help provide suggestions for future usable interfaces, yet to be implemented. It is also important to synthesize the results of the studies done into some design guidance that we can provide to interface designers (most of whom currently probably know almost nothing about haptics) so that they know what to do with this new medium in order to use it effectively to improve human-computer interaction. From the work presented in these proceedings we can see that haptics has a lot to offer HCI, the challenge is to make it happen.

Acknowledgements

We would like to thank all of our reviewers, who worked under a tight time restriction and got their reviews in when we needed them. Thanks also go to Andrew Crossan, Marilyn McGee, Ian Oakley, and Ray Yu from Glasgow for helping with the organization of the workshop. The workshop was part funded by the EPSRC grant GR/M44866 and supported by the BCS HCI group and the Glasgow Interactive Systems Group.

For more information, please refer to http://www.dcs.gla.ac.uk/haptics

March 2001

Stephen Brewster
Roderick Murray-Smith

Reviewers

Gunar Jansson, Dept of Psychology, Uppsala University
Alan Wing, Dept of Psychology, University of Birmingham
Frank Pollick, Dept of Psychology, University of Glasgow
Timothy Miller, Dept of Computer Science, Brown University
Christine MacKenzie, School of Kinesiology, Simon Fraser University
Helen Petrie, Dept of Psychology, University of Hertfordshire
Shumin Zhai, IBM Almaden Research Center
Chris Hasser, Immersion Corporation
Bob Stone, Ben Bishop, Virtual Presence Ltd
Stephen Furner, BT Advanced Communication Research
William Harwin, Dept of Cybernetics, Reading University
Roberta Klatzky, Carnegie Mellon University
Gregory Leplatre, Daniela Busse, Dept of Computing Science, University of Glasgow

Table of Contents

Psychological Issues and Measurement

Applications of Haptics

Haptic Feedback: A Brief History from Telepresence to Virtual Reality

Robert J. Stone

MUSE Virtual Presence
Chester House, 79 Dane Road, Sale, M33 7BP, UK
Tel.: (+44) (0)161-969-1155
robert.stone@musevp.com

Abstract. This paper presents a short review of the history surrounding the development of haptic feedback systems, from early manipulators and telerobots, used in the nuclear and subsea industries, to today's impressive desktop devices, used to support real-time interaction with 3D visual simulations, or *Virtual Reality*. Four examples of recent VR projects are described, illustrating the use of haptic feedback in ceramics, aerospace, surgical and defence applications. These examples serve to illustrate the premise that haptic feedback systems have evolved much faster than their visual display counterparts and are, today, delivering impressive peripheral devices that are truly usable by non-specialist users of computing technology.

1 Introduction

Some of the early developments relating to physical methods of generating haptic feedback for human-system design purposes have been well covered in historical publications by (for example) Corliss and Johnson [1], Mosher [2], Stone [3], Thring [4] and, more recently, in an excellent book by Burdea [5]. However, it is only quite recently that haptic technologies have appeared that are capable of delivering believable sensory stimuli at a reasonable cost, using human interface devices of a practical size.

This has opened up a wealth of opportunities for academic research and commercial developments, from haptic feedback systems to aid blind persons' exploration of virtual environments, through applications in aerospace and surgery, to a revitalisation of the ceramics industry. This brief paper cannot catalogue all relevant developments, but attempts to provide a potted review the history of haptic feedback from the early days of teleoperation or telerobotics to present-day developments in Virtual Reality (VR) and simulation.

Turning first to the robotics arena, most researchers now accept the definitions put forward by Sheridan when considering the systems aspects of controlling remote robotic vehicles and manipulators (eg. Sheridan [6], [7]). Until the mid-1990s, terms such as teleoperation, telepresence, robotics, telerobotics and supervisory control had been used interchangeably.

S. Brewster, R. Murray-Smith (Eds.): Haptic HCI, LNCS 2058, pp. 1-16, 2001.

Two of relevance to the emergence of haptic feedback developments are *teleoperation* – the extension of a person's sensing and manipulation capability to a remote location and *telepresence* – the **ideal** of sensing sufficient information about the teleoperator and task environment, and communicating this to the human operator in a sufficiently natural way, that the operator feels physically present at the remote site. The "Holy Grail" of telepresence also provided the motivation behind some of the early human-system interface efforts underpinning NASA's Virtual Environment Workstation, *VIEW* (eg. Fisher *et al.* [8], which included investigations of basic glove-mounted vibrotactile feedback transducers; see Fig. 1), and the commercial VR aspirations of the late VPL Inc with its flagship product, the *DataGlove*.

Fig. 1. Early US newspaper extract featuring the *DataGlove* concept and hinting at future robotic applications and haptic feedback variants.

The remote handling communities serving nuclear, subsea, space and military markets had hoped that telepresence would become the natural successor to the many remote handling systems in evidence in the 1950s. Unfortunately, even today, creating the illusion that a human operator is still present in a remote hazardous worksite or is fully immersed within a computer-generated world remains the "Holy Grail".

2   Nuclear Industry and Early Bilateral Manipulators

Bilateral Master-Slave Manipulators (MSMs) – functionally no different from today's desktop haptic feedback systems – have been prevalent in the international nuclear industry for over half a decade, permitting safe, remote handling of irradiated material under direct human control and supported by direct (lead-window) and indirect (closed-circuit TV) vision.   A master control arm is typically a mechanical reproduction of a remote slave arm (the slave gripper being replaced at the master by a scissor, pistol, or similar control grip device), the two components being linked by means of chains, cables or some other electromechanical motion system. "Mini-masters", such as that proposed in the 1980s for the original NASA Flight Telerobotic Servicer and other remotely controlled space, subsea and land vehicles are, as the name suggests, small master controllers. These may or may not be kinematically similar to the remote slave device and have met with mixed levels of success when applied to laboratory or field demonstrators.

Fig. 2. One of the Project *GROPE* workstation configurations, showing a large screen display and molecular docking application, under human control via a nuclear industry bilateral master manipulator arm.

By far the most publicised use of master control arms for Virtual Reality applications has been for molecular modelling (the well-known *GROPE IIIb* Project) and haptic interaction with electrostatic molecule-substrate force simulations and nano-level surfaces (generated from Scanning Tunnelling Microscope data) at the University of North Carolina at Chapel Hill (eg. Brooks [9]; Brooks *et al.* [10]; see Fig. 2).

Early work at UNC utilised an Argonne Remote Manipulator (ARM) system, one of two donated from the Argonne National Laboratory, and a field sequential computer screen (based on liquid crystal shutter glasses). Later, the screen was replaced with a projection display, with users of the ARM interacting with 3D images produced using polarised projection display lenses and spectacles.

Compared with mechanical MSMs, *servomanipulators* have the advantages of being mobile (cable linkages) and possessing large load-carrying capacities. The early servomanipulators were designed to incorporate ac-driven servos, connected back-to-back, to provide force reflection.

These were later replaced with dc servos, integrated within the manipulator arm, leading to a more compact form of remote handling device. One of the most popular servomanipulators - the MA-23M – was designed in a modular fashion to aid repair and maintenance, as well as provide an upgrading path for introducing automation (Vertut [11]; see Fig. 3). Selectable force feedback (also known as "force boost") ratios - 1/2, 1/4, 1/8 - were included as standard, the bilateral positioning system being provided by means of potentiometers which determined the relative positions of master and slave arms.

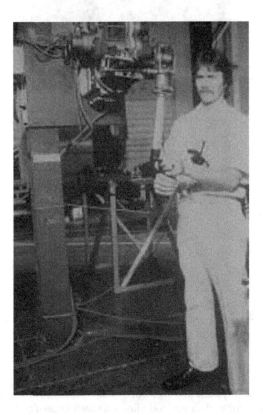

Fig. 3. MA-23M master control arm, under investigation during a human factors research programme conducted by the author and the Atomic Energy Authority (Harwell, UK) in 1986.

3   Exoskeletons

Exoskeletons originated partly as "Man Amplifiers", capable, through direct human slaving, of lifting and moving heavy loads. The early "Handyman" controller, described in Mosher [2] and Corliss and Johnson [1], was an example of a forearm-and-hand exoskeleton possessing two 10-degree-of-freedom (dof) electrohydraulic arms; the General Electric "Hardiman" was a whole-body exoskeletal frame (Thring [4]).

Until quite recently, the exoskeleton concept had been unpopular, due to limitations in the functional anatomy of the human arm. Also, force-reflecting actuators had to be mounted on the outside of the exoskeletal framework to accommodate the users' arm. Furthermore, there were concerns with such devices' small operating volume, possible safety hazards (associated with toppling and locking) and electro-mechanical inefficiency (see also Wilson [12]; Salisbury [13]). Nevertheless, thanks in part to the emergence of a range of lightweight, low-cost body systems developed under the VR banner, the exoskeleton received renewed interest in the early 1990s as a means of registering body movement in a virtual environment and, importantly, as a technique for feeding haptic data back to the immersed user (eg. Bergamasco [14]; see Fig. 4).

Fig. 4. Professor Massimo Bergamasco of the Scuola Superiore di Studi Universitari in Pisa, Italy, demonstrating the results of his early exoskeletal system, funded by the European Commission as part of an ESPRIT II project known as GLAD-IN-ART (Glove-like Advanced Devices in Artificial Reality).

However, even to this day, exoskeletons have been confined to academic research labs or industrial design organisations (eg. Zechner and Zechner in Austria; see Fig. 5) and noticeably absent from commercial catalogues. Witness the fate of the pioneering

US company Exos, sold to Microsoft in 1996, having developed such exoskeletal haptic demonstrators as *SAFiRE* (Sensing And Force Reflecting Exoskeleton) and the *HEHD* (Hand Exoskeleton Haptic Display).

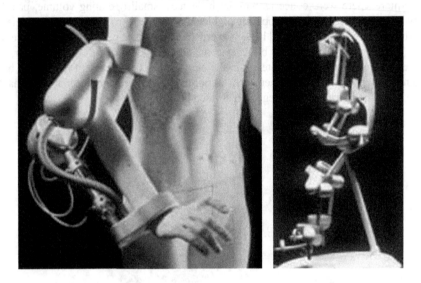

Fig. 5. Forearm and whole-body exoskeleton concepts from Sabine Zechner of Zechner and Zechner (Austria, *circa* 1993).

4   Other Haptic Feedback Attempts

As hinted earlier, there have been many attempts to recreate tactile and force sensations at the finger, hand, arm and whole body level – far more than can be covered here. However, a wealth of data on historical and contemporary devices has been compiled under the excellent Haptics Community Web Page (http://haptic.mech.northwestern.edu/database/).

The commercial haptics arena is also changing on a regular basis (witness Immersion Corporation's recent acquisition of Haptech Technologies and Virtual Technologies – home of the CyberGlove, CyberTouch and CyberGrasp). The next 5 years promise some quite exciting developments in this field, with systems becoming more widespread as costs come down and software and applications support is improved. Just a small selection of those devices with which the author's team has been involved will be covered here, before looking at a number of emerging applications fields.

Teletact was conceived in November of 1989, during one of the generic research programmes within the UK's National Advanced Robotics Research Centre in Salford. The concept of using pneumatics to provide feedback to the fingers of an operator controlling a robot originated in the 1960s, courtesy of research efforts at Northrop Grumman (Jones and Thousand [15]).

Co-developed with Airmuscle Ltd of Cranfield, the first prototype glove, employing 20 small air pockets was produced in September of 1990, and appeared on the BBC's *Tomorrow's World* TV Programme later that year, with a selection of vegetables and an Angoran rabbit as the tactile subjects!

This prototype glove was of an analogue design, supplying up to 13lb psi of air pressure per pocket (proportional control, later with inflation *and* deflation). The author recalls a period of intense legal activity in the early 1990s when, having visited Airmuscle, the developers of what was then W Industries' (later Virtuality) *Space Glove* produced a prototype tactile feedback version using remarkably similar pneumatics technology to that integrated within *Teletact*!

A more sophisticated glove - *Teletact II* (see Fig. 6) - was specified in May of 1991. This device featured a greater density of air pockets, 30 in all, with two pressure ranges. The majority of the pockets (29) were limited to 15lb psi. However, a new palmar force feedback pad was developed, receiving a maximum pressure of 30lb psi. A vacuum system was also devised to increase the step response of the glove whilst deflating.

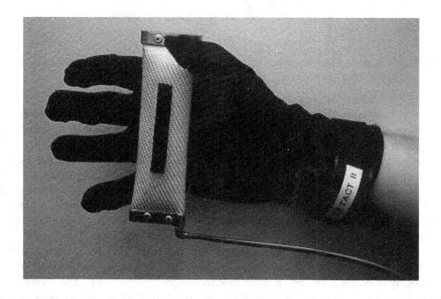

Fig. 6. The *Teletact II* pneumatic tactile feedback glove developed by the UK's National Advanced Robotics Research Centre and Airmuscle Limited, showing an early palmar feedback concept.

In contrast to the glove, the *Teletact Commander* was a simple multifunction hand controller equipped with embedded Polhemus or Ascension tracking sensors (see Fig. 7). Three *Teletact*-like air pockets were attached to the outer surface of the hand controller to provide simple tactile cues when the user's virtual hand or cursor made contact with a virtual object. These pockets were controlled either by compressor or by a single solenoid-actuated piston.

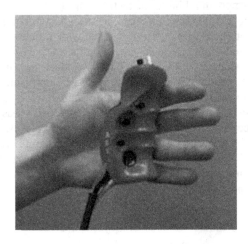

Fig. 7. The *Teletact Commander* hand controller, showing the simple layout of some of the air pockets and VR interactive control buttons.

Other haptic developments at the ARRC included a prototype minimally invasive surgery haptic feedback system, funded by the Department of Health and Wolfson Foundation (Fig. 8). This device actually pre-dated the Immersion Corporation *Impulse Engine* and used basic strain gauge, potentiometer and servomotor devices to provide position sensing and feedback to a laparoscopic instrument in 3 translational degrees of freedom, with grip/forceps actuation.

A simple wire frame cube provided the test environment, hosted on a 486 PC and allowing users to explore the inside of the cube using haptic feedback, whilst and invoking and varying such parameters such as in-cube viscosity, wall elasticity, dynamic "beating" effects and back wall "tissue" grasp and pull.

A piezo tactile feedback demonstrator system was also developed by the ARRC, in collaboration with the Electronic and Electrical Engineering Department of the University of Salford, for the Defence Research Agency (Chertsey). The project was undertaken to demonstrate the potential for future interactive technologies in the design of military vehicle workstations.

Called the *TactGlove* (Fig. 9), it consisted of a 3-digit sensory glove assembly (thumb, index and middle finger) equipped with a Polhemus Fastrak tracker and PZT piezo "sounders" to provide variable frequency tactile input. A simple VR control panel - was developed using Superscape Limited's original Virtual Reality Toolkit (VRT). Users could view the virtual control panel using either a standard monitor, or via a Virtual I-O *i-Glasses* headset (stereo or biocular modes) and could control the 3D position of a schematic "hand" (a simple 3-cylinder cursor).

On making contact between the "hand" and one of three virtual controls (a rotary knob, push-button and toggle switch), the appropriate "collision" signal was transmitted to the glove sensors, either singly or in combination. Actuating the control produced a perceptible change in the frequency of stimulation or in the case of the push-button and toggle switch, a build-up of frequency, followed by a rapid drop, to simulate breakout forces.

Fig. 8. Early picture of the UK National Robotics Research Centre minimally invasive surgery haptics demonstrator, developed under a research programme sponsored by the UK Department of Health and the Wolfson Foundation.

Fig. 9. The *TactGlove* in use with a simple Virtual Reality control panel demonstration.

Recognition of Salford University's ongoing efforts in haptic technologies should be made here, under the leadership of Darwin Caldwell, Professor of Advanced Robotics. Caldwell's team has been involved in the design, construction and testing in a virtual world of an "Integrated Haptic Experience", comprising a 7-dof arm tracking and force reflection pMA exoskeleton (Fig. 10), a 15-dof hand/finger tracker and a 5-dof force reflection hand master, together with a cutaneous tactile feedback glove providing pressure, textural, shape, frictional and thermal feedback.

Fig. 10. The University of Salford's pMA exoskeleton.

5   Four Case Studies from the VR Community

5.1   Ceramics

Recent developments in the British economy have prompted certain "heritage" industries to look very closely at their businesses and the prospects for improved productivity and growth in the early part of this new century. Companies such as Wedgwood and Royal Doulton, famous international, historical names in the production of quality crockery and figurines are turning to Virtual Reality in an attempt to embrace technology within their labour-intensive industries. Ceramics companies and groups, such as the Hothouse in Stoke-On-Trent, are experimenting with new haptics techniques and achieving some quite stunning results.

The importance of experiments like these, however, lies not only with the results but moreso in the people who actually *produce* the results. Talented sculptors –

people with incredible manual skills but *no* background in computer technology whatsoever – have, given access to Sensable Technologies Inc's *PHANToM* Desktop and *Freeform* "digital clay" products, started to produce ornate sculptures *within 3-4 days*! Then, using local industrial resources, they have used 3D printing and stereolithography facilities to convert these virtual prototypes into physical examples (Fig. 11) and high-end VR to display them in virtual showrooms and domestic settings of very high visual fidelity (Fig. 12).

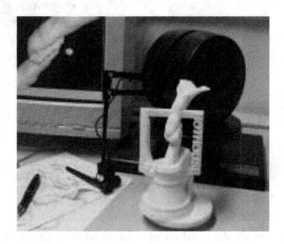

Fig. 11. An early example of the physical realisation of a Hothouse trial sculpture using a Sensable *PHANToM* and *Freeform* "digital clay".

Fig. 12. Some of the new virtually created ceramics products *in situ* within a VR domestic "show room".

5.2   Aerospace Maintenance

The use of VR to streamline design and training processes in the aerospace industry is not new (Angus and Stone [16]). However, the absence of a credible haptic feedback mechanism has forced developers to use other sensory cues to indicate collision detection between pipes, tools, limbs and so on (eg. 3D "ghosting") within a cluttered working volume (Angus and Stone, *op cit.*; see Fig. 13).

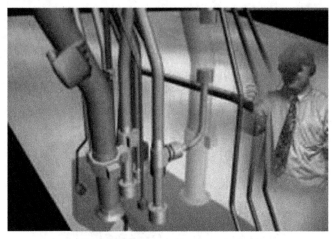

Fig. 13. Early experiments with visual cueing of haptic events, in this case showing "ghosted" pipe images used to convey collisions with adjacent aerospace engine components.

As with other engineering applications of VR, it is only recently, that the aerospace industry has revisited VR to assess its suitability for 21st Century projects and products. The European Initiative ***ENHANCE*** (ENHanced AeroNautical Concurrent Engineering) brings together the main European civilian aeronautical companies and seeks to strengthen cooperation within the European aeronautical industry by developing common working methods which govern the European aeronautical field, defining appropriate standards and supporting concurrent engineering research. One project within *ENHANCE* concerns an advanced VR maintenance demonstrator which links a virtual mannequin with PTC's DIVISION MockUp virtual prototyping software with Sensable Technologies' *PHANToM* haptic feedback system. Based on a 3D model of a conceptual future large civil airliner, the VR demonstration involves controlling the mannequin during aircraft preparation and safety procedures, and in gaining access to retracted main landing gear for the purposes of wheel clearance testing (Fig. 14).

Certain key interaction events throughout the demonstration are executed using the *PHANToM* device. In order to define these stages clearly, and to identify those procedures and events warranting the application of haptic feedback, a context-specific task analysis was carried out, as recommended in the new International Standard **ISO 13407** (*Human-Centred Design Processes for Interactive Systems*).

Fig. 14. The PTC DIVISION MockUp interface showing the *PHANToM*-controlled virtual mannequin interacting with an undercarriage safety component.

5.3   Surgery

As well as the early ARRC and Immersion Corp. "keyhole" surgery haptic feedback attempts, there have been, and still are projects with significant haptic technology components. One of these projects stems from a European Union Framework V Project called *IERAPSI*, an Integrated Environment for Rehearsal and Planning of Surgical Interventions.

An early *IERAPSI* work package relates to the human-centred definition of surgical procedures (again based on ISO 13407), specifically focusing on surgical activities underpinning mastoidectomy, cochlear implantation and acoustic neuroma resection (Fig. 15). The surgical procedures definition and task analyses (Stone [17]) were conducted in collaboration with the ENT department of Manchester's Royal Infirmary.

These exercises resulted in the selection of the *PHANToM* Desktop/1.5A for haptic and vibratory stimuli when simulating the use of pneumatic drill (through cortex and petrous bone) and a second device for irrigation and suction (possibly a *PHANToM* Desktop).

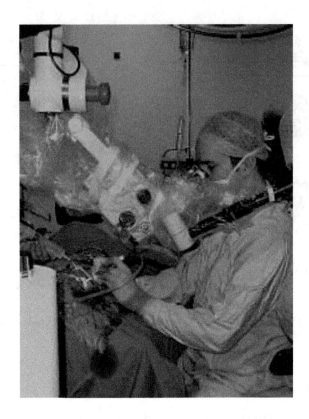

Fig. 15. Temporal bone surgery (infantile cochlear implant) in progress at Manchester's Royal Infirmary.

5.4   Land Mine Clearance Training

MUSE Virtual Presence's Paris-based subsidiary SimTeam has developed an immersive VR land mine detection training system for the French Army, using the *PHANToM* as the primary interaction device.

The system presents the trainee with a basic representation of the ground area to be investigated and, using a standard issue military probe attached to the *PHANToM*, he is required to locate potential mines by gently inserting a virtual representation of the probe into the "ground".

Once a definite contact has been made, the trainee must continue probing until a recognisable pattern of penetrations has been made (Fig. 16). In addition to the visual and haptic features of this trainer, a pattern recognition system is available which matches the trainee's penetrations with known land mine geometries. Once a pattern match has been made, a schematic of the most likely mine configuration is displayed.

Fig. 16. The *PHANToM* system in use as part of an immersive VR trainer for landmine detection and identification. The right-hand part of the figure shows how the system's pattern recognition system can be used to present the trainees with "best-fit" landmine types on the basis of ground penetration patterns.

6   Conclusions

The claims of early VR proponents that their immersive VR system was the "ultimate" in human-system interface technologies (to coin Ivan Sutherland's early phrase) were soon proven outlandish by those who bought and tried to use the products.

However, after nearly 15 years of development, we are now witnessing the evolution of the truly intuitive interface. Interestingly, it is not the visual modality *per se*. that won the race to deliver this interface, but the combined senses of vision, force and touch.

The history underlying the development of haptic technologies has, it must be said, benefited from more innovation, enthusiasm and excitement than that of the visual display industry and it is those qualities that have helped to produce the intuitive systems and stunning applications evident today. The best is yet to come!

References

1. Corliss, W.R., and Johnson, E.G.: Teleoperator Controls. AEC-NASA Technology Survey (1968) NASA, Washington DC, Ref. NASA SP-5070
2. Mosher, R.S.: Industrial Manipulators. Scientific American (1964). 211(4). 88-96
3. Stone, R.J.: Virtual Reality and Telepresence. Robotica (1992) 10. 461-467
4. Thring, M.W.: Robots and Telechirs. Ellis Horwood, Chichester (1983)
5. Burdea, G.C.: Force and Touch Feedback for Virtual Reality. John Wiley & Sons, Inc. (1996)
6. Sheridan, T.B.: Telerobotics. Plenary Presentation for 10th IFAC World Congress on Automatic Control, Munich (July, 1987)

7.   Sheridan, T.B.: Telerobotics. Automatica (1989) 25(4). 487-507
8.   Fisher, S., Wenzel, E.M., Coler, C., and McGreevy, M.: Virtual Interface Environment Workstations. Proceedings of the Human Factors Society 32nd Annual Meeting (1988)
9.   Brooks, F.P.: Grasping Reality Through Illusion - Interactive Graphics Serving Science. Proceedings of CHI '88 (1988). 1-11
10. Brooks, F.P., Ouh-Young, M., Batter, J.J., and Kilpatrick, P.J.: Project GROPE - Haptic Displays for Scientific Visualisation. Computer Graphics (1990) 24(4). 177-185
11. Vertut, J.: Advances in Remote Manipulation. Transactions of the American Nuclear Society (1976)
12. Wilson, K.B.: Servoarm - A Water Hydraulic Master-Slave. Proceedings of the 23rd Conference on Remote Systems Technology, American Nuclear Society (1975). 233-240
13. Salisbury, J.K.: Controller Arm for a Remotely Slaved Arm. United States Patent, No. 4,160,508 (1979)
14. Bergamasco, M.: The GLAD-IN-ART Project. In Proceedings of Imagina '92 (Edited by Le Centre National de la Cinematographie) Monte Carlo, France (1992). II-7 to II-14
15. Jones, L., and Thousand, J.: Servo Controlled Manipulator Device. US Patent 3,263,824; Northrop Corporation (2 August, 1966)
16. Angus, J., and Stone, R.J.: Virtual Maintenance. Aerospace (May, 1995). 17-21
17. Stone, R.J.: IERAPSI - A Human-Centred Definition of Surgical Procedures. Work Package 2, Deliverable D2 (Part 1), Revision 1.0; Framework V Contract No.: IST-1999-12175 (May, 2000)

Design Principles for Tactile Interaction

Ben P. Challis and Alistair D.N. Edwards

Department of Computer Science, University of York
York, YO10 5DD, UK
{bpc,alistair}@cs.york.ac.uk

Abstract. Although the integration of tactile feedback within the human-computer interface could have considerable benefits this channel of communication is often overlooked or, at most, employed on an ad hoc basis. One contributing factor to the reluctance of interface designers to consider using tactual feedback is the lack of established design principles for doing so. A preliminary set of principles for tactile interface design are described. These have been constructed using the findings of a study into the presentation of music notation to blind people.

1   Introduction

Although we rely on touch to perform many everyday actions, the real potential for enhancing such interaction is often neglected and, where tactile feedback is available, it is often on an *ad hoc* basis. Tactile interaction could benefit many computer based applications, whether on a stand-alone basis or in support of visual and auditory interaction. However, if this is to become a reality, then solid design principles will need to be established such that efficient design strategies can be realised. The work presented here is a first-step towards achieving this target. Using existing psychological knowledge along with results from studies into computer-based tactile interaction a number of foundation principles are outlined.

2   Background

There are many reasons why users could benefit from the inclusion of haptic interaction within a given system. Visually dominated interfaces are commonplace yet may not always be the most efficient or intuitive method for performing a given task. In the most extreme scenario the graphical user interface simply excludes visually impaired users. However, there are also instances where a user needs to control and observe a process where the process itself is already providing visual feedback (e.g. slide projector, radio-controlled equipment, stage lighting etc.). In these circumstances, the user is likely to benefit from some level of increased haptic feedback so that their visual attention can be maximised in terms of directly observing any changes being made. In certain other circumstances, using a car radio whilst

S. Brewster, R. Murray-Smith (Eds.): Haptic HCI 2000, LNCS 2058, pp. 17-24, 2001.

driving for example, a strategic shift in balance from visual toward tactile interaction could prove to be safer.

Given the amount of information that is sometimes presented within graphic displays, it could be a real asset to incorporate alternative display methods to help reduce potential confusion. Besides helping to alleviate the growing problem of overcrowded, and therefore, confusing graphic displays, haptic displays present possibilities for providing physical manipulation of controls in a more intuitive fashion. Many music applications attempt to emulate the environment that the user is likely to be familiar with by providing graphic faders, rotary knobs and push buttons. Although these look like controls that might be found on a mixing desk or synthesiser, the precision in use that is expected is often lost when trying to manipulate these graphic images using a mouse and keyboard.

The increasing availability of new force-feedback devices presents many possibilities for creating 'virtual' displays which could benefit some of the previous examples. However, similar solutions could be achieved using dedicated static displays and there is therefore a trade-off to be made according to which display approach is adopted. With virtual displays, the technology used allows the display to be instantly updated or completely altered to meet new requirements within a task. Whilst this is an obvious asset from the perspective of flexibility, this exploration method cannot provide the user with the finer levels of tactile feedback. Such feedback allows us, for example, to discriminate between many types of fine textures and tactile patterns, identify and discriminate between raised symbols and to notice even small changes in height between separate objects. This kind of feedback is available using dedicated static tactile displays although at extra cost in terms of producing each display. It is likely, therefore, that there will be design principles which will be common to both approaches along with additional principles which are specific to each display type.

3   Design Principles

The focus of this research has been on the use of static displays to enhance tactile interaction within computer-based systems. An example application for the delivery of music notation to blind people has been created [1,2]. The system, called Weasel, uses PVC tactile overlays on an Intellikeys touchpad in conjunction with speech output and audio output. Results obtained from the close observation of users working with the system have been used along with existing psychological knowledge on interaction with raised lines [1,2,9], tactile symbols [3,7,11,12] and textures [6,8,10], to create a set of fundamental design principles for tactile interaction.

Graphical music notation can present a large quantity of information which is perceived by the reader in a near parallel fashion. Often, much of this information will be redundant to a particular learning task so the reader simply ignores that data which is unwanted. Non-visual music notations (e.g. braille music and 'Talking Scores') present exactly the same information but in a serial fashion; effectively, the learner must interpret every single instruction before deciding whether it is important to the task in hand.

Besides producing large amounts of translated instructions, these alternative approaches do not assist the reader in forming an adequate mental image of the layout of the musical extract that they are working with. A page of music contains a certain number of lines of music and each of these lines will have a certain number of bars belonging to it. There may be an incomplete or 'lead-in' bar at the beginning along with indications as to where one section stops and another starts. These sections might need to be repeated and if they do there might be substitute sections (first and second time bars) for each repeat.

All of these elements are invaluable in terms of building an impression of 'shape' which the reader can easily relate to. Without this, the reader is unable to easily communicate to fellow musicians using common terms of reference such as "the third line of the first page" or perhaps "from the third bar of the top line to the second-time bars".

The aim of the Weasel Project has been to address this particular issue by presenting this aspect of music notation as a tactile overlay on a touchpad. The user can quickly gain an impression of the structural layout of a page of music and then interact directly by pressing onto the overlay to retrieve a description of the music within a particular bar. This is delivered as either musical playback or a spoken description using speech synthesis and the reader has further control over what level of detail is presented.

3.1   Initial Overlay Design

Vacuum-formed PVC overlays were used in preference to the more common method of 'swell paper'. Although the former are more complex to manufacture, they can afford considerable differences in height within the same overlay which 'swell paper' cannot. The overlays were designed using a very simple visual-to-tactile mapping such that each overlay looked like its visual counterpart (see Fig. 1).

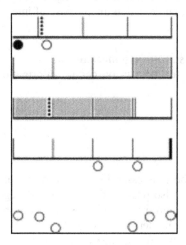

Fig. 1. An example of one of the PVC overlays used within the Weasel music notation system.

Each 'tactile page' was approximately 'legal-letter' size and was presented in portrait orientation. A 1.5mm high guideline was provided beneath each line of bars and different levels of height were used for barlines (2mm), repeat marks (4mm high dots) and the final barline (4mm). First-time and second-time bar areas were represented using textures and these were of a lower height than the guideline. Circular symbols were occasionally located just beneath the guideline to represent the presence of either a dynamic or a number of spoken descriptions. These could be pressed to retrieve the description and where more than one item was present the symbol could be double-clicked to progress to the next item in the list.

In addition, there was a control section located at the bottom of the overlay which provided access to a menuing system for changing various settings. This was designed to be controlled using the index, middle and ring finger of each hand where the left hand controlled the selected *option* and the right hand selected the *item* within that option.

Foundation Design Principles

In the initial design stage of the project, the following principles were employed:

A consistency of mapping should be maintained such that descriptions of actions remain valid in both the visual and the non-visual representations.
An example in music would be a reference to a location such as "The last bar of line two on page three". The same would apply to the relative location of on-screen controls including the directions in which they can be moved.

The tactile representation within an interface should focus on data that is static.
This was partially due to the lack of dynamic displays that can function at a tactile level. However, even if a display was dynamic there would still be a problem in notifying the user exactly where within the display a change had taken place. Reliance on visual feedback would be defeating the purpose of integrating tactile interaction in the first place.

Height should be used as a filtering mechanism.
The user should be able to home in on certain information types using height as a discriminating feature.

3.2   User Testing

The Weasel system has been assessed by a group of six users. All of the users were competent musicians who also possessed a good knowledge of the main concepts of music notation. Five of the group were sighted and were therefore blindfolded whilst using the system and the sixth member was blind.

The group was first trained to use the system using a series of five overlays which gradually introduced the various tactile components used. After this training period, each user was asked to perform a number of tasks using two completely new overlays which included all of the tactile components used previously.

The testing was in two parts. Firstly, the user was asked to explore the new overlay and systematically describe each tactile object and its meaning as they located it. After this, the user was asked to perform a number of tasks each of which involved changing various settings and then moving to specific locations within the music and retrieving a description of that particular area. Although the results of these tests were quantifiable, observation was regarded as being just as valuable from the perspective of understanding how or why certain actions might be complex or confusing to the user.

3.3   Results

The results from the testing showed that the users were capable of understanding, navigating around and interacting with the overlays. However, through general observation and comments that were made by users, there were obvious problem areas within the interface. It quickly became apparent that the simple mapping used had led to the inclusion of quite large uninformative areas. These were such that users often seemed confused as to their whereabouts within the overlay. In addition, some of the users performed a task incorrectly because they had failed to locate the topmost line of music, their actions were, however, accurate within the context of that line.

Users also exhibited problems with double-clicking which appeared to produce quite clumsy actions; this observation was reinforced from general comments on the awkward nature of performing a double-click with virtually no haptic feedback. The guideline was not as useful in establishing an exploration strategy as had been hoped. This was, again, probably partly due to the visual-to-tactile mapping that was adopted which meant that even though a guideline was available it was still necessary for the user to have to leave this to explore other areas.

These results have led to the expansion of the original three foundation design principles to now include the following additional principles:

Good design will avoid an excess of 'empty space' as this is a significant source of confusion.
The term 'empty space' is used in reference to areas on a display that do not communicate anything useful to the user. If a user can place a fingertip into a display without quickly locating a feature that gives them a meaningful cue they are effectively in 'empty space'. It might not be possible to eradicate this but it should be minimised.

A simple visual-to-tactile mapping is likely to produce many problems and is therefore unlikely to be the most efficient design strategy.
This is not in conflict with the first principle that was described. A consistency of mapping can and should be maintained but the likelihood is that the tactile display will not actually look like its visual counterpart.

Good design practice should, whenever possible, encourage a specific strategy for the exploration of a particular display.
If the display is to be used in a non-visual way then this principle becomes particularly significant. However, even when used in support to a visual display this principle remains valid. It would be undesirable for the user to have to visually monitor the tactile display to observe their progress within an action.

Double-clicking is an inappropriate form of interaction within static displays.
Without haptic feedback, double-clicking can quickly becomes inefficient leading to the user perceiving closure when it has not been achieved. Alternative methods using multiple points of contact and timed single-presses are being explored as part of the Weasel project.

A display should be sized and orientated such that users are not expected to overreach to discover the full extent of the display.
This may seem obvious but it is surprising how often users will fail to fully explore a display when they are unable to see their progress. A suitable maximum display area is approximately A4 sized in landscape orientation.

Tactile objects should be simple.
When designing objects for use within a graphic display it is possible to employ a considerable number of dimensions by which differences can be achieved. Tactile interaction can allow subtle changes within a dimension e.g. changes in height, width or texture. However, the greater the number of dimensions along which the user is expected to notice change, the more complex the object will appear to be to the user. Changes along fewer dimensions will make for a more immediately recognisable object which will in turn provide a basis for faster and more accurate interaction.

4   Future Work

A new design of the Weasel system is currently being implemented which is based around the extended set of design principles. 'Empty space' is being reduced to being no greater than the approximate size of a fingertip and this is being used to also provide a more efficient and intuitive strategy for exploration. The new overlays (see Fig. 2) are still constructed from PVC but are now presented in landscape orientation. The bar-areas and guideline are now integrated into a single strip approximately 15mm wide and 300mm long. This approach presents the user with a simple left-to-right reading strategy which will help minimise the level of exploration that is required within the overall display. The height of a normal bar-area is approximately the thickness of standard printing paper. Barlines are about the width of a fingertip and approximately 1mm high. Repeat marks are presented as 'ramps' that rise from within the bar-area up to a higher barline of 2mm.

The controls for the menuing system have not been changed as these appear to have functioned quite satisfactorily. However, the lists of *options* and *items* now 'wrap-around' rather than terminating at two extremes. Alternative methods to double-clicking are being explored within the new design. One such possibility is for the user to press and hold an 'active' area and after a short period another action (e.g. progressing through a list) will be activated automatically.

5   Conclusion

Tactile interaction is often overlooked within interface design even though it could prove to be a more appropriate approach to adopt for certain circumstances. Although tactile interaction is not unusual within many everyday actions it is still relatively novel and perhaps somewhat underused within the human-computer interface.

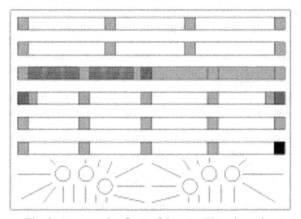

Fig. 2. An example of one of the new Weasel overlays.

Successful integration within computer-based systems is only likely to be achieved if an effective design strategy can be employed. It is hoped that the continued development of the foundation design principles, as presented here, will form an effective basis for interface designers to begin to maximise the potential for tactile interaction within their applications.

Acknowledgements

This research has been funded by the Engineering and Physical Sciences Research Council (award ref. 96309035). We would like to thank Intellitools Inc. (55 Leveroni Court, Suite #9, Novata, CA. 94949) for providing an Intellikeys touchpad to help with the practical aspects of this research.

References

1. Bentzen, Billie Louise and Peck, Alec F (1979). Factors affecting the traceability of lines for tactile graphics. The Journal of Visual Impairment and Blindness. 73(7), 264-269.
2. Berla, Edward P and Murr, Marvin J (1975). Psychophysical functions for the active tactual discrimination of line width by blind children. Perception & Psychophysics. 17(6), 607-612.
3. Berla, Edward P and Butterfield, Lawrence H (1977). Tactual distinctive features analysis: Training blind students in shape recognition and in locating shapes on maps. The Journal of Special Education. 11(3), 335-346.
4. Challis, BP and Edwards, ADN (2000). Weasel: A system for the Non-visual Presentation of Music Notation. Proceedings of ICCHP 2000, 113-120.
5. Challis, BP and Edwards, ADN. (2000). Design Principles for Non-visual Human-Computer Interaction. ACM SIGCAPH Bulletin, (Spring).
6. James, GA and Gill, JM (1975). A pilot study on the discriminability of tactile areal and line symbols for the blind. American Federation for the Blind Research Bulletin. 29,
7. Lambert, LM and Lederman, SJ (1989). An evaluation of the legibility and meaningfulness of potential map symbols. The Journal of Visual Impairment and Blindness. October, 397-403.
8. Lederman, Susan J and Kinch, Denise H (1979). Texture in tactual maps and graphics for the visually handicapped. The Journal of Visual Impairment and Blindness. 73(6), 217-227.
9. Lederman, Susan and Campbell, Jamie I (1983). Tangible line graphs: An evaluation and some systematic strategies for exploration. The Journal of Visual Impairment and Blindness. 77(4), 108-112.
10. Millar, Susanna (1985). The perception of complex patterns by touch. Perception. (14), 293-303.
11. Nolan, CY and Morris, JE (1971). Improvement of tactual symbols for blind children: Final report. American Printing House for the Blind.
12. Simpkins, Katherine E (1979). Tactual discrimination of shapes. The Journal of Visual Impairment and Blindness. 73(3), 93-101.

The Haptic Perception of Texture in Virtual Environments: An Investigation with Two Devices

Paul Penn[1], Helen Petrie[1], Chetz Colwell[1,2], Diana Kornbrot[1],
Stephen Furner[3], and Andrew Hardwick[3]

[1]Sensory Disabilities Research Unit, University of Hertfordshire
Hatfield, Hertfordshire.Al10 9AB, UK
{p.penn,h.l.petrie,d.e.kornbrot}@herts.ac.uk
[2] Now at the Knowledge Media Institute, The Open University
Milton Keynes, MK76AA, UK
[3]BTexaCT Research, Adastral Park
Martlesham Heath, Suffolk IP5 3RE, UK
{stephen.furner,andrew.hardwick}@bt.com

Abstract. The incorporation of the haptic sense (the combined effects of touch and proprioceptive information) into virtual reality (VR) has considerable potential to enhance the realism of virtual environments and make VR more accessible to blind people. This paper summarises an experiment into the haptic perception of texture in VR conducted with a Phantom haptic device. This experiment was an extension of a previous experiment involving the IE3000 haptic device in a programme of research into haptic perception in VR. On the basis of the reported work guidelines for the creation of haptic environments using textural information for both blind and sighted individuals are presented.

1   Introduction

Until recently interaction with virtual environments (VEs) was only viable via the visual and auditory senses. The absence of the haptic sense considerably limited the realism of VEs. Haptic information is the combination of what we feel through our skin (cutaneous information) and what we feel through the position and movement of our limbs and joints (kinesthetic information). Loomis and Lederman [6] noted: "touch facilitates or makes possible virtually all motor activity, and permits the perception of nearby objects and spatial layout" (pp 31-2). Furthermore, the inclusion of haptic information in VR has great potential to improve blind peoples' access to VEs and improve the accessibility of Graphical User Interfaces (GUIs). This could be achieved by providing haptic alternatives to visual components of a GUI, for example Windows borders, icons and menus

However, limitations of haptic virtual reality (VR) devices mean that users cannot simply interact with virtual objects in the same manner as with their real counterparts. The device used to relay the haptic stimulation to the user dictates the nature of the

S. Brewster, R. Murray-Smith (Eds.): Haptic HCI 2000, LNCS 2058, pp. 25-30, 2001.

presentation of and interaction with virtual objects. Consequently, one cannot assume that the findings from experiments into the haptic perception of real objects will apply to the haptic perception of virtual objects. To investigate this issue, Colwell et al [1] conducted several experiments investigating the perception of virtual objects and the virtual representation of texture using a three-degree of freedom device (i.e. one which allows three-dimensional interaction with virtual objects), the Impulse Engine 3000 (IE 3000) from Immersion Corporation (www.mmersion.com) (Fig. 1). Texture was chosen as it is a highly salient object attribute and therefore could be a useful means of representing information in virtual environments incorporating haptics.

Fig. 1. The IE3000 haptic device.

More recently, the authors have extended this work using the same methodology, but a different device: the Phantom 1.0A desktop device from SensAble Technologies (http://www.sensable.com) (Fig. 2). One goal of the further research is to assess the impact of the particular device used on the perception of virtual objects and textures.

Fig. 2: The Phantom 1.0A haptic device.

Lederman and her colleagues [2,3,4,5] have conducted extensive research on roughness perception for real surface texture. In these experiments the stimuli were metal plates with equally spaced grooves cut or etched lengthways into them. The depth profile of these plates is a periodic rectangular waveform. The textures provided by the grooves can be defined by three parameters: groove depth (amplitude), groove width and the spacing between the grooves (land width). The research has indicated that groove width is the most significant determinant of the perceived roughness of the textures. With such textures, perceived roughness increases as a function of increasing groove width [2,3,4,5].

Simulations of plates featuring rectangular waveforms such as those used by Lederman were not adopted in the current research, although this would have been a logical move, because of problems arising from the infinitesimally small virtual contact point which the interfaces to haptic VR devices entail (see Section 2.2 below). This meant that in pilot simulations, the virtual contact point kept catching in the corners of the rectangular grooves. Instead, virtual textures featuring sinusoidal waveforms were used, as these did not create any catch points. Sinusoidal waveforms are defined by two parameters: groove width (period) and groove depth (amplitude).

2   Experimental Methodology

2.1   The Methodology for Measuring Subjective Roughness

The methodology used to measure perceived roughness is a well-known psychological technique known as magnitude estimation, devised by Stevens [7]. In this technique there are a series of stimuli of known physical characteristics. Participants are asked to provide estimates of the magnitude of the roughness of the physical stimuli (e.g. textures) by assigning numbers to the roughness they perceive in relation to a baseline texture. If one stimulus seems twice as rough as another, it is given a number twice as large. So if a person calls the initial (baseline) texture "20", then one perceived as twice as rough would be would be assigned the number "40" and one half as rough would be assigned the number "10". It is well known in psychology that perception of such stimuli produces a power law such that $R = P^n$, where R is the perceived Roughness as expressed by the magnitude estimates and P is some Physical characteristic of the surface (such as such as grit size for sandpaper [8] or groove width). n is known as the power law exponent. If this law holds then log (R) will be a linear function of log (P) with slope n. Slope n provides us with an *exponent* that describes the rate at which R increases as a function of P. A positive exponent indicates that perceived roughness of the stimulus increases with increases in the physical parameter the stimuli (i.e. groove width), while a negative exponent indicates that perceived roughness of the stimulus decreases with increases in the physical parameter (i.e. groove width).

2.2   The Experimental Procedure

The experiment involved 23 participants, (13 male and 10 female). 10 participants were blind, (8 males and 2 females). Of the blind participants 5 were congenitally blind, the remaining 5 lost their sight between the ages of 8-42. The ages of the participants ranged from 19-54.

The stimuli consisted of ten virtual plates featuring an area of sinusoidal shaped parallel grooves running the entire length of the plate and measuring 4 cm. in width. The amplitude of the grooves was constant across the virtual plates at .1125mm. The virtual plates differed in their sinusoidal groove widths, which ranged from .675mm to 2.700mm in 10 equal increments of .225mm.

Interaction with the virtual textures with the Phantom device occurred via two different endpoints, a stylus and a thimble. Each endpoint gave access to a simulation of an infinitesimally small virtual contact point between the endpoint and the texture. In the previous work [1] with the IE3000 device, the participants grasped a small spherical cover that was fitted to the end of the device's arm.

The participants made magnitude estimates on the ten virtual textures after sweeping the stylus/thimble endpoint across the textured surface once only. This procedure was repeated six times for each texture and for both the thimble and stylus endpoints (the presentation order of the textures was randomly ordered by the computer and the order in which the endpoints were used was counterbalanced between participants). White noise was played to the participants via headphones throughout the duration of the experiment to prevent them from obtaining any audio cues to the dimensions of the virtual textures. This procedure replicates Colwell et al [1].

3   Summary of Results

Relationship between Groove Width and Perceived Roughness.
The relationship between the perceived roughness of the virtual textures and the geometry of those textures was, for the majority of individuals, the opposite of that found for the real textures used by Lederman and her colleagues. Lederman [2,3,4,5] found that perceived roughness increased as a function of increasing groove width (positive exponent), whereas the results of this experiment indicated that perceived roughness increased as a function of decreasing groove width (negative exponent) for the majority of the participants. Negative exponents relating groove width to perceived roughness have also recently been reported by Wall and Harwin [9]. The apparently contradictory result may well result from the fact that the contact point in virtual environments is infinitesimally small, and thus much narrower than the groove widths of the textures being investigated. Whereas in the experiments with real textures, participants ran their fingers over the plates – thus the contact point was considerably wider than the groove widths.

The Effect of the Endpoint Used.
The endpoint used with the Phantom exerted a significant effect on the rate at which perceived roughness changed as a function of given increments in groove width (the exponent in the power law). In this experiment the negative exponent was greater for the Phantoms' thimble than for its stylus endpoint for both blind and sighted participants[1].

Variation between Individuals in Perceived Roughness.
Although there was no significant difference between blind and sighted people in the perceived roughness of the virtual textures, there was a good deal of variation in the exponents relating groove width and perceived roughness in both blind and sighted participant groups.

The Effect of the Particular Haptic Device Used.
The results obtained with the Phantom haptic device differ from those obtained in the previous study with the IE3000 [1] in one important respect.   In the current experiment, more sighted participants individually demonstrated a significant relationship between groove width and perceived roughness with the Phantom device (9/13 participants, 69%) than with the IE3000 device (7/13 participants, 54 %). Such a difference was not observed with the blind participants (90% of blind participants showed a significant relationship between groove width and perceived roughness in both studies).

For the participants for whom there was a significant relationship between groove width and perceived roughness, the results obtained with the Phantom device replicate those found with the IE 3000. For example, exponents did not significantly differ between blind and sighted participants for either device. In addition, with both devices the majority of participants perceived roughness to decrease with increasing groove width.

4   Guidelines for the Implementation of Texture in Virtual Environment

The reported results have substantial implications for the implementation of textures in VEs. The fact that similar trends in the results from the Phantom and the IE3000 have emerged indicates their applicability to three degree of freedom haptic VR devices generally. Designers of haptic VEs should take note of the following points when they design VEs that include virtual textures.

1)   *To increase perceived roughness, decrease groove width.* When using textures composed of grooves of a waveform similar to that used in the reported experiment, designers need to bear in mind that increases in the groove width of

---

[1] In an earlier publication the stylus attachment was identified as having the larger negative exponent. This was an error that went unnoticed during the preparation of the manuscript.

which the virtual texture is composed is predominantly perceived as reductions in roughness.

2)   *Groove widths can remain the same for blind and sighted users.* It is not necessary to incorporate further adjustments to the increments between virtual texture grooves to produce similar results between blind and sighted users. The popular belief that blind people are more sensitive in their sense of touch does not apply significantly to these types of textures.

3)   *Sensitivity to virtual textures is better with thimble attachment.* If optimal sensitivity to the virtual textures is required for an application, given the current choice between a stylus or a thimble attachment, designers should use the thimble attachment.

4)   *Provide an adjustment facility for groove widths.* Cross platform compatibility with future devices will require the facility for the user to adjust the increment between the virtual textures groove widths to reflect the discrimination that is achievable for the individual with the specific device.

Acknowledgements

The authors gratefully acknowledge the assistance of all the blind and sighted individuals who took part in these studies. Paul Penn is a Ph.D. candidate supported by the ESRC and British Telecommunications. Chetz Colwell is also a Ph.D. candidate supported by the ESRC and MA Systems and Control Ltd, UK.

References

1. Colwell, C., Petrie, H., Kornbrot, D., Hardwick, A., and Furner, S. (1998). Haptic virtual reality for blind computer users. *Proceedings of ASSETS'98: The Third International ACM Conference on Assistive Technologies.* New York: ACM Press.
2. Lederman, S.J., and Taylor, M.M. (1972). Fingertip force, surface geometry and the perception of roughness by active touch. *Perception and Psychophysics, 12*(5), 401-408.
3. Lederman, S.J. (1974). Tactile roughness of grooved surfaces: The touching process and effects of macro- and microsurface structures. *Perception and Psychophysics, 16*(2), 385-395.
4. Lederman, S.J. (1981). The perception of surface roughness by active and passive touch. *Buletin of the Psychonomic Society, 18*(5), 253-255.
5. Lederman, S.J. (1982). The role of vibration in the tactual perception of roughness. *Perception and Psychophysics, 32*(2), 109-116.
6. Loomis, J.M., and Lederman S.J. (1986). Tactual Perception. In K.R. Boff, A. Kiuifman, and J. P. and Thomas (Eds.), *The Handbook of Perception and Human Performance* (pp. 31-31 31-41). New York: Wiley/Interscience.
7. Stevens, S.S. (1957). On the Psychophysical law. *Psychological Review*, 64(3), 153-181.
8. Stevens, S.S., and Harris, J.R. (1962). The scaling of subjective roughness and smoothness. *The Journal of Experimental Psychology, 64*(5), 489-494.
9. Wall, S.A., and Harwin, W.S. (2000) Interaction of Visual and Haptic Information in Simulated Environments. In S. Brewster and R. Murray-Smith, (Eds.) *First International Workshop on Haptic sHuman Computer Interaction.* Glasgow: University Of Glasgow.

Haptic Display of Mathematical Functions for Teaching Mathematics to Students with Vision Disabilities: Design and Proof of Concept

Frances L. Van Scoy[1], Takamitsu Kawai[1], Marjorie Darrah[2], and Connie Rash[2]

[1]Virtual Environments Laboratory
Department of Computer Science and Electrical Engineering
West Virginia University, Morgantown, West Virginia, USA
fvanscoy@wvu.edu, kawai@csee.wvu.edu
[2]Alderson Broaddus College, Philippi, West Virginia, USA
darrah@ab.edu, rash@ab.edu

Abstract. The design and initial implementation of a system for constructing a haptic model of a mathematical function for exploration using a PHANToM are described. A user types the mathematical function as a Fortran arithmetic expression and the system described here carves the trace of the function onto a virtual block of balsa wood. Preliminary work in generating music which describes the function has begun.

1   Problem Statement

It is difficult to teach some kinds of mathematics without using graphical representations of functions. In this paper we describe the design of a proposed haptic application and the implementation of a prototype using a PHANToM which will allow a blind student to feel the shape of a function being studied.

2   Related Work

Some of our previous work has been in constructing PHANToM-based haptic maps for mobility training. [1] Other VE Lab members are constructing haptic models of atoms. [2]

In addition we have done work in sonification of basketball game data [3] and geographic information systems data [4]. In those projects we have generated music designed to represent data interrelationships.

S. Brewster, R. Murray-Smith (Eds.): Haptic HCI 2000, LNCS 2058, pp. 31–40, 2001.

3   Approach

Our haptic math software package is designed to allow the input of a function, expressed as a Fortran expression such as

$$10.0 * X ** 2 -2.0 * X + 1.0 \tag{1}$$

Our package parses the textual representation of the function and then evaluates the function over an appropriate domain of values. The software then builds a 3-d model of a block of material on whose face the trace of the function is carved. The user can then use the PHANToM to follow the trace of the function. Optional commands allow the user to specify the domain and range to be displayed, the presence or absence of the axes, and major and minor tick marks on the axes and major and minor grid lines.

4   Design

We address the design of the software in two sections: the user interface and the implementation of the haptic display.

4.1   User Interface

There are two phases to using the software: (1) defining the function to be displayed and (2) exploring the function using the PHANToM. The user enters the function using the computer keyboard and explores the function with the right hand controlling the PHANToM and the left hand optionally entering keyboard commands.

Initializing the System
After launching the system, the user is prompted audibly to move the PHANToM to its reset position and press the "enter" key.

Defining the Function
Using the keyboard, the user inputs the function to be studied, expressed as a Fortran arithmetic expression. Currently uppercase letters are reserved for commands, so the user must use all lower case letters in entering the expression.

The system vocalizes the expression that has been typed so the user will know what has been typed (and therefore not inadvertently feel the wrong function due to a typographical error). The audible message "now you can feel the function" indicates when the model of the function has been "carved."

Exploring the Function
The user then explores the function using the PHANToM. In the future optional audio cues will guide the user to move the PHANToM tip to the function trace. The

shape of the function can then be followed by moving the PHANToM tip along the "carved" groove.

We assume that the user is right handed and will use the left hand on the computer keyboard to enter commands that modify preferences or trigger various audio cues.

Using the Keyboard for Optional Commands
The functions to be accessed by the left hand are those shown in Table 1.

Table 1. Keyboard Commands

Command	Meaning
A	toggle on/off audio feedback
R	vocalize ("read") expression as entered so far
C	remember entered expression (imitates ctrl+C for "copy")
V	recall remembered exprssion (imitates ctrl+V for "paste")
S	enter mode for setting lower bound of domain (X-axis)
D	enter mode for setting upper bound of domain
X	enter mode to set lower bound of range (Y-axis)
E	enter mode to set upper bound of range
Q	reset domain and range to default values
<esc>	quit the application

The letters S, D, X, and E were chosen for their relative positions on the keyboard to suggest relative position (down, up, left, right) of bounds.   When the system is in a mode in which it expects a new bound to be entered, typing a valid bound followed by "enter" causes the system to return to ordinary mode.

We anticipate adding other commands that will speak the location of the carved function with respect to the tip of the PHANToM, the (x,y) coordinates of the current location of the PHANToM tip, or the (x,y) coordinates of the nearest point in the function to the current PHANToM location.

4.2   Architecture of the Application

The major functional components of the application are the function compiler and the haptic modeler.

Function Compiler
We have used flex and bison to construct a compiler which translates the function definition provided as a character string by the user into a tree which can then be used to evaluate the function for various values in the domain. In the tree, the internal nodes are the operators and the leaves are the operands. For example, the function given in expression (1) is translated into the tree shown in Figure 1.

We support six arithmetic operations, addition, subtraction, multiplication, division, exponentiation (expressed by both ^ and **), and unary minus; the sine, cosine, and tangent functions and their inverses (sin, cos, tan, asin, acos, atan); and logarithm, absolute value and square root (log, abs, sqrt).

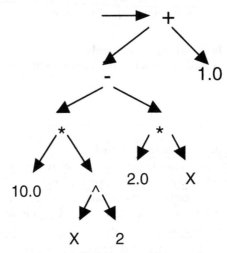

Fig. 1. Internal Tree Representation of Arithmetic Expression.

Haptic Modeler
Let f be the function the user wishes to explore hapticly. For each pair (valueX, valueY), where valueY=f(valueX), we construct five points in (x,y,z) space as follows:

   (valueX + offsetX, offsetY, 0.0)
   (valueX + offsetX, valueY + offsetY - gapY, 0.0)
   (valueX + offsetX, valueY + offsetY, depthZ)
   (valueX + offsetX, valueY + offsetY + gapY, 0.0)
   (valueX + offsetX, sizeY + offsetY, 0.0)

We then build eight triangles for each x-value. Four of them are shown in gray in Figure 2. These triangles are all co-planar.

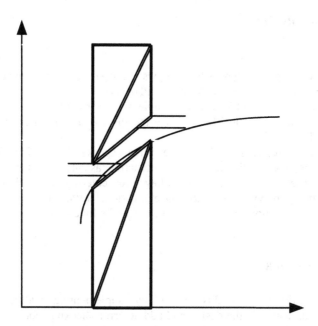

Fig. 2. Strip of Triangles Representing Uncarved Surface.

Four other triangles are constructed in the gap between the two pairs of triangles shown in Figure 2.

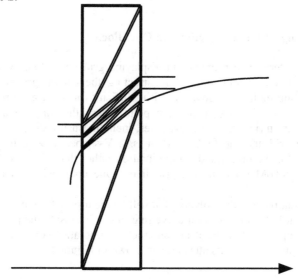

Fig. 3. Strip of Triangles in Which Middle Four Triangle Represent Carved Region.

They form a v-shaped trench below the plane of the previous triangles, which is the groove traced by the PHANToM. This is shown in Figure 3.

5   Implementation

We have a working prototype which allows the user to input a function and then explore the carving of the function using the PHANToM.

The current system includes some simple voice prompts.   Initially the system speaks, "Welcome to Haptic Math!   Place the PHANToM in its reset position and press <ENTER>."

When the user presses the "R" key, the systems speaks "Expression" followed by a character by character reading of the current function, as entered so far.

When the user presses the <enter> key after entering a function, the system responds with "Displaying the following expression," followed by a reading of the function definition, followed by "Now you can feel the function."

6   Future Work

We are currently refining this system by implementing additional keyboard commands as indicated in the design and adding error checking (for the syntax of the user's function and for domain and range values).

More substantive enhancements including adding the ability to carve multiple functions on one virtual block of wood, generating musical melodies which describe the shape of the function, and developing functionality for actual classroom use.

6.1   Carving Multiple Functions on One Block

We have encountered two problems in displaying grid lines along with the function: our initial triangle-based method of constructing the carved groove doesn't easily extend to creating multiple grooves and it is difficult for the user to recognize which direction to move the PHANToM at a point where the function and a grid line intersect.   We are trying several approaches, including using different shapes for the carving of the grid and the function (that is, a V-shaped groove for one and a U-shaped groove for the other) and using vibration rather than a carved line to indicate when the PHANToM tip is near a grid line.   One approach we have tried is the following.

1. Create a flat rectangular polygon that will be the top surface of the block.

2. Create a hole for the function curve (e.g. $f(x) = x$) inside the polygon created in step 1., by applying the Boolean subtraction operation on the polygons (the polygon(s) has its hole(s) as its attribute) as shown in Figure 4.

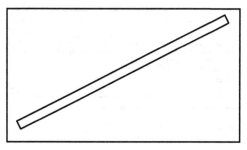

Fig. 4. Flat Rectangular Polygon with Hole for Function.

3. By applying the Boolean subtraction operation further, deform the hole shape so that it contains the X-axis shape as shown in Figure 5. (If the function curve has multiple intersections with the X-axis, the isolated part will appear inside the polygon. The algorithm allows such situations.)

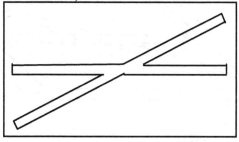

Fig. 5. Deformation of Hole to Contain X-axis Shape.

4. Apply a polygon triangulation to the polygon of the previous step as shown in Figure 6. This generates a triangle polygon set necessary to pass the shape data to the `gstTriPolyMesh` function that implements generic geometry in the GHOST library.

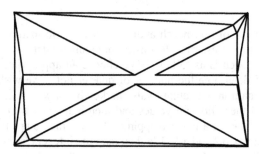

Fig. 6. Triangle Polygon Set.

5. Next, extrude the above polygon to the z-direction and create the side polygons of the groove as shown in Figure 7.

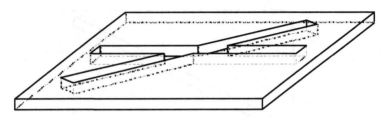

Fig. 7. Result of Extrusion of Polygon.

6. In the end, attach a rectangular polygon as a bottom of the groove as shown in Figure 7. Eventually, every appearing rectangular polygons also will be decomposed by its diagonal line into two adjacent triangular polygons and passed to `gstTriPolyMesh` function.

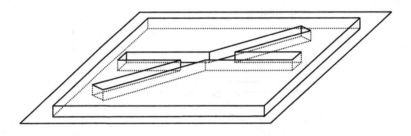

Fig. 8. Final Version of Carving.

Thus we can carve the groove using any types of strokes. The advantage of this method is that we can use various shapes for the bottom of the groove and the cross point of the groove (just adding a big rectangular polygon in the end).

6.2　Sonification

Sonification is the use of nonspeech audio to convey information [5]. Our interest is primarily in generating Western style music from numeric data.

Our general approach is as follows. We choose an appropriate domain and range for a function and determine the number of quarter notes we wish to generate. We then divide the domain into n subintervals, marked by $x_0, x_1, \ldots, x_n$, We sample the function at each of these domain values and then map each $f(x_i)$ to a numeric value between -12 and 12, using a linear mapping scheme which maps the lower and upper bounds of the range to -12 and 12. We then map the integers in the range -12 to 12 to the notes in the Western chromatic scale between the C below middle C to the C above middle C. Table 2 shows the result of such sampling and mapping for

$$f(x) = \sin(x) \tag{2}$$

The result is the music shown in Figure 9.

Table 2. Assignment of Notes to Sine Function Evaluated at 26 Domain Values between 0.0 and 6.25.

X	0.0	0.25	0.50	0.75	1.00	1.25	1.50	1.75	2.0
Y	0.0	0.25	0.48	0.68	0.84	0.95	1.00	0.98	0.91
12*y	0	3	6	8	10	11	12	12	11
Note	C	D#	F#	G#	A#	B	C	C	B

X	2.25	2.50	2.75	3.00	3.25	3.50	3.75	4.00	4.25
Y	0.78	0.60	0.38	0.14	-0.11	-0.37	-0.57	-0.76	-0.89
12*y	9	7	5	2	-1	-4	-7	-9	-11
Note	A	G	F	D	B	Ab	F	Eb	Db

X	4.50	4.75	5.00	5.25	5.50	5.75	6.00	6.25
Y	-0.98	-1.00	-0.96	-0.86	-0.71	-0.51	-0.28	0.00
12*y	-12	-12	-12	-10	-9	-6	-3	0
Note	C	C	C	D	D#	F#	A	C

Fig. 9. Music Generated from Sin(X), where $0.0 \leq X \leq 6.25$, in Radians.

Our intent is to generate such music automatically from the function, domain, and range given by the user as an enhancement to the haptic math system.

6.3 Enhanced User Interface and Curriculum Application

We continue to refine the user interface design based on consultation with teachers and others with limited vision.

There are three possible further steps for the project. We could develop a full haptic graphing calculator. Alternatively, we could add functionality for assisting in teaching specific mathematics courses. For example, we could add a front end that would allow the user to build parameterized conic sections, or we could display not only the trace of a function but also its derivative.

We are also exploring working with K-12 teachers about potential related applications to curricula in geography, statistics, and astronomy.

Acknowledgements

This work is supported by the EPSCoR programs of the National Science Foundation and the state of West Virginia and the West Virginia University Department of Computer Science and Electrical Engineering.

The authors acknowledge with gratitude the advice of William Carter, professor of education at Marshall University, on user interface issues and future curriculum uses. We also acknowledge the work of Chris Coleman, a WVU undergraduate art student and member of the VE Lab, in producing a video of the project. As part of her masters research, WVU computer science graduate student Sunitha Mutnuri is using the t2mf and mf2t packages from Piet van Oostrum at the Uniersity of Utrecht. We anticipate using her expertise to add automatic generation of music to our system. Documentation on these packages can be found at
http://www.cs.uu.nl/pub/MIDI/PROGRAMS/MSDOS/mf2t.doc.
PHANToM is a registered trademark of SensAble.

References

1. Van Scoy, Frances L., Baker, Vic, Gingold, Chaim, EMartino, Eric, and Darren Burton: "Mobility Training using a Haptic Interface: Initial Plans," PHANToM Users Group, Boston, Massachusetts, October 10-12, 1999.
http://www.sensable.com/community/PUG99/07_vanscoy.pdf.
2. Harvey, Erica, and Gingold, Chaim: "Haptic Representation of the Atom," Proceedings of Information Visualisation 2000, London, July 19-21, 2000. pp. 232-238.
3. Van Scoy, Frances L.: "Sonification of Complex Data Sets: An Example from Basketball," Proceedings of VSMM99 (Virtual Systems and MultiMedia), Dundee, Scotland, September 1-3, 1999, pages 203-216.
4. Van Scoy, Frances L.: "Sonification of Remote Sensing Data: Initial Experiment," Information Visualisation 2000, London, UK, July 19-21, 2000. pp. 453-460.
5. Kramer, Gregory et al.: Sonification Report: Status of the Field and Research Agenda, prepared for the National Science Foundation by members of the International Community for Auditory Display, 1997, available at
http://www.icad.org/websiteV2.0/References/nsf.html.

Haptic Graphs for Blind Computer Users

Wai Yu, Ramesh Ramloll, and Stephen Brewster

Department of Computing Science, University of Glasgow
Glasgow, G12 8QQ, U.K.
{rayu,ramesh,stephen}@dcs.gla.ac.uk
http://www.dcs.gla.ac.uk/~rayu/home.html

Abstract. In this paper we discuss the design of computer-based haptic graphs for blind and visually impaired people with the support of our preliminary experimental results. Since visual impairment makes data visualisation techniques inappropriate for blind people, we are developing a system that can make graphs accessible through haptic and audio media. The disparity between human haptic perception and the sensation simulated by force feedback devices is discussed. Our strategies to tackle technical difficulties posed by the limitations of force feedback devices are explained. Based on the results of experiments conducted on both blind and sighted people, we suggested two techniques: engraving and the use of texture to model curved lines on haptic graphs. Integration of surface property and auditory cues in our system are proposed to assist blind users in exploring haptic graphs.

1   Introduction

We are currently conducting an EPSRC funded project (Multivis) aimed at providing access to complex graphical data, i.e. graphs and tables, for blind and visually impaired people. A multimodal approach, using sound and touch, is adopted in this research. Traditionally, graphs and diagrams are presented in Braille, and raised dots and lines on the swell-paper. Several problems are associated with this kind of graph presentation technique. Firstly, only a small proportion of blind people has learned and uses Braille (only 26% of blind university students use it). Secondly, the resolution and the accuracy of the raised graphs and diagrams are fairly low so that blind people can only get a rough idea about the content. Thirdly, complex details on the graph are difficult to perceive and become rather confusing. Fourthly, dynamic data, which could change frequently, cannot be represented by the traditional approach. Finally, no assistance is available to blind people when exploring the graph so that this process becomes quite time consuming and tiring. Therefore, we would like to tackle these problems by using computer technology, such as force feedback devices, 3D sound and computer assistance to help blind and visually impaired people to access graphs and diagrams. In this paper we focus on the current state of our research and discuss future work on haptic graphs.

S. Brewster, R. Murray-Smith (Eds.): Haptic HCI, LNCS 2058, pp. 41-51, 2001.

1.1   Haptic Perception

Touch or haptic perception is usually considered as a secondary sensory medium to sighted people although it is very important in our daily lives. We need touch feedback to manipulate objects successfully and effectively, for instance grasping a cup of coffee and turning the door handle. Touch is even more crucial for visually impaired people and becomes their primary sensory feedback. Haptic receptors are located all over our body and have been classified into two main categories: cutaneous and kinesthetic. Cutaneous receptors reside beneath the surface of the skin and respond to temperature, pain and pressure. Kinesthetic receptors are located in muscles, tendons and joints, and correspond to the position of limbs and their movement in space [1].

1.2   Touch and Force Feedback Devices

Force feedback devices are available to provide a haptic channel of information exchange between humans and computers. Ramstein et al. have developed the PC-Access system which offers auditory information (non-verbal sounds and voice synthesis) reinforced by the sense of touch via a force feedback device called the Panograph to enhance users' productivity, increase their satisfaction and optimise their workload [2]. More recently, Grabowski and Barner have investigated the use of a combination of the sense of touch, using the PHANToM haptic device, and representative soundscapes to develop visualisation aids for blind and visually impaired individuals [3].

Most current force feedback devices can provide movements in either 2D or 3D space. Commonly, users need to insert one of their fingers into a thimble or hold a stylus attached to one end of the mechanical linkage, which is coupled with electrical motors at the other end, to feel the reaction force (Figure 1). By tracking the position of the thimble or the tip of the stylus, contact and interaction with virtual objects can be represented by the appropriate force generated from the motors. Therefore, force feedback devices are good at simulating kinesthetic sensory information but not at cutaneous sensation [4]. Only a single point contact can be produced which means that only the interaction force corresponding to users' finger tip is simulated by the devices. This is a huge bandwidth reduction on the haptic channel when compared with the number of haptic receptors in human body. By using force feedback devices, people can manipulate virtual objects, and feel their shape and weight. However, detailed and realistic texture on an object is difficult to reproduce due to the limitation of single point contact.

This limitation in the force feedback devices has a major effect on our haptic graph representation. Braille, and raised dots and lines used in the tactile graphs rely on users' sensitive and rich cutaneous receptors in the fingers. By pressing a finger on the embossed objects, the skin is deformed and gives a tactile perception of the shape and size of the objects. However, in the virtual haptic graphs, users only have a single point contact which will not give instant information about the property of the object being contacted. Therefore, constructing graphs by using embossed objects can cause various problems which will be explained in the following sections.

Fig. 1. A PHANToM device with overlaid arrows showing all possible movements. (PHANToM is a product of SensAble Technologies, Inc.).

2   Preliminary Studies

Several pilot studies have been conducted in the Department of Computing Science at the University of Glasgow [5]. These studies were to investigate the use of a force feedback device (PHANToM) to provide haptic representation of line graphs and bar charts. The main areas investigated include: (1) whether users can obtain general information about the graph, (2) effect of haptic gridlines on providing data values on the graph, and (3) whether users can distinguish different lines based on various levels of surface friction. The results have shown that users were able to get a general idea about the layout of the graph through the developed haptic interface. However, not all the users were able to use the gridlines to find the maximum and minimum points on the lines. Moreover, some users found them disturbing when exploring the graphs. The effect of different friction levels on the lines was not obvious because some users had problems distinguishing the difference. Users were often confused when exploring complex graphs and as a result an incorrect layout of the graph was perceived. This is undesirable and contradicts the aim of the haptic interface, which is supposed to be an aid to blind people.

Therefore, the haptic interface has been modified and an experiment was conducted to investigate the effect of the change on haptic graph exploration [6]. The levels of friction were reduced into two: sticky and slippery. A toggling feature was implemented on haptic gridlines so that users can turn them on/off whenever they like. The hypotheses here were:

  ! ∀ The distinctive friction key can be used to distinguish separate lines on the graphs.
  ! ∀ Toggled gridlines will provide an effective means of measurement and reference within the graphs.

2.1   Experiment Set Up

Several line graphs were created for this experiment (Figure 2). In common, two lines were displayed on a graph and they were either located separately or cross-intersecting each other. Two different friction properties were applied to the lines and they were classified as sticky and slippery. The lines were made up by cylinders, which are one of the primitive shapes supported by the GHOST programming SDK. Therefore, straight-line approximation was used to construct simple line graphs. All the lines were half sub-merged into a flat surface and thus a semi-circle cross-section was formed on all the line models. Due to the circular cross-section of cylinders, users can feel the jagged corner at the joints of the graph lines.

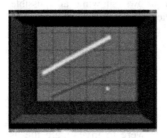 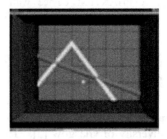

Fig. 2. Examples of the graphs used in the experiments. (They show the sticky and slippery lines, X and Y axes, and gridlines.).

Both sighted and blind people were recruited as participants for this experiment. Ten sighted participants were used and nine were male. Most of them were from a postgraduate course in I.T. Their ages range from 20 to 35. Five blind participants were invited from a local organization for blind people. Their ages were between 30 and 71 and they had different education backgrounds. It was hoped that ten blind participants could have been obtained but only five participants volunteered to take part in the event. Such a small number is insufficient to provide any statistically meaningful results but some implications can still be obtained from the experiment results.

Training was given to the participants to familiarize them with the PHANToM device and the features of the graphs. They had one minute on each of the following graphs, (1) a blank graph, (2) a graph with two parallel lines and (3) a graph with intersecting lines. Therefore they were introduced to the general layout of the graphs, friction key, toggled gridlines and the potential problems of jagged corners. The sighted participants were not allowed to see the graphs on the computer screen throughout the training and experiment sections.

The experiment was divided into two parts. Part 1 was designed to test the friction key. Participants had to explore two graphs in one minute each. Each graph had two parallel lines. At the end, participants needed to identify the sticky and slippery lines and the steeper of the two lines on each of the two graphs.

Part 2 was concerned with testing the toggled gridlines as well as further testing the friction key and general perception of the graphs. Sighted and blind participants had different designs of the experiment procedures and measurements. For the sighted participants, four minutes were given on each of the six graphs which had cross-intersected lines. During the four-minute exploration, sighted participants needed to obtain the co-ordinates of the maximum and minimum points of each line based on the gridlines. After the exploration, participants were asked to make a sketch of the perceived graph. For the blind participants, only four graphs were given with six minutes exploration time on each. This was because the number of measurements was increased and the experiment had to be kept to a reasonable length. Sketches were not required but participants had to identify and estimate the X and Y co-ordinates of the maximum and minimum values of each line. They were also asked to determine the locations where the lines crossed the axes (if different from the max/min co-ordinates) and the crossover points if there was any time left.

All the cursor activities, which are the movements of the PHANToM's stylus, were recorded and saved into a log file. They provided the traces of participants' behaviour during the graph exploration and thus became useful at the stage of data analysis.

After completing parts 1 and 2, all the participants were asked to fill out a questionnaire which was concerned with four areas:

- !∀ The perceived difficulty of the tasks
- !∀ The effectiveness of the gridlines
- !∀ The usefulness of the toggling gridlines feature
- !∀ The effectiveness of the friction key

Participants were asked to rate each area on a scale of one to ten and give any comments on the experiment and the interface in general.

2.2 Results

In the thirty tests carried out on both sighted and blind participants to distinguish the lines by their surface friction, 93.3% of the responses were correct (Figure 3). Large variation was found on participants' feedback on the questionnaire (Figure 4). The mean rating is 6.5. This difference could be because the usefulness of the friction key was hindered by other factors, such as complexity of the graphs and the line modeling technique. Despite this difference, the friction key was effective at indicating different lines on a simple graph, provided there are no other sources of confusion.

No conclusive results supported the effectiveness of the gridlines which was judged on the participant's performance in estimating the maximum and minimum values of the graph lines. Sighted participants' rating on the questionnaire matched their performance. However, blind participants gave a very high rating even though the majority performed poorly. The mean rating of the effectiveness of the gridlines was 7 out of 10 (Figure 5). The result showed that when participants were confident of the shape and layout of the graphs then the gridlines could be used effectively. However counting the gridlines is often affected by the obstruction of other lines on the graph.

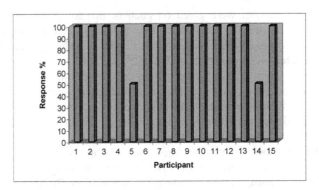

Fig. 3. Correct Distinction of Lines according to Friction in Part 1 (sighted participants: 1-10; blind participants 11-15).

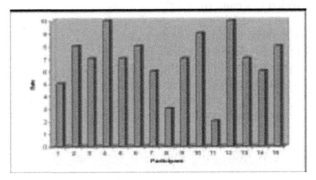

Fig. 4. Participants' rating on the effectiveness of the friction key (sighted participants: 1-10; blind participants 11-15).

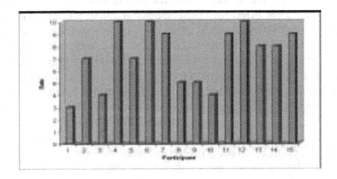

Fig. 5. Participants' rating on the effectiveness of the gridlines (sighted participants: 1-10; blind participants 11-15).

Sighted and blind participants had different ratings on the effectiveness of toggling gridlines (Figure 6). Nine out of ten sighted participants rated its effectiveness as 8 or greater out of 10. On the other hand, three blind participants chose not to use the toggling feature and thus no conclusion can be drawn. However, it was noticeable that the participants who made most use of it tended to produce the most accurate results.

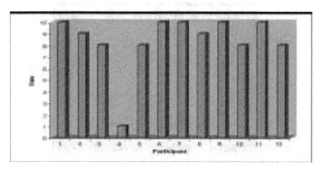

Fig. 6. Participants' rating on the usefulness of the toggling gridlines (sighted participants: 1-10; blind participants 11-15).

2.3   Discussion

Three main issues were investigated in the experiment. Using friction key was shown to be useful to distinguish different lines on a simple haptic graph but become less effective in a complex graph. Some participants were confused by the cross intersection points between two lines. They thought the graph consisted of two separate lines combining sticky and slippery parts. This can be seen from the sketch drawn by the participants after the graph exploration (Figure 7b). Effect of the friction key was hindered by the embossed cylindrical lines. The line modeling technique, which simply joined cylinder objects together, caused this confusion. Participants found it hard to keep their pointer on the line, especially at the corners and the end points of the lines (Figure 7c). This increased the difficulty of tracing the trend of the lines and instead participants struggled to figure out the shape of the line model. Therefore, this simple line modeling technique cannot provide users with effective graph exploration but obstructs users from perceiving correct information about the graph. Different line modeling techniques which can produce curved lines and smooth joints are required.

Gridlines provide an aid to find the values on a haptic graph. However, the experiment results showed that they were not very effective and not every participant could use them easily. There are four fundamental problems associated with this kind of haptic gridlines. First of all, the uneven surface caused by the raised gridlines may distract users from searching the data lines. Secondly, gridlines are often overlapped by data lines and thus become very difficult to count. Thirdly, they only provide approximate values which are not so useful when exact values are required. Finally, it is very time consuming to count the gridlines because users need to remember the counted numbers in cases of comparing different points on the lines. Therefore, it is very difficult to provide exact values of the points on graphs through the haptic interface. Another sensory modality e.g. sound, is needed to solve this problem. Synthesized speech could be used to speak out the value when users press a key on the keyboard or the switch on the PHANToM's stylus.

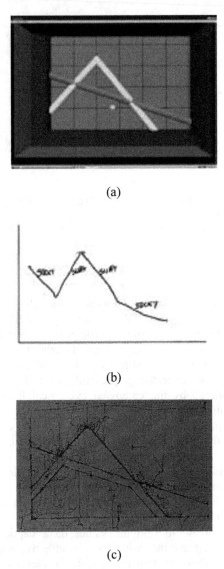

(a)

(b)

(c)

Fig. 7. (a) the actual graph, (b) participant perceived graph, and (c) cursor log of a participant's exploration trace. (problems at corners are represented by the chaotic trace of the cursor position.).

Although the number of blind participants involved in the experiment is quite small, it did raise some issues on choosing participants for future experiments. Blind people's age, educational background and knowledge of mathematics and graphs may affect their performance in the experiment. Moreover, perception of graphs may vary from people blind from birth and people blind in the later stage of their life. Therefore, the experimenter needed to explain x and y axis and co-ordinate values to participants who have congenital blindness and have not much knowledge on graphs. On the other hand, an adventitiously blind participant managed to explore the graphs quickly and locate the maximum and minimum values accurately. Therefore, a homogenous group of blind participants, who are of a similar age and have similar experience on graphs, will be required to test or to evaluate further the effectiveness of the haptic interface.

3   Future Work

Issues of future research are raised based on the implications obtained from the preliminary studies:

! ∀ Developing different techniques to model curved lines;
! ∀ Solving user confusions at intersection points between several lines;
! ∀ Using surface friction/texture to distinguish multiple lines;
! ∀ Investigating methods to provide a quick overview of graphs;
! ∀ Incorporating other sensory modalities into the haptic interface.

As shown in the experiment's results, the line modeling technique using cylinder objects, which are simply jointed together, does not give users a smooth sensation at the joints. The single point contact given by PHANToM also contributes to this problem because the user's pointer cannot stay on the surface of the cylindrical objects easily. It clearly shows that traditional emboss technique used to present text and diagrams to blind people is not suitable for force feedback devices. Instead, an engraving technique is proposed here to present line graphs on the haptic interface. Curved lines can be represented by a groove on a flat surface so that users can easily locate and follow the track of the groove (Figure 8). Techniques of modeling and joining this kind of groove segments by polygons have been developed. Initial testing showed this technique is effective and can solve the problems stated above. However, further improvement is needed in order to handle multiple lines.

The problem with intersections between multiple lines is that users get confused when they reach the crossover points. They may lose their sense of direction at the junction where two lines intersect. There are various ways to solve this problem. All the lines on the graph can be displayed selectively, therefore when the user's pointer is moving in a groove, the other lines can be automatically hidden from the user so that smooth transitions can be provided. Alternatively, different textures can be applied on the surfaces of the grooves so that users can tell which groove they are supposed to follow by distinguishing the different sensation. In addition, sound hints can be produced by giving auditory feedback when users switch between grooves.

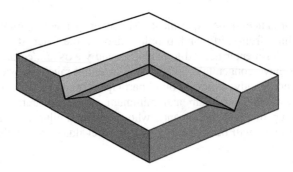

Fig. 8. Engraved line on a flat surface.

There are many different parts on a graph so that various surface textures can be applied in order to tell them apart. Since preliminary results have shown that users can distinguish different frictions applied on the lines, mixtures of friction and texture can be used as a distinctive feature of an object. Using surface texture not only can solve the confusion of multiple lines but also gives an indication of different parts of the graph so that users will know where they are on the graph. Investigation is needed here to identify which type of texture can be easily perceived by users via the PHANToM because force feedback devices are generally not good at presenting cutaneous sensation [4].

When blind people are exploring an unknown object, they often want to know the outline of the object by touching it. The same situation applies to graph exploration where blind users would like to know the boundary and dimensions of the graph before feeling the other objects in detail. As the limitation of single point contact, information received by blind users is fairly localised and restricted at that instant of time. Therefore, blind users need to spend a longer time in order to get a general idea about the layout of the line graph. An effective way of presenting the overview of the line graph will shorten the time required in this process and give blind users a better understanding about the graph. Using non-speech sound to provide this kind of quick overview is being investigated.

Using force feedback devices opens a door to graph access for blind people, however, it has some limitations, such as low accuracy and limited bandwidth, so that some information cannot be represented in haptics effectively. For blind people, hearing is another important sensory medium therefore auditory feedback can be introduced into the haptic interface to present information either explicitly by using synthesized speech or implicitly using non-speech sounds. The multimodal approach is used in this research project to provide blind people with access to graphical information.

4   Conclusion

In this paper, we introduced our research work on developing a multimodal system to make graphs accessible to the blind and visually impaired people. Some preliminary studies have been carried out to evaluate the usefulness of the PHANToM force feedback device in providing this haptic information. Issues in presenting line graphs on the developed haptic interface were discussed with the support of the results obtained from experiments. The PHANToM has been proved to be good at providing kinesthetic rather than cutaneous sensation. The single point contact provided by PHANToM is inadequate when used on embossed line graph objects. Therefore, different line graph modeling techniques, which engrave data lines on a flat surface, have been developed to solve this problem. Friction and surface textures were shown to be useful to distinguish different objects on the line graph, whereas, toggled gridlines were unable to provide approximate values on the lines easily to the users. Users could get a general idea about the layout of the line graph through the developed haptic interface. However, it also indicated that the line graph perceived by the users is often distorted and inaccurate due to the limitations of the force feedback device and the modeling technique. The implications of the preliminary studies have inspired the future development of this research work. The issues of presenting line graphs more effectively to blind people were discussed. In conclusion, haptic interface are useful to provide graph information to blind computer users, however, its limitations indicate that a multimodal approach would be more appropriate and effective for our work.

Acknowledgments

The authors would like to thank the Glasgow and Western Scotland Society of Blind for its participation in the experiments. This research work is funded by EPSRC Grant GR/M44866, ONCE (Spain) and Virtual Presence Ltd.

References

1. Klatzky, R.L., and Lederman, S.J. (1999). The haptic glance: A route to rapid object identification and manipulation. In D. Gopher and A. Koriats (Eds.) Attention and Performance XVII. Cognitive regulations of performance: Interaction of theory and application. (pp. 165-196). Mahwah, NJ: Erlbaum.
2. Ramstein C., Martial O., Dufresne A., Carignan M., Chasse P., and Mabilleau P. (1996). Touching and Hearing GUI's: Design Issues for the PC-Access System. Second Annual ACM Conference on Assistive Technologies, pp 2-9.
3. Grabowski, N.A., and Barner, K.E. (1998). Data Visualisation Methods for the Blind Using Force Feedback and Sonification. Part of the SPIE Conference on Telemanipulator and Telepresence Technologies V, Boston Massachusetts, pp 131-139.
4. Oakley, I., McGee, M.R., Brewster, S.A., and Gray, P.D. (2000). Putting the feel in look and feel. In ACM CHI 2000 (The Hague, NL), ACM Press Addison-Wesley, pp 415-422.
5. Pengelly, H.L. (1998). Investigating the Use of Force-feedback Devices in Human-Computer Interaction, Masters dissertation, Department of Computing Science, University of Glasgow, 1998.
6. Flisch A. (1999). Investigation of the Effectiveness of a Haptic Graph Interface, Masters dissertation, Department of Computing Science, University of Glasgow, 1999.

Web-Based Touch Display for Accessible Science Education

Evan F. Wies[1], John A. Gardner[2], M. Sile O'Modhrain[1],
Christopher J. Hasser[1], and Vladimir L. Bulatov[2]

[1] Immersion Corporation, 801 Fox Lane, San Jose, CA 95131, USA
chasser@immersion.com
[2] Science Access Project, Oregon State University, 301 Weniger Hall
Corvallis, OR 97331-5607 USA
john.gardner@orst.edu

Abstract. Inaccessibility of instructional materials, media, and technologies used in science, engineering, and mathematics education severely restricts the ability of students with little or no sight to excel in these disciplines. Curricular barriers deny the world access to this pool of potential talent, and limit individuals' freedom to pursue technical careers. Immersion has developed a low-cost force-feedback computer mouse. This haptic display technology promises fundamental improvements in accessibility at mass-market prices (sub-$100). This paper presents the results of an investigation into the potential benefits of incorporating haptic feedback into software intended for college and high school physics curricula.

1   Introduction

Physics, chemistry, engineering, and mathematics curricula are full of abstract principles and physical concepts, many of which are inherently dynamic in nature. Examples cross all disciplinary boundaries in the sciences and engineering, and include gravity, inertia, springs, damping, friction, momentum, fluid flow, pulleys, centrifugal force, gyroscopic motion, chemical bonding, and magnetism. Our interaction with such systems is most often mediated by direct physical contact (lifting objects against the force of gravity, rotating tools and feeling inertial forces, etc.) As such, our understanding of many dynamical systems is coupled to our haptic senses, which in turn are finely tuned to interpret dynamic properties in our environment.

This work explored the feasibility of making force-feedback simulations available to blind and visually impaired students over the World Wide Web as part of science education curricula. This included the development of enabling software technology to take advantage of a new low-cost force-feedback mouse (manufactured by Logitech under license from Immersion Corporation) and a demonstration curriculum module. A panel that included both educational experts and blind students was then recruited for a pilot study to assess this module.

S. Brewster, R. Murray-Smith (Eds.): Haptic HCI 2000, LNCS 2058, pp. 52-60, 2001.

Fig. 1. Logitech Wingman Force Feedback Mouse

2   Related Work

Though haptic feedback is a relatively new modality for HCI, its potential for providing access to GUIs for blind computer users was recognized early on and has been explored by many researchers. Broadly speaking, these efforts can be divided into two strands, projects which have concentrated on rendering the components of the 'environment', the GUI itself [1], [2], [3], and those which have focused on rendering 'content', the non-text information that might be produced by applications such as mathematical packages etc. [4], [5], [6], [7]. Two further studies have specifically addressed issues related to haptic rendering of objects and images on the World Wide Web [8], [9]. However, both differ from the present study in that they concentrate on the rendering of web page layout and address only in passing the possibility of rendering content haptically as well.

Two studies that have implications for both strands of research have focused on questions of shape and texture discrimination. Colwell studied the perception of virtual textures, shapes and objects by both blind and sighted subjects [10]. Fritz and Barner developed a method to synthesize perceptually distinct haptic textures using stochastic modeling techniques [11]. Their goal was to create a variety of textures that could then be used to display complex data plots.

3   Accessible Science Education Curriculum Development

The present project focused on the development of a prototype instruction module (curriculum module) organized around a set of didactic goals. The key features of the curriculum module were that it was accessible and Web-deployed. It used force feedback in a way that was meaningful and necessary for the blind student to understand the material presented (in conjunction with corresponding text-to-speech information).

The development and implementation of the curriculum module were carried out by the Science Access Project at Oregon State University, with Immersion Corporation providing guidance regarding force feedback paradigms. The evaluation phase of the project was conducted by Immersion, which provided evaluators with haptic devices and technical support. Finally, to collect feedback from the evaluators, educators from Oregon State University collaborated with Immersion to design a user evaluation survey.

3.1   Topic of Curriculum

Our team chose introductory electric fields as the most appropriate instruction topic for the feasibility study because it lends itself naturally to education using a force display. The purpose of the curriculum module was to demonstrate to the student experimentally the electric field due to a uniformly charged (non-conducting) sphere and to require the student to measure and analyze experimental data to find the charge on the sphere. It is a demanding laboratory suitable for advanced undergraduate physics majors or for introductory graduate students in the physical sciences.

3.2   Curriculum Module Design

The curriculum Module was designed as a sequence of tutorial web pages that guided the student through both the experimental and data analysis stages of the laboratory. The goal of the experimental phase of the module was to allow the student to gain an understanding of the behavior of electric charge on the surface of a sphere. Using the Logitech Wingman Force Feedback Mouse, the student controlled the position of a test charge "attached" to the cursor while feeling the resulting force either attracting or repelling their hand from the surface of the sphere. By clicking the mouse button at any point, the student can record data - the force at a particular radius.

Next, the students enter an analysis mode. In this mode the students can explore their collected data, select curve-fitting parameters, and feel the fit curves. This environment is designed to help the student gain a quantitative and qualitative understanding of the physical phenomena, to literally get a "feel" for the character of the data they have collected.

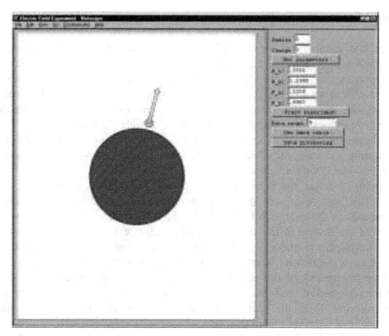

Fig. 2. Screen shot of the Experiment Mode of the electric field laboratory.

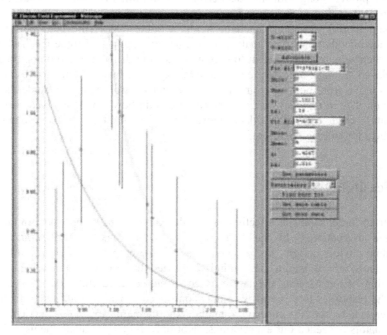

Fig. 3. Screen shot of the Analysis Mode of the electric field laboratory.

3.3   Interface Design

The principal components of the laboratory are presented as two screens, the experimental screen and the data analysis screen. In both experimental and data analysis phases, considerable care was taken to ensure that the force feedback associated with interface objects (environment) was clearly distinguishable from that associated with the electric field experiment (content) (See Appendix). The design included two frames – an interface frame (on the right side of the screen) and a content frame (on the left side of the screen). Throughout the entire laboratory, screen-reading software voiced the text and user interface items; however, a screen reader is optional if the student is not blind.

In experiment mode, the force on the test charge could be felt at the mouse pointer position. The force vector was also visible as an arrow. An audible warning indicated the boundaries of the charge field; optionally, an additional force field was available that allowed the student to feel the contour of the charge. Once the experiment phase had been initiated, the student could collect data on charge position and the force on the charge via a simple user interface. This interface provided controls to alter the size and charge parameters of the electric charge, to display the numeric values of the current cursor position and force vector, and to show the number of data points already collected. From the interface frame, the student could also view a table of collected data, or enter data analysis mode.

Having collected their data, the student entered the data analysis mode. Here their data were plotted along with statistical error bars and fitted curves. The student could zoom in on a region of the curve by drawing a rectangle over the region of interest, and could modify fitting parameters. Again, audible and tactile cues defined the workspace boundary. In data analysis mode, several regimes of force feedback were available encouraging the student to explore data from different viewpoints. Data can be displayed as single attracting points, as a curve or as a tour (i.e. the mouse could be made to move from point to point under computer control taking the student's hand along with it.) In this way, the student can ascertain how closely a given curve fits their data. Such exploratory data analysis, which has eluded blind students and researchers for so long, therefore becomes a reality.

4   Feasibility Study

In order to understand the effectiveness of the curriculum, Immersion conducted a two-stage evaluation. In the first stage, an educational expert evaluated the curriculum module design. In the second stage of the project, a panel of four experts and students, all of whom were blind, evaluated the curriculum module. Upon completion of the module, they were asked to answer a carefully designed survey. Using the responses to this survey, Immersion hoped to gather information to enable improvements to both the curriculum module and the hardware. The experience with the evaluators exceeded our expectations. Not only did they validate the use of force feedback for accessible education, they had many useful comments on technical issues that will improve our interactions with blind users in the next phase of the project.

All evaluators were quite enthusiastic about the force feedback aspects of the curriculum. Negative comments were largely focused on other important issues such as the installation procedure, curriculum module instructions, and screen reader problems. This evaluator's responses to the following questions illustrate the positive impact of force feedback:

Q. Did feeling the forces of the electric charge affect your understanding of the physical phenomena? If so, how? Why? If not, what would improve it?
A. Yes. I didn't realize that the charge would always be greatest at the boundary of the sphere. Using the control key while moving through the electric field allowed me to explore this.

Q. Did feeling the data points and the fitted plot affect your ability to interpret the experimental data? If so, how? Why? If not, what would improve it?
A. Yes. I particularly liked the "jump to point" mode, because this gave me a good feel for the relationship between the points on the graph.

Q. Overall, did force-feedback affect your ability to learn the material?
A. Yes. Feeling the behavior of a physical system in this way makes it possible for blind people to understand it, much as a quick-time movie of a simulation might help sighted students.

Q. Do you have any additional comments concerning the experience, or suggestions for the use of force feedback in educational applications?
A. Yes. I think force feedback has great potential in educational applications, particularly where it is necessary to explain dynamically changing behavior of systems.

Another evaluator had this general comment:
"I can't even begin to enumerate the possible applications, but I can see this technology being valuable across a wide range of disciplines and to students and professionals with a range of learning styles and capacities. Also, I think that there are many applications where the haptic feedback in combination with aural feedback could be potentially very useful. ... The possibilities seem almost endless -- so much so that it may be more efficient to sort out the applications where there would be limited usefulness for this technology."

An adventitiously blind evaluator felt that force feedback would be valuable regardless of students' vision status:
"When I was in high school (and had 20/20 vision) I would have loved to have something like this available that would allow me to explore various phenomena that would otherwise have been impractical to recreate in a laboratory."

In summary, the responses to the evaluation survey lead us to believe that force feedback can provide information to the blind student not available through traditional access technologies.

5   Challenges and Lessons

Creating an Internet-deployed science education curriculum module presented Immersion with new logistical and technological challenges. Unlike a laboratory environment where hardware and software configuration can be tightly controlled, our evaluators were responsible for installing software and hardware on their own systems. Force feedback software and hardware were still in the prototyping stage, adding to the complexity of the installation process. Moreover, evaluators used different screen reading software packages, which in turn interacted with the Windows operating system in subtly different ways. A large amount of effort was unavoidably devoted to ensuring that the force feedback software and hardware was properly installed on the evaluator's systems. The lessons learned from this experience have influenced the subsequent design of Immersions installation tools. In addition, it was not possible to observe closely how much time evaluators spent on the curriculum activities. Based on these experiences, future studies will take place in more controlled settings with on-site technical support.

Web deployment itself presents challenges for distribution of haptic content. Force-feedback is fundamentally high-bandwidth and computationally intensive, however we need to present complex physical phenomena on weak computers over slow Internet connections. Immersion's TouchSense technology overcomes some of these constraints through the application of an embedded controller. This embedded controller can only display a finite set of low-level primitives. For this study, we were able to leverage this architecture to display more complex effects. Over the course of this project, Immersion created new technologies that allow high-level effects, such as electric fields, to be displayed in the constrained, inexpensive realm of Internet-deployed science education.

6   Summary and Future Work

A key result of this project was the proof-of-concept curriculum module that demonstrated accessible, Web-based science education using force feedback. The curriculum module served as both a test bed for accessibility concepts and as a progressive force feedback application that demanded substantial core technology development.

Responses of evaluators to a post-evaluation survey clearly indicate that haptic feedback was a useful tool for realizing the behavior of a dynamical system and a potentially viable modality for presenting non-text content such as data plots for blind computer users. Encouraged by the results of this pilot study, the authors have begun the second phase of this project, which will include the development of a broader range of science curriculum modules and a large-scale user study with blind high school students.

Acknowledgements

The National Science Foundation supported this work through an SBIR (Small Business Innovation Research) grant, Award No. DMI-9860813. Jon Gunderson at the University of Illinois, Urbana-Champagne, provided feedback on the force feedback curriculum module and tested it with his students. Dr. Norman Lederman of the Department of Science and Mathematics Education at the Oregon State University College of Science contributed to the user evaluation survey. Several anonymous testers gave generously of their time to provide feedback on the efficacy of the curriculum module.

References

1. Dufresne, A.: Multimodal user interface system for blind and "visually occupied" users: Ergonomic evaluation of the haptic and auditive dimensions. Proceedings of Human-Computer Interaction. Interact '95 (1995) p. 163-168.
2. Ramstein, C., et al.: Touching and hearing GUIs - Design Issues in PC-Access systems. Proceedings of the International conference on assistive technologies ACM/SIGCAPH ASSETS'96, (1996) p. 2-9.
3. O'Modhrain and Gillespie: The Moose: A Haptic User Interface for Blind Persons. Proceedings of the WWW6 (1996).
4. Asghar, M.W.: Multiresolution representation of data in a haptic environment. Telemanipulator and Telepresence Technologies V. Proceedings of the SPIE - The International Society for Optical Engineering. 3524, (1998) p. 159-169.
5. Grabowski, N.A.: Data visualization methods for the blind using force feedback and sonification. Proceedings of the SPIE - The International Society for Optical Engineering 3524 (1998) p. 131-139.
6. Fritz, J.P.: Design of a haptic graphing system. Proceedings of the RESNA '96 Annual Conference Exploring New Horizons... Pioneering the 21st Century (1996A) p. 158-160.
7. Fritz, J.P.: Design of a haptic data visualization system for people with visual impairments. IEEE TRANSACTIONS ON REHABILITATION ENGINEERING 7, 3 (1999) p. 372-384.
8. Ramstein, C., and Century, M.: Navigation on the Web using Haptic Feedback. Proceedings of the international symposium on Electronic Art ISEA'96.
9. Hardwick, A.: Tactile display of virtual reality from the World Wide Web-a potential access method for blind people. DISPLAYS (1998) 18, 3 p. 153-161.
10. Colwell, C.: Haptic virtual reality for blind computer users. Proceedings of ASSETS'98. Third International ACM Conference on Assistive Technologies (1998) p. 92-99.
11. Fritz, J.P.: Stochastic models for haptic texture. Proceedings of the SPIE - The International Society for Optical Engineering 2901 (1996B) p. 34-44.

Appendix: Key Accessibility Features of the Curriculum

Many accessibility features were incorporated into the electric field laboratory. The following list describes the most important of these features. This list serves as the beginning of a design guidebook for the authoring of accessible multi-modal, Web-based multimedia. It is important to note that many of these accessibility features are unrelated to force feedback. Although force feedback is an integral aspect of the curriculum module, accessible design requires a holistic, multi-modal approach. Oregon State and Immersion Corporation were extremely sensitive to these issues.

! ∀ Two regimes of forces in experimental mode (electric force or objects) allow a blind student to clearly feel the environment of the experiment and the physical processes involved.

! ∀ Several regimes of forces in data processing mode (data points feeling, curve feeling, data point touring) give a blind student the capability to study data in a means similar to that of a sighted student using an image of data plot.

! ∀ The Web browser window is resized automatically to occupy the biggest possibly area of user the screen. This offers a bigger area for the experimental field or data plot field in the force-feedback mouse workspace. This lets the student feel force details better.

! ∀ Instructions are written in a way that allows a blind student with a screen reader to have access to the mathematical formulas used in text (via ALT text).

! ∀ User interface forms are designed for clear reading and easy navigation using a screen reader (e.g., one input field with associated caption per line).

! ∀ All essential user interface commands are available via keyboard. In particular, data collection is done via the keyboard because it was found to be too hard for a student to click the mouse button while keeping the mouse steady under external forces.

! ∀ Different sounds (when mouse pointer crosses experimental field boundaries, charged sphere boundary, or data plot boundary) allow the blind student to know   where the mouse pointer is located.

! ∀ Confirmation sounds (during data point collection and during data point enumeration) help the student to be sure about a correct program response.

! ∀ Collected and processed data are represented in editable text tables, which are accessible and allow simple navigation.

Communicating with Feeling

Ian Oakley, Stephen Brewster, and Philip Gray

Department of Computing Science, University of Glasgow
Glasgow, UK, G12 8QQ
{io,stephen,pdg}@dcs.gla.ac.uk

Abstract. Communication between users in shared editors takes place in a deprived environment – distributed users find it difficult to communicate. While many solutions to the problems this causes have been suggested this paper presents a novel one. It describes one possible use of haptics as a channel for communication between users. User's telepointers are considered as haptic avatars and interactions such as haptically pushing and pulling each other are afforded. The use of homing forces to locate other users is also discussed, as is a proximity sensation based on viscosity. Evaluation of this system is currently underway.

1 Introduction

Synchronous shared editors provide a canvas on which multiple distributed users can simultaneously create content, for instance a shared whiteboard or textual document [1, 13]. Despite the prevalence of full duplex audio and video links in implementations of these systems, communication between collaborators still occurs in a deprived environment. A person is removed from the rich multi-sensory environment of the real world and required to work in a complex, often social, setting through the primitive communicative medium of a window, or several windows, on a screen.

One of the most critical deprivations in these environments is that of the awareness [5, 15]. Gutwin *et al.* [9] define workspace awareness to include:
"...knowledge about who is in the workspace, where they are working, what they are doing and what they intend to do next."

Awareness refers to the background, low fidelity, knowledge of the positions, actions and intentions of other people. In real world interactions we gather this information through casual glances at other workers, our peripheral vision, or through the sounds others make as they work. We gather awareness information from the world around us in a host of subtle and sophisticated ways and weave this rich tapestry of information into a background picture of what, and where, work is going on.

Coupled strongly to this concept of awareness is that of observed attention [11]. This refers to the ability to know what another person is focusing on or referring to simply by observing their behaviour. This ability, typically characterised in the real

S. Brewster, R. Murray-Smith (Eds.): Haptic HCI 2000, LNCS 2058, pp. 61-68, 2001.

world by the ability to see where someone is looking or pointing, makes talking about complex information simpler by providing a straightforward way of ensuring all participants are referring to the same object.

Information pertaining to gestures is also beneficial. Gestures in communication are of two types. Firstly gestures to aid the flow of a conversation, for instance eye contact and secondly bodily gestures, typically of the hands or arms, to illustrate, or re-enforce, the information presented in the conversation. Eye contact is important in conversation not only because it aids token passing but also because it is the medium for the transmission of a large amount of important emotional content [12]. Tang & Minneman stress the importance of bodily gestures [17]. In observational studies of several group drawing activities they concluded that hand gestures are used regularly and productively in groups to :

"...act out sequences of events, refer to a locus of attention, or mediate their interaction...."

It is clear that gestural information of both kinds is important in communication.

Many solutions to address these issues have been put forward. Typically they involve trying to enhance one of the existing communication channels. For instance video can be improved if it allows participants to maintain eye contact [11]. Non-speech audio feedback has also been shown to be effective [8]. A variety of on screen graphical widgets, such as telepointers and radar views have also been shown to help reduce these problems [9]. Telepointers are local cursors representing each remote user. They allow basic graphical gesturing and provide some measure of awareness information. Radar views provide a small map of the workspace including a small telepointer for each user.

In this paper we present a novel approach to address these issues in the form of the relatively unexplored area of haptic communication. Although there is little work on this topic, the work that does exist is promising. Brave & Dahley [2] state:

"Touch is a fundamental aspect of interpersonal communication. Whether a greeting handshake, an encouraging pat on the back, or a comforting hug, physical contact is a basic means through which people achieve a sense of connection, indicate intention, and express emotion."

The majority of work on haptic communication has reflected this statement and focused on intimate interpersonal communication.

Perhaps the first communicative haptic environment was Telephonic Arm Wrestling [18] which was an art exhibit consisting of a pair of spatially separated robot arms which allowed two remote users to arm wrestle with one another. Several devices have been developed on a similar theme. The shaker in Feather, Scent and Shaker [16] allowed users to shake a device in their hand and have this represented as vibration in another users coupled device. The Bed [4] attempted to create a distributed bed and used haptics to create a sensation of the remote partner breathing. inTouch, [2, 3] is a device consisting of three rollers. Moving a roller causes a similar movement in a connected device. This provides a richer feedback than the previous systems as each roller can be manipulated, either clockwise or anticlockwise, independently of the others. These systems are characterised by a lack of reported evaluation of any sort.

Perhaps the most sophisticated device in this area is HandJive [7], which was developed as a toy to support people's desire to fidget when listening to a group presentation such as a lecture. It consisted of a pair of cylinders, joined together at the centre. Each cylinder could rotate around this joint to lock into one of five discrete positions (including straight). A change in position of the device was reflected in other coupled devices. HandJive differs from inTouch in that a pair of users could only move the device along opposite axes, meaning that users could not fight over the position of the device. The researchers suggest that two users could co-operatively construct "dances", or perhaps play simple games using the device. This device was developed iteratively and although no formal evaluation took place the authors report that users of the various prototypes were positive about the device and the interactions that it afforded.

It is possible that haptics can have more impact than simply acting as a conduit for interpersonal communication. Durlach & Slater [6] speculate that the sense of touch may be vital to the sense of presence that users perceive in Collaborative Virtual Environments (CVEs). They reason that the ability to feel objects or other users would enhance feelings of interaction and direct manipulation which have been linked with an increased sense of presence. They also refer to touch not being a "distance sense" – if we are to feel something it must be close to us, making a simulation more compelling. Finally, they suggest that users are unused to receiving illusions of touch and are continually bombarded with artificial visual and auditory stimuli, and therefore haptic simulations are more likely to draw users in and increase their subjective experiences of presence. This last effect would obviously hold only while haptic simulations are a rarity.

In a companion paper to the one described above Ho *et al.* [10] discuss how both performance and a sense of "togetherness" are increased with the addition of haptics to a simulation of the physical task of co-operatively steering a ring along a wire. While these results were statistically significant, they were over a small sample of users and were based on an unvalidated questionnaire. Furthermore the ecological validity of testing user performance with and without haptics in a physical task is questionable. The authors admit that this work is non-conclusive and ongoing.

The sum total of this research is that, while little of it is formal, it does seem that haptics can be advantageous to communication. Observational reports in a number of papers suggest that touch does enhance a users sense of interaction and presence. Users enjoy the experience of communicating through touch in a variety of situations and feel confident interacting with one another through this modality.

2   Haptics in Shared Editors

Given the discussion of some of the problems of shared editors – awareness, attention and gesturing – the question arises as to how haptics be applied to solve these problems. This paper presents the idea of enabling haptic cursor interactions between collaborators. Telepointers are transformed from being a simple graphical representation of position to physical avatars in the virtual space that can haptically influence one another. Five types of interaction between these avatars have been implemented.

Firstly, the telepointers can push one another around the workspace. As one cursor encroaches on another both can feel a force pushing them apart, or if one cursor intersects another at speed then the other cursor will be pushed away. We hypothesise this would be used as a warning, for instance if a user was about to perform some disastrous action another user might attempt to push the first user aside in order to prevent this. Another potential use would be to catch another user's attention, the remote equivalent of a tap to the shoulder. This interaction is reminiscent of others in the literature – for instance both the arm wrestling simulation [18] and inTouch [2] are basically mechanisms that allow distributed users to push against one another. In this instance, however, the pushing simulation is much more complex, as it is embedded within the context of a spatial workspace – to push a user you must first locate that user, and as you push them they can retreat away from you. Currently the push effect is implemented with each cursor being represented by a frictionless sphere. A consequence of this is that it is difficult for cursors to push each other uniformly; they tend to slip and slide off each other. A more complex haptic simulation, including friction, or possibly even an attractive force between cursors involved in a push interaction might prove more useful.

Secondly, to extend the technique of gesturing with telepointers, a telepointer can haptically take hold of another by moving over it and depressing a button. Once held subsequent movements are played back haptically to the other cursor until the button is released. This operation has the effect of grabbing a pointer and then making it follow your path. While this is far from directly analogous to how gestures are perceived in reality, it does considerably extend and make concrete the basic gesturing function of telepointers. You can firmly and interactively transmit a complex spatial pattern to a remote user, without words.

There were some problems in implementing the gesture. The basic algorithm involved storing key points along the path of the gesture, based upon the distance of the current point to the previous key point. This distance was small, typically within 5 mm, to maintain the fidelity of the gesture. When the gesture begins an attractive force towards the first point in the gesture is applied to the user. The magnitude of this force increases with the range from the user to the point. When the user comes within a certain target range of the point the focus of the gesture moves on to the subsequent key point. Again to maintain the fidelity of the gesture this target range was kept small: 1 cm. This procedure iterates for all the points in the gesture. This is summed up in Figure 1.

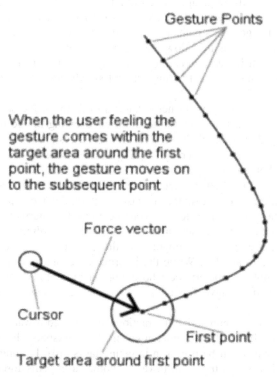

Gesture Points

When the user feeling the gesture comes within the target area around the first point, the gesture moves on to the subsequent point

Force vector

Cursor

First point

Target area around first point

Fig. 1. Depiction of a gesture.

However, we noticed that using this system, users experienced difficulties – they became lost and unable to follow the gesture. We attributed this to the fact that forces of attraction used are relatively weak and become weaker as a user approaches a target area, making it difficult to locate these areas. There were several solutions to this problem. As we had mapped larger forces to greater distances we did not want to simply increase the magnitude of the forces when users became close to a point. Nor did we want to increase the size of the range at which a user is said to have reached a point as doing this would reduce the fidelity of the gesture – small perturbations would not be recorded. We also felt that it would be easier for users to detect changes in the direction of a force rather than just its magnitude.

To achieve these goals we smoothed the gestures. As time went by without the user reaching the currently active key point in the gesture the target area around that point would increase. Eventually it would encompass the user, at which stage the simulation would turn it's attention to the subsequent point in the gesture, with a small active range once more. Moving the simulation along the path of the gesture even while the user remains stationary means that the magnitude and direction of the force applied to the user will continually change. A further consequence of this is that if a person ignores the forces from a gesture then eventually all they will feel is a force to the last point of the gesture – the details would have been smoothed away. This algorithm has the benefits of initially presenting the user with an accurate representation of the gesture and then gradually reducing its resolution. In this reduction of resolution it also ensures that a user is presented with vectors of varying magnitude and direction while remaining on the gesture's path. The algorithm also only reduces resolution as it needs to – if a person begins to follow the gesture closely after losing it for a short time, the resolution will increase once more. A temporal aspect to the gesture is also added. If you ignore the gesture for long, it will slowly lose detail and eventually vanish.

Finally, this gesture effect was further enhanced to factor in the speed of the user recording the gesture. The force applied to the user receiving the gesture was varied according to the speed at which the person recording the gesture was moving, above a certain minimum. This allows users to highlight or emphasise certain parts of a gesture by varying their speed.

The third interaction between the telepointers is designed to provide some simple awareness information. The resistance to movement of the workspace is made to change when another user draws near to your position. Or alternatively, if you are stationary when another approaches, a small vibration is applied. This provides a haptic proximity sense and is analogous to the physical sensation of presence perceived when close to another. While the information content of this effect is low, for instance it will not help determine who is approaching, nor from what direction they hail, it is hoped to have the advantage of being obvious while remaining unintrusive.

The remaining two communicative interactions are focused towards the awareness problem of being unable to locate other users in the workspace. Previous work on haptics has shown that it can be useful in targeting tasks [14]. Finding homing force on their cursor which would tug them towards another user. This force is applied at two levels. Initially a small force is applied, which allows a user to determine in what direction another user is located. After a brief time this force is increased to actually guide the user towards the other's position. The final interaction is an inverse version of the locate effect. This grab interaction allows users to turn on a homing force which pulls all other users in the workspace towards their position. This allows a user to request other users to come to some location in the document without being burdened by having to describe that location. It was hoped that these two effects would facilitate easier navigation and co-ordination between users in the workspace.

A final consideration in the design of this haptic communication was how intrusive it could be. A user working on a diagram, for instance, would probably not appreciate the application of arbitrary forces by other users. The push, gesture, and grab interactions allow a user to haptically influence another user with intrusive forces and the grab interaction in particular does this without any associated visual feedback. Modes are a potential solution to this problem. Three modes are suggested – working, communication and observation. In the working mode a user can interact with the canvas and can create content, but cannot be haptically influenced by another user. In the communication mode, users cannot interact with the canvas but have access to the haptic communication. In the observation mode, users can neither communicate haptically nor access the canvas. In our current use of a two-dimensional canvas and three-dimensional haptic device (the PHANToM from SensAble Technologies), these three modes are mapped to the z-axis of the device. Closest to the canvas is the working mode, beyond that the communication mode and, furthest away, is the observation mode. We feel that this mapping supports the physical metaphor of the canvas. You must be on the canvas to work, near the canvas to interact with other workers and when far from the canvas, you can simply watch.

Acknowledgements

This research was supported under EPSRC project GR/L79212 and EPSRC studentship 98700418. Thanks must also go to the SHEFC REVELATION Project, SensAble Technologies and Virtual Presence Ltd.

References

1. Baecker, R., Glass, G., Mitchell, A., and Posner, I. *Sasse: The Collaborative Editor.* in *Proceedings of CHI'94.*(1994), Boston, United States, ACM Press, 459-460.
2. Brave, S. and Dahley, A. *inTouch: A Medium for Haptic Interpersonal Communication.* in *Proceedings of CHI'97.*(1997), ACM Press, 363-364.
3. Brave, S., Ishii, H., and Dahley, A. *Tangible Interfaces for Remote Collaboration and Communication.* in *Proceedings of CSCW'98.*(1998), Seattle, Washington, ACM Press, 169-178.
4. Dodge, C. *The Bed: A Medium for Intimate Communication.* in *Proceedings of CHI'97.*(1997), Atlanta, GA USA, ACM Press, 371-372.
5. Dourish, P., and Bellotti, V. *Awareness and Coordination in Shared Workspaces.* in *Proceedings of CSCW'92.*(1992), Toronto, Canada, ACM Press, 107-114.
6. Durlach, N., and Slater, M., *Presence in Shared Virtual Environments and Virtual Togetherness*, in *BT Presence Workshop,*(1998), http://www.cs.ucl.ac.uk/staff/m.slater/BTWorkshop/durlach.html
7. Fogg, B.J., Cutler, L.D., Arnold, P., and Eisbach, C. *HandJive: A Device for Interpersonal Haptic Entertainment.* in *Proceedings of CHI'98.*(1998), Los Angeles, CA, ACM Press, 57-64.
8. Gaver, W., Smith, R.B., and O'Shea, T. *Effective Sounds in Complex Systems: the Arkola Simulation.* in *Proceedings of CHI'91.*(1991), New Orleans, LA, ACM Press, 85-90.
9. Gutwin, C., Roseman, M., and Greenberg, S. *A Usability Study of Awareness Widgets in a Shared Workspace Groupware System.* in *Proceedings of CSCW'96.*(1996), Boston, MA USA, ACM Press, 258-267.
10. Ho, C., Basdogan, C., Slater, M., Durlach, N., and Srinivasan, M.A. *An Experiment on the influence of Haptic Communication on the Sense of Being Together*, in *BT Presence Workshop,*(1998), http://www.cs.ucl.ac.uk/staff/m.slater/BTWorkshop/TouchExp/index.html
11. Ishii, H., and Koyayashi, M. *ClearBoard: A seamless Medium for Shared Drawing and Conversation with Eye Contact.* in *Proceedings of CHI'92.*(1992), Monterey, CA USA, ACM Press, 525-532.
12. Mantei, M.M., Baecker, R.M., Sellen, A.J., Buxton, W.A.S., and Milligan, T. *Experiences in the Use of a Media Space.* in *Proceedings of CHI'91.*(1991), New Orleans, LA, ACM Press, 203-208.

13. Minneman, S.L. and Bly, S.A. *Managing a Trois: a Study of a Multi-user Drawing Tool in Distributed Design Work*. in *Proceedings of Conference on Human Factors and Computing Systems*.(1991), New Orleans, LA USA, ACM Press, 217-224.
14. Oakley, I., McGee, M.R., Brewster, S.A., and Gray, P.D. *Putting the feel into look and feel*. in *Proceedings of CHI'2000*.(2000), The Hague, NL, ACM Press, 415-422.
15. Pedersen, E.R., and Sokoler, T. *AROMA: abstract representation of presence supporting mutual awareness*. in *Proceedings of CHI'97*.(1997), Atlanta, ACM Press, 51-58.
16. Strong, R., and Gaver, B. *Feather, Scent & Shaker*. in *Proceedings of CSCW'96*.(1996), Boston, MA, USA, ACM Press, 363-364.
17. Tang, J.C., and Minneman, S.L., *VideoDraw: A Video Interface for Collaborative Drawing*. ACM Transactions on Information Systems, (1991). **9**(2): 170-184.
18. White, N., and Back, D., *Telephonic Arm Wrestling*, 1986),
http://www.bmts.com/~normill/artpage.html

Improved Precision in Mediated Collaborative Manipulation of Objects by Haptic Force Feedback

Eva-Lotta Sallnäs

Interaction and Presentation Laboratory
Royal Institute of Technology, S-100 44 Stockholm, Sweden
evalotta@nada.kth.se

Abstract. The extent that haptic force feedback affects people's ability to collaborate in a mediated way has not been investigated much. In this paper an experiment is presented where collaboration in a distributed desktop virtual environment with haptic force feedback was studied. A video analysis of the frequency of failures to lift cubes collaboratively in a haptic condition compared to a condition with no haptic force feedback was conducted. The frequency of failures to lift cubes collaboratively is a measure of precision in task performance. The statistical analysis of the data shows that it is significantly more difficult to lift objects collaboratively in a three-dimensional desktop virtual environment without haptic force feedback.

1   Introduction

In this paper results are presented from an experimental study of interaction in a collaborative desktop virtual environment, where the independent variable was haptic force feedback. Haptic sensing is defined as the use of motor behaviours in combination with touch to identify objects [1]. The PHANToM (SensAble Technologies Inc. of Boston, MA), a one-point haptic device was used for the haptic force feedback, and a program especially developed for the purpose provided the collaborative virtual environment. The program enables for two individuals placed in different locations to simultaneously feel and manipulate dynamic objects in a shared desktop virtual environment. The aim of this paper is to present results from an analysis of the video recorded collaboration between subjects. The focus of the analysis was to investigate how haptic force feedback affected the precision in manipulating objects collaboratively in the desktop virtual environment.

In an earlier analysis of data from this experiment it was shown [7] that haptic force feedback significantly increases task performance, which meant that the tasks were completed in less time in the haptic force feedback condition. All pairs of subjects succeeded in completing all tasks, which proves that it was possible to manipulate the PHANToM satisfactorily in both conditions. Results from a questionnaire that measured perceived performance showed that the subjects in the haptic feedback condition perceived themselves as performing tasks significantly better. Results also showed that haptic force feedback significantly improves perceived virtual presence in the collaborative distributed environment, measured by a questionnaire. Virtual

S. Brewster, R. Murray-Smith (Eds.): Haptic HCI 2000, LNCS 2058, pp. 69-75, 2001.

presence was in this experimental study defined as the subjective experience of being in one place or environment, even when one is physically situated in another. Finally the results showed that haptic force feedback did not increase perceived social presence significantly, also measured by a questionnaire. The definition of social presence in this experimental study was feeling that one is socially present with another person at a remote location.

The results from the analysis in this paper show in more detail how performance is affected by haptic force feedback for joint manipulation of virtual objects.

2   Background

A small number of studies have investigated interaction with haptic force feedback interfaces. Gupta, Sheridan and Whitney [4] investigated the effect of haptic force feedback in one study were the task was to put a peg in a hole, simulating an assembly task. Two PHANToM's were employed for haptics in order for the user to be able to grasp objects with the thumb and the index finger. Results showed that haptic force feedback shortened task completion times. Also, Hasser, Goldenberg, Martin and Rosenberg [5] showed in their study that the addition of force feedback to a computer mouse improved targeting performance and decreased targeting errors.

These studies did not investigate collaborative performance but single human computer interaction. However, in one study, subjects were asked to play a collaborative game in a virtual environment with one experimenter who was an "expert" player. The players could feel objects in the common environment. They were asked to move a ring on a wire in collaboration with each other in such a way that contacts between the wire and the ring was minimised or avoided. Results from this study indicate that haptic communication improves task performance [2, 3]. Results from another study suggest that if people have the opportunity to "feel" the interface they are collaborating in, they manipulate the interface faster and more precisely [6]. The experimental task in this study required one subject to hand over a virtual object to another subject.

3   Method

3.1   Subjects

Twenty-eight subjects participated in the experiment. The subjects performed the experiment in pairs and there were 14 pairs, each consisting of one woman and one man (Fig. 1). The subjects, who were students from Lund University in Sweden, were between 20-31 years old and their mean age was 23 years. The subjects did not know each other and did not meet prior to the experiment. During the experiment the subjects were located in different rooms, unaware of each other's physical location.

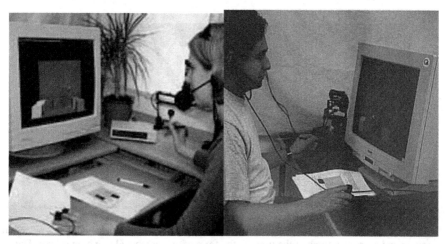

Fig. 1. Subjects are doing tasks using two versions of the PHANToM, on the left a "T" model and on the right an "A" model.

3.2   Apparatus

The haptic display system used in this investigation was a PHANToM (Fig. 1), from SensAble Technologies Inc. of Boston, MA. Two PHANToMs, placed in two different rooms linked to a single host computer, were used for the experiment. Both PHANToMs were identical in operation, but were of different models. One was attached to the table (the "A" model) and the other was attached hanging upside down (an older "T" model). Two 21-inch computer screens were used to display the graphical information to the users, one for each user in the different locations. The screens, attached via a video splitter to the host computer, showed identical views of the virtual environment. Headsets (GN Netcom) provided audio communication via a telephone connection. The headsets had two earpieces and one microphone each. A video camera was used to record the interaction from one of the locations and a tape recorder recorded the sound at the other location. The angle of video recording was from behind the subject and slightly from the side so that the computer screen and the hand with which the person was controlling the PHANToM were visible.

3.3   Independent Variable

The collaborative desktop virtual interface was the independent variable in the experiment and there were two conditions, one three-dimensional visual /audio/haptic interface and one three-dimensional visual/audio interface. The only variable feature was haptic force feedback. The haptic environment consisted of a room with constraining walls, ceiling and floor and it contained eight dynamic cubes that initially were placed on the floor (Fig. 2).

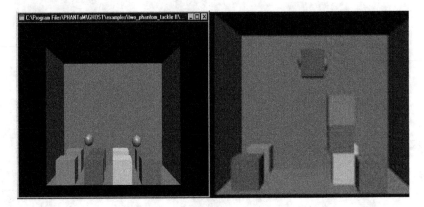

Fig. 2. Two views of the collaborative virtual environment with eight dynamic cubes placed in the room and representations of the users in the form of one green and one blue sphere. The right picture shows two subjects lifting a cube together.

The cubes were modelled to simulate simplified cubes with form, mass, damping and surface friction, but lacked e.g. the ability to rotate. The cubes were identical in dynamic behaviour, form and mass but were of four different colours (green, blue, yellow and orange, two of each) to make them easily distinguishable. The subjects could lift the cubes in two different ways. Either the users collaborated in lifting the cubes by pressing into the cube from opposite sides and lifting upwards simultaneously, or a single user lifted a cube by pressing it against the wall and pushing it upwards. The subjects were represented by spheres in the graphical environment which were distinguishable by colour (one was blue, the other green). In the version without haptic force feedback the PHANToM functioned solely as a 3D mouse, as the user could feel neither the cubes, nor the walls, nor the other user in the environment.

3.4   Tasks

In the experimental study each collaborating pair of subjects was presented with five tasks (A-E). All pairs of subjects managed to complete all tasks. For the analysis in this paper, data on the frequency of failures to lift the cubes collaboratively were collected for two of the five tasks. These were task A and task C which both required subjects to lift cubes in order to complete the task. Task A consisted of lifting eight cubes together in order to build one cube, without getting a visual illustration. Task C consisted of lifting eight cubes together in order to build two piles. Both subjects in each pair got a visual illustration for task C (Fig. 3).

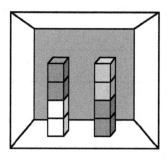

Fig. 3. The visual illustration of task C.

The subjects tried all the important features in the environment for approximately two minutes in order for them to establish an understanding of how the environment functioned.

4   Video Analysis

The video recordings generate reliable data about the navigation and manipulation of cubes of both subjects in the virtual desktop environment. Both subjects' behaviour in the three dimensional environment can thus be studied. In both conditions but especially in the condition without haptic force feedback, the subjects did not always manage to lift or transport the cubes. Reasons for these failures were that they did not position their representations (with their PHANToM) correctly or that they could not co-ordinate joint movements appropriately. In this study the video recordings were analysed in order to collect the frequency of failures to lift the cubes collaboratively as a measure of precision in task performance. The operational definition of failure to lift a cube were, that two subjects positioned their representations beside one cube and tried to lift it, but failed to lift or transport the cube in order to proceed one step in performing the task. Data on the frequency of failures to lift the cubes collaboratively were only collected for task A and task C.

5   Results

Frequencies of failures to lift cubes together were analysed with ANOVA (analysis of variance). Results show that there is a significant difference (Table 1) between conditions regarding subjects' ability to lift cubes in task A (p=0.003) and in task C (p=0.011). In the haptic force feedback condition subjects failed to lift cubes on average 4 times in task A, and 7 times in task C. In the condition without haptic force feedback subjects failed to lift cubes on average 12 times in task A, and 30 times in task C.

Table 1. Frequency of failures when lifting cubes together in pairs, in a haptic and non-haptic condition respectively.

Failure to lift cubes together			Haptic feedback	No haptic feedback
Task A (n=14) F=15	p= 0.003 **		M=4	M=12
Task C (n=14) F=9	p=0.011*		M=7	M=30

* = significant at 95% level
** = significant at 99% level

This should be compared to the results that show that there was no significant difference between conditions regarding how many successful lifts the subjects performed in order to complete task A (p=0.32) and task C (p=0.67).

6   Conclusions

The results of this study are consistent with the earlier results that show that haptic force feedback improves performance when the task is to lift cubes collaboratively [7]. The earlier results suggested that it took significantly longer time to perform tasks in the condition without haptic force feedback. In the earlier analysis subjects also judged their performance as significantly better in the haptic environment. The analysis that is presented in this paper show that it is significantly more difficult to coordinate actions with the aim of lifting objects in a three-dimensional desktop virtual environment without haptic force feedback. These results show that a major part of the difference regarding time to perform tasks can be explained by the fact that subjects' precision when lifting cubes without haptic force feedback is significantly lower.

It should be noted that even in the haptic condition manipulation of virtual cubes was not effortless and subjects did fail a number of times even with haptic force feedback. But subjects performed the actions that they had planned more consistently and they did not shift strategy in the collaborative task as often because of failure to lift a cube.

Acknowledgments

Kirsten Rassmus-Gröhn and Calle Sjöström are gratefully acknowledged for the contribution of the software that made it possible to use the PHANToMs collaboratively, and for the assistance in managing the PHANToM hardware. Without their work this experiment would not have been possible to perform. I would also like to thank Kerstin Severinson-Eklundh for her valuable comments and suggestions.

References

1. Appelle, S. (1991). Haptic perception of form: Activity and stimulus attributes. In Heller, M., Schiff, W. (Eds), The psychology of touch. New Jersey: Lawrence Erlbaum Associates, Inc. 169-188.
2. Basdogan, C., Ho, C., Slater, M., and Srinivasan, M.A. (1998). The Role of Haptic Communication in Shared Virtual Environments. Proc. of the PHANTOM™ User Group.
3. Durlach, N., and Slater, M. (1998). Presence in shared virtual environments and virtual togetherness. BT Presence Workshop.
4. Gupta, R., Sheridan, T., and Whitney, D. (1997) Experiments Using Multimodal Virtual Environments in Design for Assembly Analysis. Presence: Teleoperators and Virtual Environments. 6(3), pp. 318-338.
5. Hasser, C.J. Goldenberg, A.S., Martin, K.M., and Rosenberg, L. B. (1998). User Performing a GUI Pointing Task with a Low-Cost Force-Feedback Computer Mouse, DSC-Vol. 64, Proc. of the ASME Dynamics and Control Division, pp. 151-156.
6. Ishii, M., Nakata, M., and Sato, M. (1994). Networked SPIDAR: A Networked Virtual Environment with Visual, Auditory, and Haptic Interactions. Presence: Teleoperators and Virtual Environments. 3(4), pp. 351-359.
7. Sallnäs, E-L., Rassmus-Gröhn, K., and Sjöström, C. (In press). Supporting Presence in Collaborative Environments by Haptic Force Feedback. Accepted for publication in ACM Transactions on Computer-Human Interaction.

Hand-Shaped Force Interface for Human-Cooperative Mobile Robot

Riku Hikiji and Shuji Hashimoto

Humanoid Research Institute, Waseda University
3-4-1 Okubo, Shinjuku-ku, Tokyo 169-8555, Japan
{riku,shuji}@shalab.phys.waseda.ac.jp
http://www.phys.waseda.ac.jp/shalab/

Abstract. Aiming at realization of direct and intuitive cooperation between human and robot, we develop an interface system for a mobile robot that can take physical communication with its user via hand-to-hand force interaction. The hand-shaped device equipped on the robot with a flexible rubber-made arm can sense the intentional force exerted by its user. The finger part can be actuated in 1 DOF to achieve haptic force feedback. The robot also has bumper sensors and ultrasonic sensors around the body. The balance of the intentional force and the environmental condition determines the robot's motion. In this research, we design simple algorithms for both human-following and human-leading motions, and devise experiments with human users. Qualitative and quantitative evaluations of the experimental results are also presented.

Keywords. Human-machine interface, human-cooperative robot, haptic interface, "Kansei", human-following, human-leading, force interaction.

1 Introduction

Until recent days, tasks of robots had been mostly limited to heavy labors and repetitive works in industrial factories, extreme circumstances and so on. From now on, however, robots are required to hold more and more works in fields of nursing, aiding, communication, entertainment, etc. Their operational opportunities in human environment are increasing significantly, and the stance of robots is shifting from "in place of human" to "with human".

An operation in human environment, in most cases, requires massive transactions of dynamic environmental recognition, sound recognition, linguistic recognition and motion planning. There are many technological problems to be overcome for self-controlled autonomous mobile robots that work without acquiring any support from others. It seems to require more time until the appearance of such robots. On the other hand, robots that can work as acquiring support from human are considered to be more practical at present. Studies on human-cooperative robots are drawing considerable attention of robotics researchers.

S. Brewster, R. Murray-Smith (Eds.): Haptic HCI 2000, LNCS 2058, pp. 76-87, 2001.

In human-robot cooperation, it is important to develop an interface system that affords direct and intuitive interactive communication. There are papers on transferring task by cooperation of multiple mobile robots [1] or on cooperative carrying task by a human and a manipulator robot [2,3]. Human-following experiment with biped humanoid robot is reported as well [4]. In our laboratory, some studies have been proposed to realize haptic interaction between users in distance [5,6]. All of the above utilize force information in achieving cooperative tasks or communication, but very few of them are essentially designed to be human interface. Efficient interface system for human-robot cooperation must afford, or appeal to "Kansei" of, human users to interact with the robot. "Kansei" is a human ability of achieving perception in non-logical way [7]. The study of interface system utilizing force [8] suggests that handling, safety and impression are also important factors. By the way, one of our most natural and well-regarded communication ways is to take hands of each other. Hand-to-hand interaction provides direct physical force information as well as an effect on mental side in terms of togetherness, amiability, and security. It seems efficient to utilize haptic interaction in an interface system of human-cooperative robot.

Thus we propose the hand-shaped force interface for the autonomous mobile robot that is designed to take physical communication with the user via haptic/force interaction. The hand-shaped device has 1 DOF at the finger parts and is capable of gently grasping a human hand when it is actuated. The force information is acquired by the strain gages that are attached on the flexible rubber-made arm physically supporting the hand. The robot's motion is determined by the force input and/or the environmental condition. Fundamental obstacle recognition is achieved by using bumper sensors and ultrasonic wave sensors around the body. The robot informs the user of obstacles he/she is not aware of by changing the route regardless of the intentional force. Simple algorithms for both human-following and human-leading tasks are designed. We devise experiments with human users, presenting qualitative and quantitative evaluation to examine the system's efficiency.

In the future, the system can be applied to a guide robot to be used in various scenes, a communication robot for children and elders, and a performance robot in achieving interaction with a human such as dance.

2   System

This section explains the structure and function of the interface system in application to the human-cooperative mobile robot. First, we introduce the base mobile robot. Then, we view the whole system and function of the proposed force interface.

2.1   Robot Body

The robot we use in this research is two-wheeled mobile robot that can move forward/backward and rotate clockwise/counter-clockwise. Equipped obstacle sensors are bumper sensors and ultrasonic wave sensors. The bumper sensors are equipped in front and on the tail of the body and can sense obstacle contact in six different directions. The ultrasonic sensors are mounted to detect obstacles in front of the robot without touching.

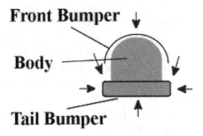

Fig. 1. Equipment of the bumper sensors and directions of obstacle sensing (Top View).

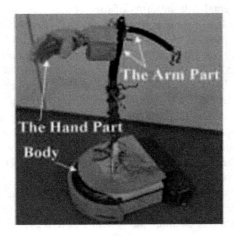

Fig. 2. Outlook of the robot with the Hand-Shaped Force Interface.

2.2   Interface Structure

Appearance of the whole robot is shown in Fig.2. The haptic, or force, interface system is composed of the hand-shaped device supported by the flexible arm. The hand part is made of a plastic skeleton covered with a rubber glove, and is capable of gentle grasp with 1 DOF at the fingers. When the hand part is grasped, it is actuated to grasp back the human hand. The arm part is made of two rubber sticks, one vertically fixed on the top of the robot body and the other horizontally on top of the vertical one.

2.3   The Arm Part and Force Sensing

The arm part physically supports the hand part, and since it is rubber-made, it can easily be bent as an intentional force is exerted to the hand part. Flexibility of the arm thus provides a structural compliance to the system.

With the use of bridged strain gauges, the arm part also functions as a force sensor. We adopt the Four Active Gage Method for measuring the force/torque. Each set of the two bridges (one on the vertical part of the arm and the other on the horizontal part) provides an independent output corresponding to the bend in a particular direction, that is, either forward/backward or clockwise/counter-clockwise (Fig.3). Independence as well as linearity of the force sensor output is confirmed in experiment as shown in Fig.4.

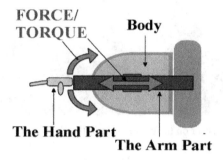

Fig. 3. Decomposition of the intentional force exerted to the arm part (Top View).

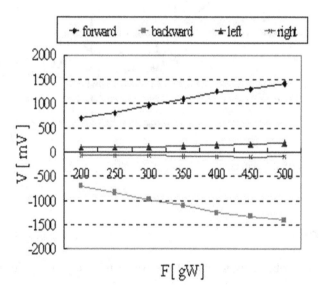

Fig. 4. Bend sensor output for force exerted either forward, backward, to the left, or to the right.

2.4   The Hand Part and Grasping

On the bottom side of the hand is a micro-switch as a human grasp sensor (Fig.5). When the hand part is grasped, the micro-switch is turned on, and the fingers are actuated to gently grasp back the human hand. We implemented an electro-thermal actuator (BMF250, Toki Corporation [9]). It is made of threadlike Shaped Memory Alloy (SMA). It contracts like muscles when electric current flows, and it elongates when cooled. The 1 DOF fingers are directly attached to the actuator as shown in Fig.6.

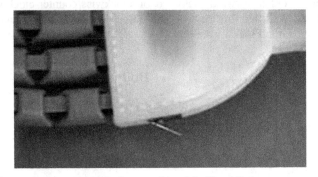

Fig. 5. The micro-switch sensor on the bottom side of the Hand Part.

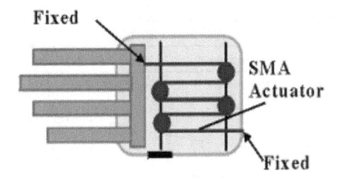

Fig. 6. Structure of SMA actuator.

3   Control

This section describes how to control the whole robotic system with the proposed interface.

3.1   Control Structure

The intentional force exerted to the interface system gives the set point of the robot's mobilization control. Fig.7 shows the entire structure of the motion control system. The algorithm is described in the following section.

Control of the grasp mechanism is open-looped, and strength of the grasping is determined experimentally.

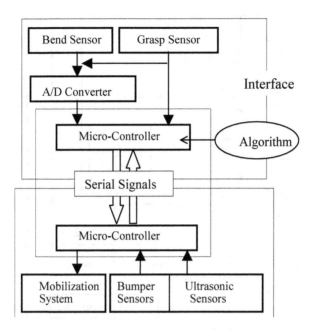

Fig. 7. Diagram of the whole control structure of the robotic system.

3.2   Algorithm

We have developed two different algorithms, one for human-following task and the other for human-leading task. With the human-following algorithm, the robot moves so as to cancel out the intentional force exerted to the hand-shaped interface (Fig.8). With the human-leading algorithm, route of the robot's leading task is pre-programmed, and the robot executes the task unless excessive counter-directional force is exerted (Fig.9). When the human follower pulls the robot's hand toward opposite direction of the leading motion, the robot stops until the intentional force ceases, meaning the follower can catch up delay. In both algorithms, when the robot touches obstacle, it executes "obstacle avoidance motion (Table 1)" regardless of the intentional force input by the human partner. Since the robot and the partner are taking hands of each other, force information can be directly communicated, and thus the robot can provide the obstacle information to the partner. The robot and the human can avoid obstacles cooperatively even in case of the human not aware of obstacles.

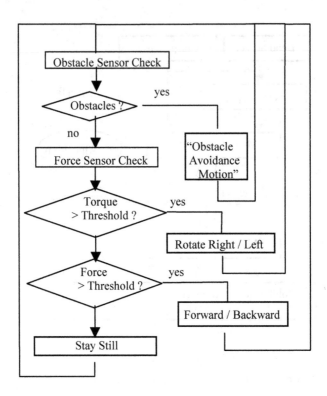

Fig. 8. Algorithm flow chart of human-following task.

In complex environment, it is possible that robot finds obstacle in different direction at the same time. When two or more conflicting "obstacle avoidance motion" occurs, for example when both right and left bumper sensors find obstacle, the robot will stay still for a second and wait for human assistance so that it can avoid vibratory motion.

Table 1. Font sizes of headings.

Direction of force/torque	Respective motion of the Robot
front left-front right-front	move backward for about 1[sec]
left	rotate counter-clockwise for 30[deg]
right	rotate clockwise for 30[deg]
tail	move forward for about 1[sec]

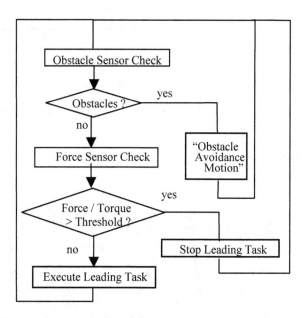

Fig. 9. Algorithm flow chart of human-leading task.

4   Experiment

In order to examine efficiency of the proposed interface, 3 experiments are devised.

4.1   Human-Following Experiment

In this experiment, the human user leads the robot from the start point to the goal point in two-dimensional static environment. A motion capture system is used to acquire the fluctuation of the distance between them during the task (Fig.10) and the trajectories of the human and the robot (Fig.11). These results support the achievement of elementary human-following task.

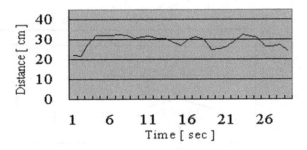

Fig. 10. Fluctuation of distance between the user and the robot in human-following task.

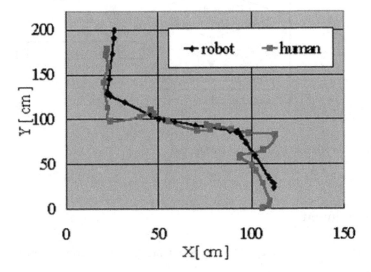

Fig. 11. Trajectories of the human and the robot in the Human-Following Experiment.

4.2   Human-Leading Experiment

In this experiment, the human volunteers are requested to follow the robot's lead with an eye mask on. The robot is programmed to execute the human-leading task in the experimental environment as shown in Fig.12. The average goal time of the human-leading tasks of 10 volunteers is comparable to the goal time of the robot moving by itself without human follower (Table 2). This suggests that an effective human-leading task is achieved. Result of the questionnaire after the experiment supports our proposition as well (Table 3)

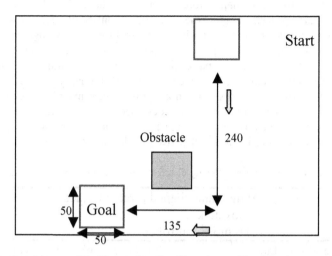

Fig. 12. Environmental map of the Human-Leading Experiment (Top View)

Table 2. Goal time of the tasks with and without human follower

Average goal time of 10 volunteers when led by the robot	29 [sec]
Goal time of the robot, when moving by itself without human follower	23 [sec]

Table 3. Questionnaire answers of the Human-Leading Experiment

	Yes	No
was able to feel the intentional force from the leading robot	10	0
felt securely lead to the goal	8	2

Comparative Experiment

In order to evaluate the efficiency of the interface system, a comparative experiment is also held with the help of the same 10 volunteers. Two other different types of the existing interface devices along with the hand-shaped force interface are used in comparison. In the same experimental environment as shown in Fig.12, this time, the volunteer users are requested to lead the robot from the start to the goal. Two of the existing interface devices are a digital joystick and a remote controller. Each interface device, including the hand-shaped force interface, is handed to the user without any instruction. Leading tasks begin when the user confidently feels that he/she has learned enough to handle the robot with each interface. The average goal time of all users suggests that the hand-shaped force interface is useful in executing such task (Table 4). Afterwards, questionnaire on qualitative evaluation is held. In each category, users must rank the interfaces in order of quality. Scores are given in integers from 3 (best) to 1 (worst), and none of the scores must be repeated more than once. The result supports that the newly designed interface excels in all factors of human interface, especially in affordance, or "Kansei" appeal, and impression. Handling seems also as efficient as other two (Table 5).

Table 4. Average goal time of using different interfaces in comparative experiment.

(a) the hand-shaped force interface (b) joystick (c) remote controller			
type of Interface	(a)	(b)	(c)
average goal time	39	30	45

Table 5. Comparative evaluation in terms of scores from the questionnaires.

CATEGORY	(a)	(b)	(c)
Was able to handle with intuitiveness ("Kansei" appeal)	2.6	1.9	1.5
Handling of the whole robot was good enough (Handling)	2.1	2.0	1.9
Felt affinity, amiability or friendliness (Impression)	2.9	2.0	1.1

5   Conclusions

In this paper, the hand-shaped force interface for human-cooperative mobile robot is proposed. By utilizing hand-to-hand force interaction, profuse communication with intentional force between a human and a robot is achieved. In the human-following task, the robot not only follows the human user to the direction in which the intentional force is exerted, but also recognizes obstacles and communicates that information to the user. In the human-leading task, the robot moves as it is pre-programmed. It stops when the human follower exerts intentional force to the opposite direction of its motion. As for evaluation of the proposed robotic system, we experimented on both tasks in real human-robot cooperation. Efficiency of the system as a human interface is also testified in comparison to other interface systems. The experimental results suggest that the proposed system fulfill the important requirements of human interface.

Now, we are planning to apply a velocity/acceleration control to the robot for achieving more smooth motion. We are also considering on supplementing utilization of sound information for more informative communication between a human and a robot in order to develop multi-modal robot interface.

References

1. J. Ota, Y. Buei, T. Arai, H. Osumi, and K. Suyama, "Transferring Control by Cooperation of Two Mobile Robots", Journal of the Robotics Society of Japan, Vol.14 No.2, 263-270, 1996 (in Japanese)
2. K. Kosuge and N. Kazamura, "Control of a Robot Handling an Object in Cooperation", Proc. of IEEE International Workshop on Robot and Human Communication, 142-147, 1997
3. R. Ikeura and H. Inooka, "Variable Impedance Control of a Robot for Cooperation with a Human", Proc. of 1995 IEEE International Conference on Robotics and Automation, 3097-3102, 1995
4. J. Yamaguchi, S. Gen, S.A. Setia Wan, and A. Takanishi, "Interaction between Human and Humanoid through the Hand Contact", Proc. of 16th Conference of the Robotics Society of Japan, 951-952, 1998 (in Japanese)
5. K. Ouchi and S. Hashimoto, "Handshake Telephone System to Communicate with Voice and Force", Proc. of IEEE International Workshop on Robot and Human Communication, 466-471, 1997
6. Y. Fujita and S. Hashimoto, "Experiments of Haptic and Tactile Display for Human Telecommunication", Proc. of the 8th IEEE International Workshop on Robot and Human Interaction (RO-MAN'99), 334-337, 1999
7. S. Hashimoto, "KANSEI as the third target of information processing and related topics in Japan", KANSEI The Technology of Emotion AIMI International Workshop proceedings, 101-104, 1997
8. J. Yokono and S. Hashimoto, "Center of Gravity Sensing for Motion Interface", Proc. of IEEE International Conference on Systems, Man and Cybernetics, 1113-1118, 1998
9. Toki Corporation Official Website. Available at http://www.toki.co.jp/BioMetal/_index.html.

Can the Efficiency of a Haptic Display Be Increased by Short-Time Practice in Exploration?

Gunnar Jansson and Anna Ivås

Department of Psychology, Uppsala University
Box 1225, SE-751 42 Uppsala, Sweden
gunnar.jansson@psyk.uu.se, annaivas@hotmail.com

Abstract. The main aim was to investigate if short-term practice in exploration with a PHANToM can improve performance. A second aim was to find out if some exploration modes are more successful than other modes. Ten participants practiced exploration of nine blocks of 24 virtual objects distributed over three days. The result was that the performance for a majority improved during this practice, but that there were large individual differences. It was suggested that one of the modes has some advantage. A main conclusion is that there is a high risk that studies of displays with users without practice underestimate the usefulness of the displays.

1 Introduction

An ideal computer display should present information in such a way that a user immediately, without any special practice, can pick up the information it makes available. Concerning visual and auditory displays this goal is reached in many cases. For haptic displays this requirement is much more difficult to achieve.

One explanation of this contrast between displays for the different senses is probably that the eyes and ears can explore many common displays in a way very similar to their natural ways of exploring the environment. This is not the case with the hands exploring the haptic displays presently available.

1.1 Restriction to One Point of Contact at a Time between User and Virtual Object

The exploration methods accessible for a commercially available haptic display, such as the three-degrees-of-freedom versions of the PHANToM (Sensable Inc.), are restricted by the construction fact that there is only one point of contact between user and virtual scene at a time. Normal haptic exploration is usually quite different. When all fingers and both hands can be used there are many points of contact between the exploring hand and the virtual scene, and there are a number of different ways of exploring an object [9]. A six-degrees-of-freedom device, such as a recently

S. Brewster, R. Murray-Smith (Eds.): Haptic HCI 2000, LNCS 2058, pp. 88-97, 2001.

developed PHANToM, increases the available information but it is still far from the natural situation.

For the contact between the user and the virtual scene there are two standard options with a PHANToM, one with a finger put into a "thimble" and one with several fingers holding a stylus. As the number of fingers involved and ways of contact are quite different in the two cases, it may be expected that the one with more fingers would be more efficient. However, in an experiment where the two options were compared there were no significant differences, neither in proportion of correctly identified forms, nor in exploration time [6, 7]. This indicates that the critical factor is their common feature, the restriction to one point of contact at a time.

1.2   The Efficiency of Haptics in Real and Virtual Contexts

Haptics is typically a sense that picks up information serially. Even if it is sometimes possible to pick up information by one grasp of an object, it is much more common to explore the object by moving it in the hand or moving the hand over it. Manipulation takes time, and there is seldom the (nearly) immediate correct identification possible with vision. This is especially apparent in virtual contexts. In an experimental study with PHANToM objects in dimensions between 10 and 100 mm it was found that the means of exploration times varied between 10 and 23 sec [8]. Even if one of the forms, the sphere, could be correctly identified in 100 % of the cases, other simple forms had lower identification proportions, as well as longer exploration times.

However, this result does not reflect the capacity of haptics. In an experiment, where the form of virtual and real objects in dimensions between 5 and 9 mm was identified, it was found that the form of real objects explored naturally were always correctly identified within a mean exploration time of 2 sec [6, 7]. The identification of virtual objects of the same forms and with the same dimensions was much slower (means down to 25 sec as best) and much less accurate (approaching 80 % as best).

There are at least two components that may be responsible for the difference in efficiency of identification between virtual and real objects. One is the earlier mentioned difference in exploratory movements accessible; another is the availability of extended skin area at the point(s) of contact between the user's skin and the virtual object. That the latter component is important was demonstrated in experiments where only one point of contact and no extended skin area were available during haptic exploration of real objects [10].

1.3   Changing the Display or the User?

The difference in identification results between real and virtual objects indicates that the capacity of haptics is not the main problem. An improvement of these results has instead to be sought in factors of importance for the interaction between haptic display and user and include changes of at least one of them. In principle, changing the display in such a way that it is better adapted to haptics' way of functioning would be an excellent solution. The development of a six-degree-of-freedom PHANToM is an effort in this direction. However, the development of displays of such a complexity as those considered here is a most demanding task, from both a technical and an economic point of view. This fact is a good reason also to consider the option of changing the user.

Human beings have in many contexts demonstrated an admirable capability to adapt to new environments, including artificial ones in technical contexts, especially after long-time practice[1]. This adaptability has been utilized to a very large degree in the development of new technology. As an evident example, consider the development of transportation means: bikes, cars, airplanes, and moon rockets. Human beings have been able to adapt relatively well to such devices and use them successfully. However, the many accidents with many of them indicate that there are limits in the adaptation potentials of the users. User adaptation has often been relied upon as a main solution for the device-user interaction, but its limits should also be considered. This said, it may be stated that adaptation of the user may be a factor contributing to a solution, especially when adaptation of a device so complex and expensive as in the case of haptic displays.

1.4   Accentuation of Haptic Exploration Problems when Vision Is not Available

When vision and haptics are used simultaneously to explore the same part of the environment haptics is to a large extent guided by vision. Vision has an immediate overview of the scene that haptics has not and can therefore guide the observer to the object to be explored and to parts of the object of special interest. When vision is not available during haptic exploration, for instance, when the exploring person is blind, haptic exploration problems are accentuated. In such situations an efficient interaction between a haptic display and its user is especially important.

2   Experimental Problems

2.1   Can the Efficiency of Exploration with a Haptic Device Be Increased by Short-Term Practice?

Most human skills can be improved by practice. Even if it is not possible to utilize all the biologically given capacities of haptics when using a device such as a PHANToM, there is a high probability that the efficiency in exploration with this display will be improved with practice. However, it is not known what level of performance it is possible to reach and how much practice is needed to attain specific levels. The main aim with the experiment to be described was to investigate the effect of practice on the efficiency in using a haptic display during a rather short period.

---

[1] A discussion of the potentials of learning computer use from a cognitive point of view was provided by Mayer [11].

More specifically, the main experimental problem was to study if short-term practice in exploration of objects with the stylus of a PHANToM can increase proportion of correctly identified object forms and decrease exploration time used?

2.2 Are there Differences in Efficiency between Ways of Holding the Stylus?

It is known from studies in other contexts where haptic exploration is used that ways of exploring is important for efficiency, for instance, concerning tactile maps [1, 4]. It is a reasonable hypothesis that this is the case also concerning the use of haptic displays.

One aspect of exploration with a PHANToM stylus is the way of holding the stylus. Even if the activities are different there are similarities with holding a pen during writing. A pen is held in many different ways. There are a number of differences in the grip of the pencil, including number of fingers used and distance between pencil point and the tips of the fingers, as well as in the rotation of the wrist. There are also important changes during the development of children's writing [3, pp. 87-94].

Informal observations indicate that users choose several different ways of holding the PHANToM stylus during exploration when no specific instruction is given. A second aim of the present experiment was to get preliminary indications of ways of holding the stylus that are successful and less successful, respectively. It may be hypothesized (1) that participants change their way during practice in order to be more efficient, and (2) that there are differences between more successful and less successful participants.

3   Method

3.1 Participants

Five men and five women, all sighted, with a mean age of 25 years (SD = 3 years) participated. They were paid and all of them except one were university students. No participants had any experience in using a PHANToM.

3.2 Haptic Display

A PHANToM 1.5 A (Sensable Inc.) was used with the stylus option. (See www.sensable.com for details.)

3.3 Virtual Objects

The virtual objects consisted of four simple geometric forms (cube, sphere, cylinder and cone) in six different sizes (dimensions being between 5 and 15 mm and all three dimensions of each object having the same length). The objects were rendered with the program ENCHANTER based on GHOST^{TM} SDK and written by Fänger and König in cooperation with the first author of this paper [2].

In order to avoid problems for the participants to find the object to be explored, it was rendered in the center of a cubic room with dimensions 2 mm larger than those for each of the objects. At the start of each trial also the end of the PHANToM arm was located within the same room. The minimum distance between a part of the object and the surrounding room was thus minimum 1 mm. In order to simplify for the observer to judge if the object or the inner walls of its surrounding room was touched, the object and the room were given different friction values, the former very low values and the room walls higher.

3.4   Spatial Arrangement

The PHANToM was placed at the edge of a table with its arm extending in free space. The participant was sitting in front of the device with the center of the virtual objects roughly in the sagittal plane and at the height of the elbow. The stylus was grasped with the participant's preferred hand and his/her forearm was approximately horizontal.

3.5   Procedure

The participants were first informed about the functioning of the PHANToM, the procedures of the experiment, and safety aspects. Then their eyes were covered and they were equipped with headphones providing white noise masking environmental sounds. For safety reasons they wore a standard head protective device common in industry.

The participants were instructed that their task was to identify the form of the object explored by saying the name of the form within a maximum time of 1 min. There was no specific instruction about how to hold the stylus; the participants were only advised to hold it in a way they considered most suitable. They were told that it was important both to be accurate and to answer without unnecessary delay.

Before the experiment proper the participants were shown four real objects (dimensions 25 mm) to be explored with a hand, each with one of the forms included in the experiment. This should eliminate any terminological misunderstanding. Next, they were presented four virtual objects (dimensions 52 mm) to be explored with the Phantom stylus.

The objects were displayed one at a time in blocks consisting of all the 24 objects. The order was randomized differently within each block. In total nine blocks were explored by the participants during three different days, three blocks each day with a few minutes rest between the blocks. The number of objects each day was thus 72 and in total each participant explored 216 objects. The time for each daily session was about one hour. The time between the experimental days was maximum a week. At the end of each day session the participants were informed about their total result that day.

Time used for the exploration of each object, from the start of the exploration until the beginning of the response was registered, and all sessions were videotaped.

4   Results

4.1   Proportion of Correct Identifications

The mean results for Proportion of correct identifications over the nine blocks of practice are presented in Fig. 1 (left). A three-ways ANOVA for the whole group demonstrated highly significant (p<.001) effects of the factors block, size of object and form of object. However, there were large individual differences. A minority of the participants (N=3) had results close to chance level from start and they did not show any improvement. Their results were remarkably different from those of a majority (N=7) whose mean result for the ninth block was about the double of that for the first block. The most successful of the participants reached a result for the ninth block (.88) that was more than five times that of a low level result for the first block (.17).

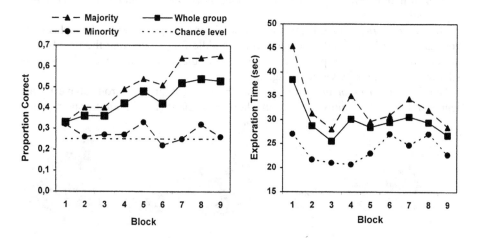

Fig. 1. Means of Proportion of Correct Identifications (left) and Means of Exploration Time (right) for each block, Blocks 1-3 during Day 1, Blocks 4-6 during Day 2 and Blocks 7-9 during Day 3. Separate curves are given for Whole group, Majority, and Minority, as well as Chance level in the left part of the figure.

Among the forms the sphere was most easily identified, a result in agreement with that in earlier experiments [8]. The cone and the cylinder were most difficult to identify. There was a clear tendency for accuracy to increase with size of object, but the increase was not monotonous.

4.2   Exploration Time

The mean results for Exploration times over the nine blocks of practice are presented in Fig. 1 (right). A three-ways ANOVA for the whole group demonstrated significant effects of the factors block ($p<.001$), size of object ($p<.001$), and form of object ($p<.01$). However, as in the case of the Proportion correct, there were large individual differences. The same two groups could again be identified. The minority (N=3) performed the task in a much shorter exploration time than the other participants and their time was nearly the same during the first and the ninth block. The majority (N=7) decreased their exploration time during the course of the experiment. There was also a tendency to decrease the time for the blocks within each of the three days.

4.3   Differences in Ways of Holding the Stylus

4.3.1   Two Main Modes Were Used
Nine of the participants used their right hand, one her left hand. In most cases the stylus was held closer to a horizontal plane than to a vertical plane. The stylus was grasped in mainly two ways that can be called *Palm-Vertical* and *Palm-Horizontal*, respectively.

The *Palm-Vertical* mode is similar to a precision grip [12, p. 86]. The stylus is in most cases held by the index finger and the middle finger opposing the thumb with the top end of the stylus protruding between the thumb and the index finger. The palm was approximately vertical (Fig. 2, left).

The *Palm-Horizontal* mode means that the stylus is grasped from above by all fingers and the palm mainly oriented in a horizontal plane (Fig. 2, middle and right)

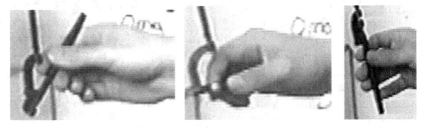

Fig. 2. The two main modes of holding the stylus during exploration with the PHANToM: the Palm-Vertical mode (left) and the Palm-Horizontal mode (middle). The photo to the right shows a temporary vertical orientation of the latter mode demonstrating the grip (photos grabbed from video).

4.3.2   Typically, One Mode Was Used throughout
Most of the participants chose one type of grasp at the start and used it through the whole experiment but three participants changed between them. Two of these changed one time (during the beginning of the third day) from Palm-Horizontal to

Palm-Vertical; one participant changed a few times but used the Palm-Vertical mode during a much longer time.

4.3.3   Advantage for the Palm-Vertical Mode?

There was no clear-cut difference in the use of the two modes between the majority and the minority mentioned above. Both modes were represented in both groups. However, it can be noted that in the successful majority the Palm-Vertical mode was used by three of seven participants throughout the whole experiment, one changed to it during the third day and one used it most of the time.

4.4   Location of Grasping on Stylus

From the videotapes it was also studied where along the stylus it was grasped. Typically, it was held within the middle third of its length with only small variations during the experiment and between participants. No conclusion about optimal way of grasping in this respect can be drawn from the analysis.

5   Discussion

5.1   Increased Efficiency for a Majority of the Participants

The performance of the majority group of participants demonstrates that the proportion of correct identifications of virtual objects can be increased during short-time practice without any specific instruction. In the experiment the mean proportion of correct identifications for this group was approximately doubled. There is a tendency to an asymptote having been reached during the third day. No participant reached a level of 100 % correct identifications, however, which is often reached with natural exploration of real objects [6, 7].

5.2   No Improvement for a Minority of the Participants

The factors responsible for the results of the minority group, proportions of correct identifications close to random and identifications without improvement, are uncertain. Their generally relatively short exploration times may indicate, however, that they, contrary to the instructions, gave more emphasis to speed than to accuracy[2].

---

[2] One participant in the minority group grasped the stylus rather close to its top much of the time, which may have been a factor contributing to her result, as such a grasp probably decreases precision.

5.3   Efficiency of Different Ways of Holding the Stylus

The analysis of the participants' ways of holding the stylus did not produce material for unequivocal conclusions. However, some suggestions can be found. Some results indicate that the Palm-Vertical mode has some advantage. However, more research is needed to reach sure conclusions.

It should be noted, however, that it is also possible that the way of holding the stylus is not a very important parameter. Such a statement would be in line with the no-difference result obtained when the thimble and the stylus options for the PHANToM were compared [6, 7]. The dominating factor may be the one-point-of-contact-at-a-time component of the haptic display.

5.4   Relevance for Visually Impaired People

One context where haptic displays may be useful is the rendering of 3D representations readable for visually impaired people [5]. That performance can be increased substantially by short-term practice would greatly simplify this application.

6   Conclusion for Evaluations of Haptic Displays

There is a high risk that evaluations of haptic display aiming to find an *absolute* level of performance and utilizing people without practice in using the device underestimate its usefulness. A few days practice in exploration may mean substantial improvements[3].

Acknowledgements

This study is a follow-up of projects made possible by grants from the Swedish Council for Research in the Humanities and Social Sciences and from the Swedish Transport and Communications Research Board. The authors are indebted to Lars-Erik Larsson for technical assistance.

References

1. Berlá, E.P.: Haptic perception of tangible graphic displays. In W. Schiff and E. Foulke (eds.): *Tactual Perception: A Sourcebook.* Cambridge University Press, Cambridge, England (1982) 364-386.
2. Fänger, J., and König, H.: *Entwicklung einer Modellierungs- und Experimentierumgebung für eine Kraftrückskopplungsgerät* (Development of a form production and experiment

---

[3] This problem is not so great if the aim is to find performance differences *between* experimental conditions.

environment for a force feedback device). Praktikumsdokumentation. Institute for Simulation and Graphics, Magdeburg University, Germany (1998)

3. Hyldgaard, L.: *Spatial accuracy and temporal efficiency in children's tracing with a pencil.* Ph.D-thesis. Uppsala University, Department of Psychology, Uppsala, Sweden (ISBN 91-506-1406-1) (2000)

4. James, G.A.: Mobility maps. In: W. Schiff and E. Foulke (eds.): *Tactual Perception: A Sourcebook.* Cambridge University Press, Cambridge, England (1982) 334-363

5. Jansson, G.: Can a haptic display rendering virtual 3D objects be useful for people with visual impairment? *Journal of Visual Impairment and Blindness* **93** (1999), 426-429

6. Jansson, G.: The importance of available exploration methods for the efficiency of haptic displays. In: *Abstracts. Symposium on Multimodal Communication.* Linköping University, Linköping, Sweden (1999)

7. Jansson, G., and Billberger, K.: The PHANToM used without visual guidance. In: *Proceedings of the First PHANToM Users Research Symposium (PURS99).* Deutsches Krebsforschungszentrum, Heidelberg, Germany (1999). Also available at http://mbi.dkfz-heidelberg. de/purs99/proceedings/jansson.pdf

8. Jansson, G., Billberger, K., Petrie, H., Colwell, C., Kornbrot, D., Fänger, J., König, H., Hardwick, A., and Furner, S.: Haptic virtual environments for blind people: Exploratory experiments with two devices. *International Journal of Virtual Reality,* **4** (1999) 10-20

9. Lederman, S., and Klatzky, R.L.: Hand Movements: A Window into Haptic Object Recognition. *Cognitive Psychology* **19** (1987), 342-368

10. Lederman, S.J., and Klatzky, R.L: Sensing and Displaying Spatially Distributed Fingertip Forces in Haptic Interfaces for Teleoperator and Virtual Environment Systems. *Presence* **8** (1999), 86-104.

11. Mayer, R. E.: From novice to expert. In M. Helander, T. K. Landauer, and P. Prabhu (eds.): *Handbook of Human-Computer Interaction.* Sec. compl. rev. ed. Elsevier, Amsterdam (1997) 781-795

12. Pheasant, S.: *Anthropometry, Ergonomics and the Design of Work.* Sec. ed.. Taylor and Francis, London (1996)

Implicit Accuracy Constraints in Two-Fingered Grasps of Virtual Objects with Haptic Feedback

Frank E. Pollick[1], Chris Chizk[2], Charlotte Hager-Ross[2], and Mary Hayhoe[2]

[1]Department of Psychology, Glasgow University
frank@psy.gla.ac.uk
[2]Center for Visual Science, University of Rochester
{chizk,mary}@cvs.rochester.edu
charlotte.hager-ross@rehabmed.umu.se

Abstract. Using virtual objects that provided haptic feedback we studied two-fingered movements of reaching to grasp and lift an object. These reach-grasp-lift movements were directed to objects of identical physical size but with the different physical properties of mass, and coefficient of friction between the floor and object. For each condition, the resulting forces and kinematic properties of movements were recorded after a brief amount of practice with reaching to grasp and lift the object. It was found that for conditions where the object was more stable to perturbation, such as large mass or high friction, the contact force with the object was greater. This suggests that the stability of the object is quickly and easily learned and subsequently influences the accuracy of the movement. The possibility is discussed that such programming of contact force is incorporated into the planning of grasps and how this would interact with the execution of grasps to virtual objects with and without haptic feedback.

1   Introduction

Reaching out to grasp and lift an object involves the problem of not only controlling the arm as it moves towards the object but also controlling the arm plus the object after contact.   This continuous action of reach-grasp-lift has commonly been examined primarily as two separate problems of 1) reaching to grasp and 2) lifting. Research into these two problems have indicated that expectation and learned models of the arm, hand and environment contribute significantly to the regularities observed in both actions.   In the present research, we focus on how learned models of the object to be grasped influence impact with the object in the transition from reach to lift in the continuous motion of reach-grasp-lift.   Our examination of the reach-grasp-lift movement was done using a virtual environment including haptic feedback that enabled us to synthesize virtual objects with both visual and haptic properties and study interaction with these objects.

In an earlier study examining grasps to virtual objects that did not provide haptic feedback it was found that, in comparison to grasps with real objects, the grasps to virtual objects had longer deceleration phases and were more variable in their endpoint position [1]. It was conjectured that this difference was mainly due to the

S. Brewster, R. Murray-Smith (Eds.): Haptic HCI 2000, LNCS 2058, pp. 98–107, 2001.

lack of impact with an object at the end of the reach to grasp movement, namely that contact with the object is used strategically to assist in braking the motion of the hand. Support for this view comes from studies in pointing movements where it has been found that contact forces are incorporated in the programming of pointing movements [2]. In grasp, although it is generally accepted that preprogrammed grasp movements incorporate aspects of the size and distance to the object [3, 4, 5, 6], there is not abundant evidence that grasping motions are sensitive to the dynamics of the object to be grasped. However, evidence exists that surface texture and other intrinsic properties of an object modulate the reach to grasp motion [7, 8].

In the present experiment we wished to explore whether contact forces were influenced by the properties of the object to be grasped. We examined this by having participants grasp virtual objects simulating different masses and friction relations between the object and floor. By performing 10 practice trials participants became acquainted with the object properties and then data was taken of the reach-grasp-lift motions. It was predicted that contact forces would be learned implicitly, and be related to the accuracy constraints demanded by interaction with each object. Specifically that heavy objects stuck tightly to the floor would be struck with significant force while light objects on a slippery floor would be struck lightly. Positive results would not only suggest a role for the programming of contact forces in the planning of reach to grasp movements, but would also indicate possible advantages of incorporating haptic feedback for interactions with virtual objects.

2   Methods

2.1   Apparatus

Both the visual stimuli and the force feedback upon contact were programmed within a virtual environment constructed with a graphics computer, head-mounted display and haptic interface device. At the heart of this virtual environment is a graphics generation system run by a Silicon Graphics Onyx processor equipped with four R10000 processors and an Infinite Reality rendering engine. In addition to generating the graphics, the Onyx is equipped with a high-speed serial board capable of simultaneous communication with the head-tracker and haptic interface device. The head mounted display used was a Virtual Research V8 composed of two 1.3" LCD panels which were capable of producing a true 640X480 VGA display. The haptic interface was obtained with two extended-range Phantom haptic feedback devices from SensAble Technologies that allowed the thumb and index finger to be tracked and force feedback applied. The workspace of the combined Phantoms is approximately 400 X 600 X 800mm. The DC motors powering the Phantoms were capable of exerting over 20 N of force to the fingers. The ability of the Phantoms to collect data of position and force at the fingertips varied with the computational load upon the system, and was 400 Hz on average.

2.2   Stimuli

The visual stimuli consisted of spheres representing the fingertip positions and a flat sheet which served as the floor upon which the cube to grasp was placed. The dimensions of the cube were 35 X 35 X 50mm, with grasps directed across the 50 mm side. The spheres representing fingertip positions had a radius of 5 mm. The flat sheet had dimensions 300X 400mm and appeared at the level of the table upon which the fingers rested. Taking the origin of this sheet to be at its center, and the close left corner to have coordinates of (-200, 150), the fingers of the right hand started their movements at position (75, -150) and the object was located to have its center at position (-65, 95). In addition there was a small sphere of radius 5 mm placed 130 mm above the center of the cube, which served as a visual signal of the height to which the object should be lifted. All the objects were rendered using lambertian shading and diffuse and point light sources.

The haptical properties were varied to obtain cubes of different weight and different frictional relations with the floor. These manipulations resulted in cubes of different weight that due to friction with the floor were more or less sensitive to displacement forces. The friction between the fingertips and the cube was held constant. For the experiment 3 object weights were used simulating mass (M) of 50, 100 and 200 grams. Four static coefficients of friction (μ_s) were used, simulating values of 0.12, 0.30, 0.65 and 1.0. The dynamic friction coefficients (μ_d) corresponding to these 4 values were 0.12, 0.12, 0.48 and 0.82 respectively. The experiment consisted of a weight series of the 3 weights with the coefficient of friction held constant at 0.65 for static and 0.48 for dynamic, and a friction series of the 4 frictional values with the mass held constant at 68 grams. A summary of these values is presented in Table 1.

The visual properties of the object to be grasped were held constant except for the color of the object which was varied to serve as an indicator that the cube to be grasped was the same or different from previous cubes.

Table 1. Mass and friction values for the 7 different experimental conditions. The rightmost column of $\mu_s M$ provides an estimate of the different relative amounts of force required to move the object.

condition	M (grams)	μ_s	μ_d	$\mu_s M$
1	50	0.65	0.48	32.50
2	100	0.65	0.48	65.00
3	200	0.65	0.48	130.00
4	68	0.12	0.12	8.16
5	68	0.30	0.12	20.40
6	68	0.65	0.48	44.20
7	68	1.0	0.82	68.00

2.3   Procedure

The experiment consisted of examining reach-grasp-lift motions towards objects in the 7 different simulated conditions (consisting of the weight series of 3 conditions and the friction series of 4 conditions). For an individual trial, a participant began with their thumb and index finger at the start position. At the go signal they reached out to grasp the cube and then lifted it to a height of 13 cm and held it steady before placing it back down on the floor and returned their fingers to the start position. Each trial was self paced and approximately 8 seconds of data were recorded for each trial.

The 7 different conditions were blocked so that participants could become accustomed to each experimental condition. For each block a participant performed 20 lifts, of which the first ten served as practice and the last ten were recorded for subsequent data analysis.

Data was recorded from 3 participants, all of whom were naive to the purpose of the experiment. The entire experiment took approximately 45 minutes.

3   Results

Data from individual reach-grasp-lift records were analyzed using software written in Matlab. This processing of data included a preliminary step of preprocessing, followed by extraction of relevant forces and kinematic markers to characterize the movements. The preprocessing involved first using linear interpolation to have each record evenly sampled at a rate of 500 Hz. Following this, the interpolated data were filtered with a 2nd order dual pass butterworth filter with a lowpass cutoff of 8 Hz. First and second derivatives of the position and force data were obtained through the use of central difference equations.

Estimates of the startpoint of the movements were found by averaging together the velocity of the two fingers and finding the first 3 points which had greater tangential velocity than 5% of the maximum velocity. Estimates of the endpoint of the movements were taken from the time that the first finger hit the object. The time of impact was taken as the time of the first peak of the first derivative of force for either finger. Examination of the first derivative of force was limited to between time of maximum aperture and time of maximum vertical position of the lifted object.

3.1   Kinematics

Reach to grasp movements are typically thought of as involving the relatively independent components of transport and preshape [3]. The maximum velocity, acceleration and deceleration of the wrist characterize the transport component, and the maximum aperture between the two fingers characterizes the preshape component. Since in the current study there were no measurements of the motion of the wrist we used the average velocity of the two fingers to estimate properties of the transport component. The magnitudes of these kinematic markers are shown in Figure 1 and their temporal sequencing of is shown in Figure 2 where time has been normalized so that time=1 is equivalent to the first touch of the object. Visual inspection of Figures 1 and 2 indicate slight deviations between the weight series and the friction series as well as within each series.

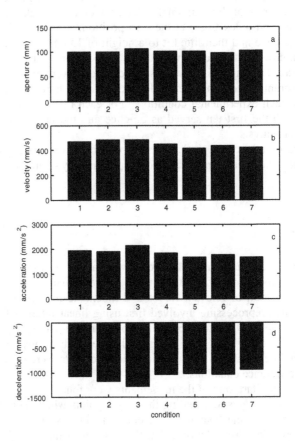

Fig. 1. Values of the a) maximum aperture, b) maximum velocity, c) maximum acceleration and d) maximum deceleration for the 7 different experimental conditions.

Closer examination of the results was obtained by performing, for each combination of participant and kinematic marker; a one factor repeated measures ANOVA that examined the effect of object condition on the kinematic marker. Result of these analyses showed that at a $p<0.05$ level of significance, condition had an effect on maximum velocity for all three participants, maximum aperture for two participants, maximum acceleration for one participant and maximum deceleration for none of the participants. Further statistical analysis was performed on the average data of all three participants and it was found that there were statistically significant effects of condition for these kinematic markers, which involved higher order interactions with participants. However, possibly due to the small number of participants, these individual differences appeared to fall into no regular pattern.

3.2   Contact Forces

Of primary interest for the current research was an estimate of the contact force with the object. Estimation of a contact force is problematic in the sense that there are two fingers involved in hitting the object and contact of the two is possibly simultaneous. Our definition of contact force was taken to be the maximum difference between the two finger forces that occurred in the first 100ms after contact of the first finger on the object. For this measure we only considered forces in the horizontal plane, ignoring the vertical component of force. We restricted our analysis to these horizontal forces since our primary interest was in forces which would displace the object and thus make it more difficult to initiate a lifting motion. An example of this measure is shown in Figure 3. The rationale for this choice was that the 100ms time window should be short enough to avoid sensory feedback while still long enough to indicate whether the object was being met simultaneously with near equal forces or nonsimultaneously with a large collision force by one of the fingers.

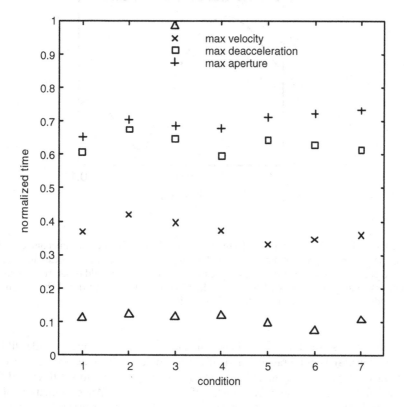

Fig. 2. Temporal sequencing of the kinematic parameters for the 7 different experimental conditions. Time is normalized so that first contact with the object corresponds to the time of 1.

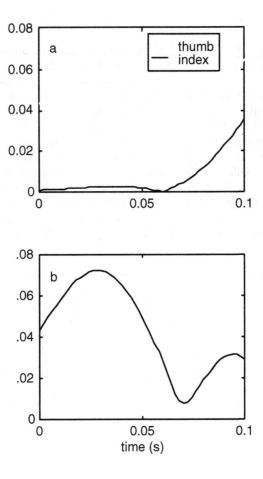

Fig. 3. Example of the calculation of contact force. In (a) we see the timecourse of force measurements for both the thumb and the index finger. In (b) we see the difference between these two curves. The corresponding estimate of the contact force would be approximately 0.07 Newtons as found on the peak of the curve shown in (b). For both (a) and (b) time of zero corresponds to contact of the first finger with the object.

Our hypothesis was that the various simulated conditions would provide different accuracy constraints for grasping and lifting the object. In other words, we would expect that the measured contact forces should be proportional to the threshold force with which the object could be struck before it moved. An examination of this hypothesis is shown in Figure 4 where we have plotted the measured contact force versus $!_s$ M. It can be seen that the relationship between these two factors is consistent with the hypothesis that objects that can withstand a greater contact force before moving will receive a greater contact force.

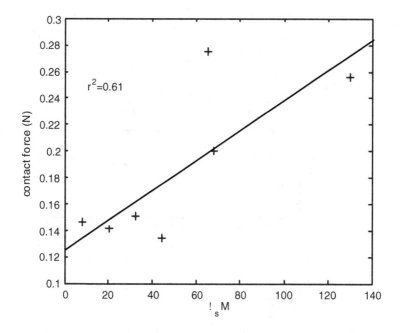

Fig. 4. A plot of the measured contact force versus the quantity $!_s M$ for each of the 7 experimental conditions. A linear regression was performed on the points and the resulting line is shown on the graph as well as, r^2, the percentage of variance accounted for by the linear relationship. The predicted relation is that contact force should increase for experimental conditions with higher values of $!_s M$.

Finally, we wished to examine the previously mentioned kinematic markers to see if the kinematic values obtained could have been related to the contact force. Figure 5 shows the maximum aperture, maximum acceleration, maximum velocity and maximum deceleration versus the contact force for each of the 7 conditions. As can be seen there was a general trend for the maximum aperture to increase with increasing contact force. Similarly, as for increasing contact force there was a tendency for the movement to accelerate quicker, reach a higher maximum velocity and then decelerate quicker.

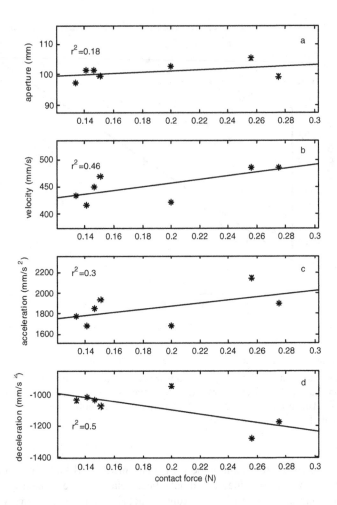

Fig. 5. The four different kinematic markers of a) maximum aperture, b) maximum velocity, c) maximum acceleration and d) maximum deceleration are plotted versus the measured contact forces. Each graph includes the resultant linear regression line and the corresponding value of r^2.

4   Discussion

The results were consistent with the hypothesis that contact forces would increase as the virtual object was more stable and thus capable of absorbing greater force before moving. In addition to these differences in contact forces it was found that the standard kinematic parameters used to describe grasp were found to covary with the contact force. The grasps to these more stable objects had apparently larger apertures and greater velocities - kinematic values which are characteristic of low accuracy grasps [9]. It thus appears that the programming of contact force with an object is intrinsically involved in the planning of grasp accuracy.

The results suggest that incorporating haptic interaction with objects would be useful for obtaining natural interactions with virtual objects. Without haptic feedback we can conjecture that the grasp kinematics would tend towards the values required when nearly zero contact force must be applied to the object. Thus, for high precision grasps there might be little effect of haptic feedback in modulating the kinematics of grasp. However, for grasps to stable objects we would expect that haptic feedback is key in providing deceleration forces to the hand. Thus, with no haptic feedback grasps to stable objects would likely appear unrealistic.

Acknowledgements

We thank Peter Giblin for helpful suggestions.

References

1. Pollick, F.E.: Virtual Surfaces and the Influence of Cues to Surface Shape on Grasp. Virtual Reality **3** (1998) 85~101

2. Teasdale N., Schmidt, R.A.: Deceleration Requirements and the Control of Pointing Movements. Journal of Motor Behavior **23** 1991 131~138

3. Jeannerod, M.: The Neural and Behavioral Organization of Goal-Directed Movements. Clarendon Press, Oxford (1988)

4. Jeannerod, M.: The Cognitive Neuroscience of Action. Blackwell, Oxford (1997)

5. Mackenzie, C.L., Iberall, T.: The grasping hand. Elsevier-North Holland, Amsterdam (1994)

6. Smeets, J.B.J., Brenner, E.: A New View on Grasping. Motor Control, **3** (1999) 237~271

7. Fikes, T.G., Klatzky, R.L., Lederman, S.J.: Effects of Object Texture on Precontact Movement Time in Human Prehension. Journal of Motor Behavior **26** (1994) 325~332

8. Savelsbergh, G.J.P., Steenbergen, B., van der Kamp, J.: The Role of Fragility Information in the Guidance of the Precision Grip. Human Movement Science **15** (1996) 115~127

9. Wing, A.M., Turton, A., Fraser, C.S.O.: Grasp Size and Accuracy of Approach in Reaching. Journal of Motor Behavior **18** (1986) 245~260

Interaction of Visual and Haptic Information in Simulated Environments: Texture Perception

Steven A. Wall and William S. Harwin

The Department of Cybernetics, University of Reading
Whiteknights, PO Box 225, Reading RG6 6AY, UK
Facsimile: +44 (0) 118 931 8220

s.a.wall@reading.ac.uk, w.s.harwin@reading.ac.uk
http://www.rdg.ac.uk/~shr97saw

Abstract. This paper describes experiments relating to the perception of the roughness of simulated surfaces via the haptic and visual senses. Subjects used a magnitude estimation technique to judge the roughness of "virtual gratings" presented via a PHANToM haptic interface device, and a standard visual display unit. It was shown that under haptic perception, subjects tended to perceive roughness as decreasing with increased grating period, though this relationship was not always statistically significant. Under visual exploration, the exact relationship between spatial period and perceived roughness was less well defined, though linear regressions provided a reliable approximation to individual subjects' estimates.

1. Introduction

It is generally the case that our perceptions of the world arise as a combination of correlated input across several of the senses. Our experiences are not based upon selective stimulation of certain receptors, as may arise in a laboratory situation. Consider the act of haptically exploring an object. Touching an object's surface often simultaneously yields information regarding the compliance, texture, shape and heat conductive qualities of the object. The touching process may also be perceived aurally, for example, a tap or scrape, and is usually supported by visual stimulus regarding the object's global structure and surface properties. Indeed, it is this correlative information that has led researchers to hypothesise that touch is more of a "reality sense" than the other four human [1]. In truth, it is likely not only the touch sensations themselves that give rise to this impression of "reality", for as our simple example has shown, several other senses are intrinsically involved. Our perception of something touched as being somehow more "real" may also be a result of the fact that, historically, sensory illusions have rarely appealed to the sense of touch. Visual illusions have existed in some form for centuries, from sleight of hand tricks to modern day computer generated cinema images. Audio signals are readily stored and reproduced with a high clarity. Yet, touch sensations have proved impossible to replicate until the advent of haptic interfaces. Even with the current state of available

S. Brewster, R. Murray-Smith (Eds.): Haptic HCI 2000, LNCS 2058, pp. 108-117, 2001.

technology, we are limited to simulations of "remote" contact via a probe or intermediary link, rather than direct stimulation of the fingerpads.

Information regarding object properties has been shown to be differentially salient under conditions of pure haptic exploration, and haptic and visual exploration. When visual information is readily available, global shape and structural cues become the defining properties of an object. Conversely, under purely haptic exploration, material cues such as texture and compliance have a greater significance. It was hypothesised that this was a result of the ease of encoding these properties [2]. Thus, shape information is easily extracted by visual means, whereas to gather this information haptically requires execution of the "contour following" exploratory procedure (EP) [3], which puts a large demand on the observer's memory for integration of temporally varying signals, and is also time consuming to perform. In contrast, the optimal EPs for extraction of compliance and texture - pressure and lateral motion, respectively, are simple and fast to execute.

However, despite the apparent importance of material qualities under haptic exploration, there is scant provision in current interfaces for texture representation .Thus, low bandwidth haptic interfaces necessitate that the operator adopts a "visually-mediated" method of object identification. That is to say, that performance must rely on visual stimuli provided by a suitable display (e.g. monitor, headset), or that the user must haptically gather information regarding object properties that are more readily encoded by vision, such as size and shape. However, even this method is obviated, as typical interfaces operate on a principal of point interaction, which places considerable constraints on performance of contour following EPs and totally occludes enclosure. It has been shown that exploration via a probe is deleterious in tasks requiring the extraction of large scale geometric data, in terms of response times [4].

What are the implications of these facts for haptic interface technology? Given the bewildering level of sensitivity in the human cutaneous system, it seems unfeasible at present to suggest a mechanical skin interface that can relay information regarding object material properties. Currently, we can only strive to provide perceptual impressions that are merely discriminable [5], or else provide simulation of object properties, such as roughness, rather than exact tactile replicas of real life materials. Most haptic interface applications, with the obvious exception of those designed for the visually impaired, seem to be augmented by visual feedback. To remove the visual interface would render the application useless, in most cases. It is evident, in their present state of development, haptic interfaces are dependent on existing HCI devices, such as the monitor, and to a much lesser extent, audio cues. However, given that interactions in the real world often incorporate information from several sensory modalities, this does not seem an unjust criticism. Despite this, until provision is made for greater accessibility to object properties, haptic interfaces will be largely dependant on existing HCI devices. Indeed, individual difficulties are often encountered in purely haptic simulations [6,7], and qualitative differences in perception between subjects is not uncommon.

This paper describes experiments relating to the perception of simulated textures using both the visual and haptic senses. Experiments are described pertaining to the perception of the roughness of "virtual gratings" displayed using a PHANToM haptic interface, and a graphical representation. The study aims to assimilate any differences in the method by which roughness is perceived between the visual and haptic senses in a virtual environment. We first consider the relevant cues by which roughness is perceived in real and simulated environments.

2. Perception of Roughness

The relevant literature regarding perception of roughness can be subdivided in to three categories. Bimodal perception is concerned with perception of real textures via visual and haptic channels simultaneously. Remote contact, as opposed to direct contact with the fingerpad, involves perception via a probe, finger sheath or other rigid link. It is possible to draw a direct analogy between sensations encountered in this mode, and when using a haptic interface. Finally, perception of roughness in a simulated environment is discussed.

2.1 Bimodal Perception

During the development of haptic applications, there has been little study with regards to the interaction of the various senses and their effects on perception, though some research exists concerning the effects of audio and visual cues on stiffness perception [8,9].

Several studies have addressed this issue in the real world. Early studies [10,11] implied that vision was somehow superior to touch. However, these results focussed on perception of object shape, which is necessarily image mediated due to the difficulties inherent in extracting this information haptically. Similar studies on intersensory conflict during perception of texture [12] showed that, when conflicts in the visual and cutaneous senses arose, the overall perception experienced by the subject was of a compromise between the two senses. It is not the case that one sense dominates the other, as an impression of roughness is easily obtainable by both the haptic and the visual sense, thus, one sense does not take precedence over the other. The two above examples illustrate that there is no strict hierarchy to the senses, and one is not necessarily more "significant" than the others. The relative importance of sensory information is dictated by the properties we are searching for in an object, and the prevailing exploratory conditions.

Heller [13] describes a series of experiments investigating the interaction of visual and haptic senses in perception of surfaces. Vision and touch produced similar levels of accuracy in the perception of roughness, however, bimodal perception proved to be superior for texture judgements. It was proposed that vision aids the perception of roughness by allowing an active explorer to guide their hand movements in a more efficient manner.

2.2 Remote Contact

It has been proposed [4] that probe exploration in the real world represents a very simple form of teleoperator system acting on a remote environment, therefore the psychophysical data obtained regarding intermediary links has especial relevance to the design of haptic interfaces and teleoperation systems.

During direct haptic exploration with the fingerpad, spatially distributed cues provide the main percept for subjects' judgements of surface properties. However, when exploring a remote environment, spatially distributed cues on the fingerpad do not correspond to the surface geometry at the distal point of the interface, rather, they correspond to the geometry of the probe itself. The user is therefore forced to adopt vibrational cues transmitted via the probe or link in order to make judgements regarding the properties of the surface [14]. Katz concluded that it is possible to judge the roughness of a surface with the same accuracy while using a probe as when using direct contact with the fingertip [15]. Performance was greatly deteriorated when the probe was "damped" using a cloth. Lederman, Klatzky and colleagues performed a series of investigations regarding the psychophysical effects inherent in remote contact. Subjects estimated the "perceived roughness" of surfaces by indicating a quantitative numerical estimate of the magnitude. It was observed that subject's estimates of perceived roughness decreased with increased inter-element spacing. An increase in contact diameter of the probe used caused a corresponding decrease in perceived roughness. When the speed of exploration was varied, an increase in speed correlated with a decrease in perceived roughness. For small inter-element spacing, roughness estimates were also larger with probes than with the bare finger, though it was also confirmed that roughness discrimination is improved using direct compared to remote contact. This was attributed to the differences in neural responses to surface characteristics during the two modes of contact. Direct contact facilitates provision of spatially intensive coding of surfaces contacting the fingerpad. However, for remote contact, spatial variation of signals on the fingerpad does not correspond to surface geometry at the distal point of the probe, hence, the primary method of encoding surface properties is via vibratory signals transmitted through the probe i.e. a temporally varying signal. Observations showed that performance using a rigid finger sheath was considerably below that achieved with more probe-like intermediary links, which are closer to the finger in terms of supporting discrimination accuracy. This was possibly a result of the larger contact area afforded by the rigid sheath. To concur with this, magnitude estimations of roughness with the rigid sheath were highly linear and had no downturn. However, the perceived roughness would be expected to drop if sufficiently wide inter-element spacing were introduced to the test stimuli.

2.3 Perception of Simulated Surfaces

Jansson et al [6] showed that the PHANToM can be used to display "virtual sandpapers" by modelling the normal and tangential forces recorded during exploration of a real sandpaper. Perceived roughness was unanimously greater for the virtual sandpaper for all grit values employed in the investigation. The difference, however, did not appear to be significant, though it was inferred that it may prove to be so should a greater number of test subjects be employed. The results showed that the real and virtual sandpapers were perceived in a similar fashion. In a related test using an Impulse Engine (www.immersion.com), both blind and sighted subjects estimated the roughness magnitude of virtual gratings with a sinusoidal profile. The spatial period of the gratings ranged from 0.375 to 1.5mm, with a fixed amplitude of

0.0625mm. There was a highly significant relationship between the perceived roughness magnitude of the virtual surface and its spatial period. The majority of the participants perceived wider groove widths to be rougher, although some perceived the narrower groove widths as rougher. All the blind participants showed a meaningful relationship between spatial period and roughness, but only 5 of the 13 sighted subjects showed a significant relationship. Thus, it was concluded that the virtual surfaces employed in the study were only suitable for visually impaired users.

Minsky and Lederman [16] investigated the perception of surface textures using only lateral forces with a 2 degree of freedom (D.O.F.) joystick, using the "sandpaper" system, whereby the users hand is pulled towards low areas and away from high areas on a texture height map, using virtual spring forces [17]. The amplitude of surface features was varied between 0.7 and 10mm, and lateral forces from 18 to 382g. Perceived magnitude of roughness was predicted almost entirely by the amplitude of the lateral force exerted on the subject's hand. There was no significant variation of estimated roughness with grating feature size.

Siira and Pai [18] describe a stochastic method in which textures are approximated by a Gaussian distribution, the parameters of which are dependant on measured surface properties. Given restrictions imposed on computation time, and the limits of human tactile perception, it was deemed that a realistic approximation of surface texture may produce the desired psychophysical impression. A virtual surface was implemented combining normal constraint forces with normal and tangential texture impulses. It was observed that a higher variance of Gaussian distribution gave a higher estimate of perceived roughness.

Fritz and Barner [5] reproduced Gaussian texture effects in 3D using a PHANToM. It was found that simple textures could be rendered from a multivariate probability density function (PDF, e.g. Gaussian, uniform), and that by combining a number of PDFs, more complex surfaces could be portrayed. Perceived roughness of simulated surfaces increased with increasing variance of the Gaussian distribution.

West and Cutkosky [7] described experiments investigating the point at which individual peak or valley features on a sinusoidal surface gave way to an overall sensation of "roughness" or "smoothness". At higher frequencies, performance was improved by using a stylus, as opposed to the fingerpad. It was surmised that this was due to the fact that the stylus could fall between features that are too small for the fingertip. It was noted that average error rates were higher for virtual walls than for physical walls, especially at low amplitudes. It was concluded that in order to improve performance at low amplitude and high spatial frequency it would be necessary to improve the bandwidth of the haptic device employed.

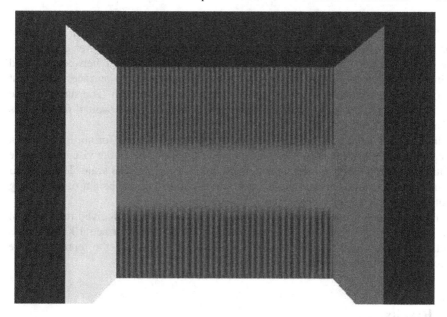

Fig. 1. Sample visual environment. Top grating is standard, spatial period = 2mm. Lower grating is test, with spatial period = 2.5mm.

2.4 Summary

It is clear that perception differs in the three modes considered. Relationships between perception and the simulated properties of virtual surfaces are less well defined than their real life counterparts, however, investigations have focussed purely on haptic perception of these surfaces. The following section describes an experiment investigating both visual and haptic perception of a simple, simulated surface.

3. Experimental Procedure

The subjects employed in the investigation were 12 students from the University of Reading, 11 male and 1 female, aged between 22 and 27. Subjects were presented virtual gratings of a sinusoidal profile under two stimulus conditions, "haptic" and "visual". In the haptic condition, the gratings were displayed using a PHANToM haptic interface. In the visual mode, a graphical representation of the virtual environment and the gratings were displayed on a standard monitor.

During each iteration of the test, the subject was presented with 2 virtual gratings on the "wall" of the workspace. The gratings were vertically aligned, and each constituted an area of height 30mm and length 100mm. There was a 30mm vertical gap between the two gratings, such that the user could readily distinguish between the two.

The uppermost grating was the "standard" surface, and remained at a constant spatial period of 2.0mm throughout the whole investigation. The lower grating was the "test" surface. The spatial period of the test surface varied between 0.5 and 3.5mm, in increments of 0.125mm, this giving a test set of 25 surfaces. Each test surface was presented once per subject in each stimulus condition. The surfaces were randomly ordered during each of the tests. The height of the sinusoidal profiles was 2.5mm peak to peak.

In the haptic condition, gratings were represented by checking for collisions with a sinusoidal surface of the appropriate height and spatial period. In the visual mode, the gratings were represented as textures defined in 2D, using an RGB scale. The R and G values were constant, whereas the B value was dependant on the height of the grating profile. A sample virtual environment is illustrated in Figure 1.

The magnitude estimation technique was used to assess the perceived roughness of the gratings. Subjects were instructed to assign the standard surface 100 roughness units, and were asked to provide a number for each test surface the represented the perceived roughness relative to the standard.

4. Results

The spatial period and roughness magnitude estimate data for each subject was converted to logarithmic scales and a linear regression analysis was then performed. The results are summarised in Table 1, for the haptics mode and Table 2 for the visual mode. The tables show the x-coefficient for the linear regression calculated for each subject, which corresponds to the slope of the graph, the standard error for this value, and the t-stat and P-value, corresponding to the statistical analysis of the significance of the results.

For the haptics condition, 3 of the 12 subjects did not display a significant relationship between spatial period and roughness magnitude. However, all the subjects showed a significant relationship when the visual stimulus was employed. Using haptic cues, 2 of the subjects had a positive co-efficient, thus, roughness increased with spatial period, however, for the remaining 10 subjects, the co-efficient was negative, indicating that roughness increased for narrower groove widths. In the visual modality, the split was more equal, with 7 out of the 12 subjects showing a positive co-efficient, which included the 2 subjects who displayed this trend in the haptics condition.

5. Discussion

It is evident from the differences in the results that the nature by which roughness is perceived under visual and haptic exploration differs, given the constraints imposed by the equipment and simulated environment that has been employed in the current investigation. Positive and negative co-efficients for haptic roughness magnitude estimates related to spatial period has been noted in a previous study [6], so it is therefore poignant that this effect should also occur under visual exploration, as well.

	X - Coefficient	Standard Error	t Stat	P-value
Subject 1	1.218	0.183	6.647	8.8E-07
Subject 2	-1.010	0.116	-8.702	9.8E-09
Subject 3	-0.819	0.099	-8.259	2.5E-08
Subject 4	0.266	0.244	1.091	0.28678
Subject 5	-0.162	0.219	-0.740	0.46701
Subject 6	-0.556	0.050	-11.201	8.6E-11
Subject 7	-0.775	0.105	-7.413	1.5E-07
Subject 8	-1.172	0.201	-5.839	6E-06
Subject 9	-0.678	0.054	-12.511	9.6E-12
Subject 10	0.344	0.277	1.243	0.22643
Subject 11	-0.553	0.052	-10.597	2.5E-10
Subject 12	-0.647	0.083	-7.787	6.8E-08

☐ **Table 1.** Summary of relationship between perceived roughness and spatial period during haptic perception.

	X - Coefficient	Standard Error	t Stat	P-value
Subject 1	1.113	0.223	4.998	4.69E-05
Subject 2	-0.788	0.125	-6.325	1.87E-06
Subject 3	1.352	0.278	4.862	6.57E-05
Subject 4	1.782	0.396	4.499	0.000162
Subject 5	-1.323	0.202	-6.539	1.13E-06
Subject 6	-0.462	0.067	-6.898	4.94E-07
Subject 7	-0.571	0.100	-5.716	8.04E-06
Subject 8	1.939	0.393	4.929	5.56E-05
Subject 9	1.003	0.211	4.759	8.49E-05
Subject 10	1.633	0.393	4.157	0.000381
Subject 11	-0.460	0.095	-4.847	6.82E-05
Subject 12	1.219	0.239	5.109	3.56E-05

☐ **Table 2.** Summary of relationship between perceived roughness and spatial period during visual perception.

It is hypothesised that the main reason for these discrepancies in perception is that the representation of the surfaces employed in the study, in both the visual and haptic mode, are both approximations to real life surfaces, rather than exact physical replicas. The most obvious example of this is that all perturbations due to the gratings in the haptic condition are normal to the surface, whereas a real surface would also provide some frictional components tangential to the surface. Also, auditory and thermal cues are omitted, which could also provide some cues as to the nature of the surface.

Subjects responses tended to agree on a negative co-efficient under the haptic condition. Lederman and colleagues modelled the relationship between perceived roughness and spatial period when exploring via a probe as a quadratic function, which showed an increasing perceived roughness over the spatial periods of interest. Lederman and Klatzky argued that "one possible reason for the shift (in relationship between spatial period and perceived roughness) might be due to the fact that as probe size increases, so too does the minimum value of inter-element spacing at which the probe can penetrate between the raised elements and drop down to the underlying surface". The PHANToM based simulation utilises a point interaction model of contact, thus, the user can always penetrate between the raised elements of the grating, within the resolution limits of the device. Hence, perception in the current study is equivalent to the downturn phase of the quadratic function.

It was unclear whether a positive or negative co-efficient was the dominant case for visual stimulus, however, all subjects showed a meaningful relationship between spatial period and corresponding roughness estimates. The discrepancies in the results likely arise due to the fact that roughness is infrequently judged using visual stimulus alone, without tactile information. As Heller [13] stated, "people may have learned that visual texture does not provide reliable information about surface irregularities and consequently depend upon touch". Examples of this are a photograph, a painting, or a visual display unit.

6. Conclusion

To conclude the results presented in this paper, haptic perception of texture is important in simulated environments, as roughness is naturally a "haptically-mediated" dimension, that is to say, it is more easily encoded using the tactile senses. However, progress still needs to be made in order to develop superior models for textured surfaces, as inaccuracies in the simulated haptic sensations could account for the lack of a significant relationship between roughness and spatial period displayed by some subjects. Frictional cues and simulation of finite diameter (as opposed to point based) interaction models are two possible methods by which a more realistic representation may be achieved. There was a greater amount of disagreement with regards to the relationship between spatial period and perceived roughness during the visual simulation. However, subjects easily related the simulation to a roughness scale, as all subjects displayed a significant relationship between the surfaces physical parameter and estimated roughness.

The immediate future work pertaining to these results is to combine visual and haptic display in order to investigate the effects of bimodal perception. It is hypothesised that this will combine the benefits of both a significant linear relationship between spatial period, while helping to standardise subjects' responses to a negative co-efficient trend.

Acknowledgements

This work is supported by EPSRC GR/L76112 "Determining Appropriate Haptic Cues for Virtual Reality and Teleoperation".

References

1. Taylor, M.M., Lederman, S.J., Gibson, R.H.: Tactual Perception of Texture. In Carterette, E. and Friedman, M. (Eds.), Handbook of Perception. Vol. III. New York: Academic Press (1973) 251-272.
2. Klatzky, R.L., Lederman, S.J., Reed, C.: There's more to touch than meets the eye: The salience of object attributes for haptics with and without vision. Journal of experimental psychology, Vol. 116, (1987) 356 - 369.
3. Lederman, S.J., Klatzky, R.L.: Hand Movements: A Window into Haptic Object Recognition. Cognitive Psychology, Vol. 19 (1987) 342-368.
4. Lederman, S.J., Klatzky, R.L.: Feeling Through A Probe. Proc. ASME Intl. Mech. Eng. Congress: Dynamic Systems and Control Division (Haptic Interfaces for Virtual Environments and Teleoperator Systems), DSC-Vol. 64 (1998)127-131.
5. Fritz, J.P., Barner, K.E.: Stochastic Models for Haptic Texture. Proceedings SPIE International Symposium on Intelligent Systems and Advanced Manufacturing Vol. 3901 (1996) 34-44.
6. Jansson, G., Petrie, H., Colwell, C., Kornbrot, D., Fanger, J., Konig, H., Billberger, K., Hardwick, A., Furner, S.: Haptic Virtual Environments for Blind People: Exploratory Experiments with Two Devices. Intl. Journal of Virtual Reality Vol. 4 (1999) 10-20.
7. West, A.M., Cutkosky, M.R.: Detection of Real and Virtual Fine Surface Features with a Haptic Interface and Stylus, Proc. ASME Intl. Mech. Eng. Congress: Dynamic Systems and Control Division (Haptic Interfaces for Virtual Environments and Teleoperator Systems) DSC-Vol. 67 (1997) 159-166.
8. DiFranco, D., Beauregard, G.L., Srinivasan, M.A.: The Effect of Auditory Cues on the Haptic Perception of Stiffness in Virtual Environments. Proc. ASME Intl. Mech. Eng. Congress: Dynamic Systems and Control Division (Haptic Interfaces for Virtual Environments and Teleoperator Systems), DSC-Vol. 61. (1997)
9. Srinivasan, M.A., Beauregard, G.L., Brock, D.L.: The Impact of Visual Information on Haptic Perception of Stiffness in Virtual Environments. Proc. ASME Intl. Mech. Eng. Congress: Dynamic Systems and Control Division (Haptic Interfaces for Virtual Environments and Teleoperator Systems), DSC-Vol. 58 (1996) 555-559.
10. Rock, I., Victor, J.: Vision and Touch: An Experimentally Cheated Conflict Between the Two Senses. Science 143 (3606), (1964) 594-596.
11. Rock, I., Harris, C.S.: Vision and Touch. Scientific American 217, (1967) 96-104.
12. Lederman, S.J., Abbott, S.G.,: Texture Perception: Studies of Intersensory Organization Using a Discrepancy Paradigm, and Visual Versus Tactual Psychophysics. Journal of Experimental Psychology: Human Perception and Performance 7(4) (1981) 902-915.
13. Heller, M.A.: Visual and Tactual Texture Perception: Intersensory cooperation. Perception and Psychophysics 31(4) (1982) 339-344.
14. Kontarinis, D.A., Howe, R.D.: Display of High Frequency Tactile Information to Teleoperators. SPIE Vol. 2057 (1993) 40-50.
15. Krueger, L.E.: David Katz's der Aufbau der Tastwelt (The world of touch): A synopsis. Perception and psychophysics 7(6) (1970) 337-341.
16. Minsky, M., Lederman, S. J.: Simulated Haptic Textures: Roughness. Proc. ASME Intl. Mech. Eng. Congress: Dynamic Systems and Control Division (Haptic Interfaces for Virtual Environments and Teleoperator Systems), DSC – Vol. 58 (1996) 421-426.
17. Minsky, M., Ouh-Young, M., Steele, O., Brooks jr., F.P., Behensky, M.: Feeling and Seeing: Issues in Force Display, Proceedings of Symposium on Interactive 3D Graphics (1990) 235-243.
18. Siira, J., Pai, D.K.: Haptic Rendering – A Stochastic Approach. Proceedings of 1996 IEEE International Conference on Robotics and Automation, Minneapolis, Minnesota, (1996) 557-562.

The Effective Combination of Haptic and Auditory Textural Information

Marilyn Rose McGee, Phil Gray, and Stephen Brewster

Multimodal Interaction Group, Glasgow Interactive Systems Group
Department of Computing Science, University of Glasgow
mcgeemr@dcs.gla.ac.uk
Tel - (0141) 330 3541
http://www.dcs.gla.ac.uk/~mcgeemr

Abstract. With the increasing availability and quality of auditory and haptic means of interaction, it is not unusual to incorporate many modalities in interfaces rather than the purely visual. The user can be powerfully affected however when information presented in different modalities are combined to become multimodal. Providing interface designers with the means to implement haptic-audio interfaces might result in adverse effects to interaction unless they are also equipped with structured knowledge on how to select effective combinations of such information. This work introduces `Integration of Information´ as one important dimension of haptic-audio interaction and explores its effects in the context of multimodal texture perception. The range and resolution of available textures through force feedback interaction is a design consideration that might benefit from the addition of audio. This work looks at the effect of combining auditory and haptic textures on people's judgment of the roughness of a virtual surface. The combined haptic-audio percepts will vary in terms of how congruent they are in the information they convey regarding the frequency of bumps or ridges on the virtual surface. Three levels of integration (*conflicting*, *redundant*, or *complementary*) are described and their possible implications discussed in terms of enhancing texture perception with force-feedback devices.

Keywords: Haptic, audio, force-feedback, texture perception, multimodal information processing, intersensory integration.

Introduction

Motivations

Multimodal Interfaces involve the use of multiple human modalities in the interaction (input, output, or both) between the human user and the computer. Haptic-audio interfaces therefore involve the use of both haptic and audio means of interaction (see Table 1. for definitions). In particular, the term haptic-audio interfaces is used here to refer to the communication of certain information to the user through an interface using a combined haptic and audio representation of this information rather than a

S. Brewster, R. Murray-Smith (Eds.): Haptic HCI 2000, LNCS 2058, pp. 118-126, 2001.

single modality representation. The advances in both haptic and audio technology have resulted in such haptic-audio interfaces becoming increasingly realistic to implement in a wide range of applications yet we have little organized knowledge on how best to design them. This work contributes to a body of knowledge on how to effectively combine haptic and auditory information.

The way we integrate information from different sensory modalities is complex (Wickens *et al*, 1983) and can seriously contribute to the quality of interaction in multimodal interfaces. The term `integration of information´ is used to refer to the information processing involved in combining two (or more) different modalities presented together to convey the same piece of information. Two modalities can be combined and the resulting multimodal percept may be a weaker, stronger, or altogether different percept. The effects of combining haptic and audio information must therefore be systematically explored to realize the potential of haptic-audio interfaces as well as to avoid creating interfaces that afford poor interaction.

There are specific interaction issues emerging from the increasing use of haptic interfaces, which could potentially be solved using careful addition of audio. One such interaction issue is that of haptically representing texture. In particular, force feedback devices are being used to convey texture by perturbing the user's hand or finger movements kinesthetically rather than cutaneously as with tactile devices (e.g. Lederman, 1999; West and Cutkosky, 1997). This often relies on much larger forces than those typically experienced on the skin during real texture perception (Katz, 1989). We have found in our previous work that such gross textures can perturb the users' movements so much that the ability to stay on the textured surface is adversely affected (Oakley *et al* 2000).

Goals
This work discusses and empirically evaluates the dimension of `Integration of Information´ in the specific context of haptic-audio texture perception. The goals of the ongoing work are to: (a) explore the effects of combining haptic and audio information at varying levels of integration and (b) determine the potential benefits of using haptic-audio percepts of texture to overcome the limitations of presenting texture through force feedback alone.

Previous Research
Within multimodal research, there have been distinct areas of specialized interest emerging. It has become clear from the research that exploring how our sense modalities behave in interaction should allow us to choose appropriate combinations of modalities according to the devices being used, the population of users, the environment, and the nature of the task.

Much of the work to date has focused on coordinating multimodal input for example (e.g. Oviatt, 1997), or the coordination of multimodal output for a specialized population such as visually impaired or physically disabled users (e.g. Mynatt, 1997; Stevens *et al*, 1997). Less work exists on the systematic study of how the combination of multimodal output of information could be better designed to coincide more closely with human information processing capabilities during multimodal interaction. In addition, little work exists on matching these information-processing capabilities to the nature of the interaction device(s) being used.

Visual displays have dominated interface research in the past but more recently auditory displays have been developed and tested (e.g. Brewster, 1997; Mynatt, 1997). With the lack of touch in interfaces now being strongly challenged, haptic technologies have also emerged at a rapid rate (Srinivasan, 1997). With the visual, auditory, and haptic channels (see Table 1. for definitions) all now technically available, multimodal interfaces can reach wider populations, increase the potential realism of displays, and generally increase the quantity and quality of information we can convey through the interface.

In human sensing and manipulation of everyday objects, the perception of surface texture is fundamental to accurate identification of an object (Katz, 1989). In a virtual world also, haptic texture information can both increase the sense of realism of an object as well as convey informational content regarding what the object is, where it is, what it is for and so on (Jansson et al, 1998).

Textures might be used in human and veterinary virtual medicine to assist in diagnosis of certain conditions. The texture of a tissue might indicate how well scarred tissue is healing for example. Using texture in the visualization of data could allow areas of interest to be 'textured' in the same way as colours are used in graphical visualization. Different textures could indicate different keys on a graph or chart for example. Being able to discriminate between various virtual textures in the textile industry might also prove beneficial. With an increasing number of customers shopping online for a variety of products, being able to convey different textures of objects will become crucial. For a variety of reasons it is desirable to be able to represent textures as effectively as possible in virtual environments.

There has been considerable previous work investigating the perceptual aspects of real surface textures. Lederman et al. (1974) suggest that texture perception is mediated by force cues created by spatial geometry of the surface. It is also possible that surface texture perception uses vibratory cues generated by the repeated and regular stimulation of mechanoreceptive afferents as the finger is moved across a surface (Katz, 1989). In fact, it is possible that both kinds of cues are involved, depending on the task to be executed (Weisenberger and Krier, 1997). Far less is known about the perceptual response to virtual surfaces. The physical properties of textures are very complex and are proving difficult to reproduce for virtual textures. For example, is a rough surface characterized by irregular or regular surface elements? What effect does inter-element spacing have on perceived roughness? Representing texture with force feedback devices in particular has proved problematic.

Force feedback devices detect changes in the device's configuration and then use mechanical actuators to apply appropriately calculated forces back to the user. Importantly, the interaction relies on kinesthetic information being conveyed to the user rather than cutaneous information (see table 1). These devices often simulate textures with larger forces than those experienced in real texture perception. In our previous work for example we found that the gross textures implemented perturbed users' movements making it hard for them to stay on a desktop target (Oakley et al., 2000).

Table 1: Definitions (Oakley, McGee, Brewster and Gray, CHI 2000).

Haptic	Relating to the sense of touch.
Kinesthetic	Meaning the feeling of motion. Relating to sensations originating in muscles, tendons and joints.
Cutaneous	Pertaining to the skin itself or the skin as a sense organ. Includes sensation of pressure, temperature, and pain.
Tactile	Pertaining to the cutaneous sense but more specifically the sensation of pressure rather than temperature or pain.
Force Feedback	Relating to the mechanical production of information sensed by the human kinesthetic system.

It could perhaps be argued that texture is more suitable to production by tactile devices. Despite the early perceptual and physiological arguments for a spatial code to texture, three-dimensional force feedback interfaces are able to simulate surface texture (Weisenberger and Krier, 1997). It is the degree of fidelity and realism achievable with such devices that is of primary interest. The interaction issue then is how to overcome any limitations of using force feedback devices alone to represent texture.

The display of a convincing haptic percept such as texture should not necessarily be limited to the haptic modalities. Audio and visual cues can be associated with a haptic display to contribute to the realism or informational content of the display (Rosenberg, 1994). The current work investigates the conditions under which audio cues do and do not enhance force feedback based texture perception.

Current Work

It would be beneficial to know the extent to which we can affect peoples' perception by coupling auditory and haptic percepts in a systematic way. In doing so we can establish ways in which to manipulate what the user will perceive at the interface. In particular, we could use this information to overcome limitations of a device. For instance, the addition of audio information to force feedback virtual surfaces might increase the range and/or resolution of textures available to the designer. Likewise, this information could be used to avoid coupling percepts that result in perceptual or cognitive conflict and which in turn might adversely affect the processing of that information.

In the current work, haptic and auditory textures will be rated by a group of participants to establish how rough each stimuli is in terms of each of the other stimuli. This will result in a set of haptic and audio textures identifiable along the dimension of increasing roughness. These haptic and audio stimuli can then be combined to produce multimodal haptic-audio roughness percepts in the main study. The combined textures will be either congruent or incongruent in terms of the information each modality conveys regarding the number of ridges/bumps on the virtual surface. Resulting multimodal percepts might provide *redundant, complementary*, or *conflicting* haptic-audio information. The effects of the different levels of congruency and resulting levels of integration of the information will be discussed.

Device

The PHANToM 1.0 force feedback device by SensAble Technologies will be used to create the haptic virtual surfaces (see Fig. 1). Force feedback devices have optical sensors that detect changes in the device's configuration. The device then uses mechanical actuators to apply forces back to the user calculated from the positional information and the stored algorithmic models of the objects with which the user is interacting. The interaction relies on kinesthetic information being conveyed to the user rather than cutaneous information (see table 1).

Fig 1: The Phantom 3D force feedback device from SensAble Technologies.

Subjects interact with the device by holding a pen-like stylus attached to a passive gimbal. The user is instructed to scrape the probe of the PHANToM back and forth across the textured area to produce the haptic and/or auditory feedback regarding the roughness of the surface. The stylus switch on the probe of the PHANToM is used to select any response a participant has to make.

Haptic and Auditory Textures

Neither haptic nor auditory textures are designed to necessarily model physically accurate or optimum representations of a rough surface. Rather, they are designed to give feedback approximate to that obtained when real textures are explored. In this way, the actual effects of experiencing such feedback multimodally as opposed to unimodally can be explored.

The haptic textures are generated as sinusoidal gratings on a rectangular patch on the back wall of the workspace. Forces are modeled as a point contact in the z-direction. The resulting profile depends on the amplitude and frequency of the 'wave'. The haptic textures will have a fixed amplitude of 0.5mm and frequency (cycles per fixed length of surface) can have one of 6 values - 10, 15, 20, 25, 30, or 35 cycles.

The auditory textures will consist of a sound played to indicate contact with a ridge/bump on the haptic virtual surface. The number of contact sounds can be matched to the number of ridges/bumps experienced haptically (congruent) or provide more or less contact sounds than there are haptic bumps/ridges (incongruent). The exact effect of this congruency/incongruency on the perceived level of roughness of a percept is the subject of investigation.

Manipulating Congruency

Congruency/Incongruency are determined by the information provided by each modality relating to the number of bumps/ridges encountered on a virtual surface. If the number of contact sounds matches the number of haptic bumps/ridges then they are defined as congruent. Incongruency occurs when the number contact sounds does not match the number of haptic bumps/ridges.

Incongruency however has directionality. Audio information might indicate more or less bumps/ridges than the haptic information. In this case, the incongruency could act to move the level of perceived roughness of a surface up or down the roughness dimension. The direction of incongruency will depend on how frequency of the haptic bumps/ridges, and frequency of contact sounds, unimodally map to level of perceived roughness.

Measuring Perceived Roughness

Surface roughness is one of texture's most prominent perceptual attributes. The precise physical determinants of roughness however are not exactly clear (e.g. Lederman, 1974). Because there is still debate over the actual parameters that determine roughness, users' *perception* of virtual roughness (regardless of the underlying physical model) is an increasingly important issue in virtual haptic interaction.

Participants will make a fixed choice response regarding a pair of surfaces. The roughest surface can be on the left, the right, or they can be judged as the same roughness. The proportion of times a surface is judged as rougher than each of the other surfaces can be obtained and the surfaces can then be placed along the roughness dimension.

Task and Procedure

The haptic-audio surfaces will be presented in pairs as rectangular patches on the back wall of the workspace (see Fig. 2). Participants will be instructed to scrape the probe of the PHANToM back and forth across the stimulus surface to form an impression of how rough the surface seems to them. They will be asked to try to maintain the same speed throughout the experiment. The participant will then be asked to make a judgment regarding their comparison of the two surfaces. They make their response by clicking the appropriate button on the screen with the stylus switch on the probe of the PHANToM.

Clicking the button labeled 'next' will present the next pair of surfaces. When the participant has completed all the trials they will be given a message indicating that they are finished the experiment and a summary file for their responses will automatically be stored for that participant.

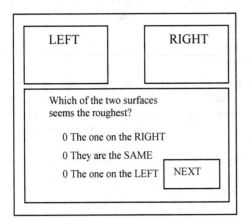

Fig. 2: Diagrammatic view of interface.

Hypotheses and Implications

Integration of Information

Haptic-audio percepts of texture may reduce, increase, or completely alter the informational content of the percept being conveyed multimodally. The exact effects of the haptic-audio coupling will depend on the level at which the information is integrated. The level at which the multimodal information is integrated will depend, in part, on the level of congruency between the haptic and audio stimuli.

Participants will experience congruent and incongruent pairings of haptic and audio textures. The level of integration of these combinations can be *conflicting, redundant,* or *complementary,* each of which has the potential to affect perception and resulting interaction in different ways.

H1 - *Conflict*: If information processed by multiple modalities attempts to convey conflicting information is some way then the resulting multimodal percept may become distorted or completely lost in the process. Alternatively, the judgment of the multimodal percept might change in some unpredictable way.

If the audio stimulus and haptic stimulus are incongruent and conflicting then multimodal (haptic-audio) judgments of roughness will move along the roughness dimension but in the opposite direction predicted by the direction of the incongruency.

H2 - *Redundancy*: People might process only one modality of information from the many available to them in a multimodal percept. The modality employed may depend on physical/perceptual ability, personal preference, or the nature of the task for example. The actual effects of providing redundant information are somewhat difficult to predict. Redundant information might increase the mental representation of the information. This may in turn lead to increased confidence or reliability of judgments without necessarily altering the content of the information.

If the audio stimulus and haptic stimulus are congruent and redundant then with or without the auditory information, perceptual judgments of a virtual surface will be essentially the same. That is, the unimodal (haptic) and multimodal (haptic-audio) judgments of roughness will be at the same level along the roughness dimension.

H3 - *Complementarity*: A percept composed of multiple modalities might combine to in fact give more than the sum of the individual parts. That is, two unimodal percepts, when combined, produce some additive effect not possible with either unimodal percept alone. Such complementary pairings of haptic and audio stimuli might act to increase the quality and/or quantity of information available through a haptic-audio interface.

If the audio stimulus and haptic stimulus are incongruent but complementary then multimodal (haptic-audio) judgments of roughness will move along the roughness dimension in the direction predicted by the direction of the incongruency. That is, when an audio and haptic stimulus are combined such that the audio stimulus is more rough than the haptic stimulus then the multimodal judgment of roughness is moved along the roughness dimension in the direction of increasing roughness. Likewise, when an audio stimulus and haptic stimulus are combined such that the audio stimulus is less rough than the haptic stimulus then the multimodal judgment of roughness is moved along the roughness dimension in the direction of decreasing roughness.

Future Work

Perceptual judgments of the unimodal stimuli are currently being gathered in preparation for combining them to produce the haptic-audio percepts. The next stage of the work will be to combine the haptic and audio textures to produce the congruent and incongruent multimodal percepts. This work will shed light on the ability of audio stimuli to alter the effect of haptic virtual stimuli and the different levels at which the haptic-audio precepts are integrated.

Work is underway to conduct an applied experiment of haptic-audio integration during force feedback texture perception. Veterinary simulation and visualization for the blind are being considered as possible applications areas. Results from the current study will serve to provide predictions regarding the effects of coupling haptic and audio information in a more applied example of force-feedback texture perception. Future work will also include a more in depth exploration of the levels at which we integrate haptic and audio information and how such organised knowledge would aid interface designers in the effective combination of haptic and audio information.

Acknowledgments

This research is supported under EPSRC project GR/L79212 and EPSRC studentship 98700418. Thanks also go to the SHEFC REVELATION Project, SensAble Technologies and Virtual Presence Ltd.

References

1. Brewster, S.A. (1997). Using Non-Speech Sound to Overcome Information Overload. *Displays*, 17, pp. 179-189.
2. Jansson, G., Fanger, J., Konig, H., and Billberger, K. (1998). Visually Impaired Person's use of the PHANToM for Information about texture and 3D form of Virtual Objects, *Proceedings of the Third PHANToM Users Group Workshop*, Cambridge, MA: Massachusetts Institute of Technology.
3. Katz, D. (1989). *The World of Touch*, (Translated by Krueger, L.E.), Erlbaum, Hillsdale, NJ. Original work published in 1925.
4. Lederman, S.J. (1974). Tactile roughness of grooved surfaces: the touching process and effects of macro- and microsurface structure, *Perception and Psychophysics*, 16, 2, pp. 385-395.
5. Lederman, S.J., Klatzky, R.L., Hamilton, C.L., and Ramsay, G.I. (1999). Perceiving Roughness via a Rigid Probe: Psychophysical Effects of Exploration Speed and Mode of Touch, *Haptic e-journal*, 1,1, (http://www.haptics-e.org).
6. Mynatt, E.D. (1997). Transforming graphical interfaces into auditory interfaces for blind users. *Human-Computer Interaction*, 12, PP. 7-45.
7. Oakley, I., McGee, M.R., Brewster, S., and Gray, P. (2000). Putting the Feel in 'Look and Feel', *In Proceedings of ACM CHI 2000*, The Hague, ACM Press, Addison-Wesley, pp.415-422.
8. Oviatt, S.L. (1997). Multimodal interactive maps: Designing for human performance. *Human -Computer Interaction*, 12, pp. 131-185.
9. Rosenberg, L.B. (1994). Design of a Virtual Rigid Surface: Haptic/Audio Registration, *CHI' 94*, April 24-28, pp. 257-258.
10. Srinivasan, M.A., and Basdogan, C. (1997). Haptics in Virtual Environments: Taxonomy, Research Status, and Challenges, *Computers and Graphics*, 21, 4, pp. 23-34.
11. Stevens, R.D., Edwards, A.D.N., and Harling, P.A. (1997). Access to mathematics for visually disabled students through multimodal interaction. *Human-Computer Interaction*, 12, pp. 47-92.
12. West, A.M., and Cutkosky, M.R. (1997). Detection of Real and Virtual Fine Surface Features with a Haptic Interface and Stylus, *Proceedings of the ASME Dynamic Systems and Control Division*, 61, pp. 159-166.
13. Wickens, C.D., Sandry, D.L., and Vidulich, M. (1983). Compatibility and Resource Competition between Modalities of Input Central Processing, and Output, *Human Factors*, 25, 2, pp. 227-248.
14. Weisenberger, J.M., and Krier, M.J. (1997). Haptic Perception of Simulated Surface Textures via Vibratory and Force Feedback Displays, *Proceedings of the ASME, Dynamic Systems and Control Division*, 61, pp.55-60.

Cursor Trajectory Analysis

Hilde Keuning-Van Oirschot and Adrian J.M. Houtsma

IPO, Center for User-System Interaction
P.O. Box 513, 5600 MB Eindhoven, The Netherlands
Tel: +31 40 2475234
h.keuning@tue.nl

Abstract. To create non-disturbing tactual feedback in human-computer interaction we want to predict the user's goal, so that the user is helped toward the target and away from non-targets. In this paper we describe an exploration of cursor movements with an amplitude of 250 pixels, in eight different directions and with three different control devices (a mechanical mouse, an optical mouse and an optical trackball) to find characteristics of the cursor path which could be used to create a prediction algorithm on direction. The focus was on the mean curvature of and the variability between the paths in each direction.

It can be concluded that on average cursor paths are rather straight in all eight directions and with all three devices. The variability of the paths depends on (1) direction; (2) friction of the control device; (3) user.

1 Introduction

As computers evolve to be basic tools in work and home, improving the human-computer interaction is critical for the user's acceptance. Among the criteria that can be listed, a system must be comfortable and efficient. This means, for example, that a computer must give the user fast and clear feedback on his or her actions. For example, recently a sensation of touch can be given to the moving hand via the control device. In controlled experimental environments tactual feedback devices, indeed, turned out to facilitate the user's target acquisition task ([7], [1] and [5]). In these experimental environments, however, only one visual object was instructed as being the target. So, there was only one object which could activate the touch feedback mechanism. In typical human computer interaction several objects are on the screen which are non-targets, but which still activate the touch feedback mechanism when entered. In such an environment with non-targets, it would be more convenient and effective if the feedback works for the user's target only. This is not possible, as long as the system doesn't know where the user wants to go. The obvious solution is to predict the user's goal from an early part in the trajectory. After predicting the target the computer system can aid the user to reach the target without getting distracted by touch feedback on non-targets.

S. Brewster, R. Murray-Smith (Eds.): Haptic HCI 2000, LNCS 2058, pp. 127–134, 2001.

2   Purpose of this Experiment

The general purpose of this study is to make a prediction algorithm based on characteristics of the initial part of the cursor trajectory. Therefore, it is necessary to know what trajectory characteristics can give useful information for a reliable target prediction. One aspect of a trajectory is its path. This is the spatial time-independent shape of the trajectory. The other aspect is the time dependence along the path ([6]).

In the first experiment we focused on the path. We investigated what movement paths look like in different directions and with different devices. The main questions were whether a constant curve could be detected, how much paths varied around the mean path and whether curvature and variability related to direction, device or user.

The device might influence the trajectory in two ways. First, there may be a biasing influence as a result of mechanical track wheels. When these are positioned in x- and y-directions it could be more difficult to move a mouse in a straight oblique than in horizontal or vertical direction. Second, the general friction of a device could influence the trajectories. When friction within the device is increased, spatial inaccuracies caused by tremors or unwanted movement components (9-12Hz) are damped out, whereas, the contribution of corrective movement actions to movement variance increases [4].

Procedure

The task of the subjects was to move the cursor to a certain target, in one of eight directions, using a certain control device. The direction from the starting point to the targets was horizontal, vertical or diagonal. So, a target could be projected in every 45 degree angle. As all targets were at the same distance and had the same width, the index of difficulty ([3]) was the same for each trial. This was done because 'direction' and 'device' were planned to be the only within subject factors in this first exploratory experiment. The control devices were a mechanical mouse, an optical mouse and an optical trackball.

Participants could start whenever they were ready. A 'start' button was shown in the middle of the screen (see fig 1). When pressing the space bar, while the cursor was on the start button, a black circle (one of the eight possible targets) appeared and the button disappeared. Meanwhile the cursor was repositioned on specified coordinates, so that each trial started exactly at the same position. The participants were instructed to reach the target in a 'normal' way, as they were used to in working on a computer. When the target was reached subjects had to wait 200 msec until the target disappeared and the 'start' button re-appeared. Then the cursor could be moved back to the start button again. After pressing the space bar the next trial started.

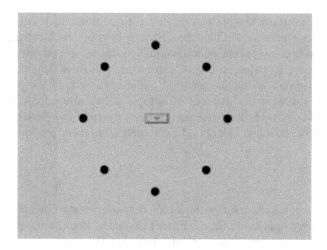

Fig. 1. All possible targets.

Design

The experiment was divided in three sessions, each with one of three control devices; a normal mouse, an optical mouse or an optical trackball. The order in which the devices were used was random. Each session consisted of a practice and an experimental part. In the experimental part each target was randomly presented ten times.

Measurements

During each trial x- and y-coordinates (in pixels) and the system time were sampled. This was done at 50 Hz, because the input devices had a default frequency of 50Hz.

Subjects

Subjects were ten employees at IPO, seven male, three female. Mean age was 29.8 years. All of them were experienced with a mechanical mouse, but not with an optical mouse or trackball.

Analysis

Because sampling was time controlled, velocity influences the spacing between the samples. To calculate the curvature of a path, however, we want equal distances between the samples, because then every part of the path contributes equally to the calculation of the curvature. Therefore, for each trajectory, new samples were calculated, by interpolation, for every 1% of total traveled distance (distance of the path itself).

To assess the *curvature*, the paths were first rotated until start and end positions were on the positive x-axis. Then the distance between each calculated coordinate and the x-axis was taken, which is equal to the accompanying y-coordinate, both with respect to value and sign. Curvature was then defined as the mean value of this distance along the path ([2]. The *variability* of the paths is represented by the standard deviation of all sample points around the mean path of the ten trajectories performed per person per direction and device.
The standard deviation is calculated over each 10-percent section of the whole path.

Results

To give an idea of what cursor paths look like, paths created by one subject with each devices are displayed in fig. 2. From this figure, it can already be seen that the mean paths must be rather straight and that the optical trackball leads to more variability than the two mice.

Figure 3 shows the mean paths and standard deviation in every direction over the three devices.
 It can be seen that the mean paths are rather straight. A statistical t-test of the mean curvature against a curvature of zero shows that the overall paths are slightly but significantly curved (p< .01). Figure 4 shows the same as figure 3, but for each device separately. Only the vertical paths (downward in the figure) created with the optical mouse and the optical trackball are visibly curved. A non-parametric test(Friedman test) was performed per device to test for differences in curvature between direction. This test showed that only for the optical mouse a difference in curvature between directions existed ($\chi^2 = 15.4, p = .031$). Specifically, it showed that moving in a vertical direction toward the body (180 decrees) resulted in a high ranking score. With a repeated measure ANOVA also, a significant effect of 'user' was found ($F_{1,9} = 13.245, p = .005$). Another two ANOVA's per user on device and direction, respectively, showed that some users were influenced by the device; especially the optical trackball resulted in more curved paths.
 Obviously, most variability is present at the paths created with the optical trackball. It also shows that the standard deviations between adjacent targets do not overlap. This means that with this target resolution every intended target should be highly predictable. With a prediction requirement of 69% correct (i.e. an angular target separation of one standard deviation) the resolution could be about 30 equally-spaced targets for the two mice and about 20-25 for the optical trackball.

 Figure 5 shows variability as a function of direction pooled over all subjects and sample points. It can be seen that the optical mouse leads to the least variability around the mean paths and the optical trackball to the most variability.

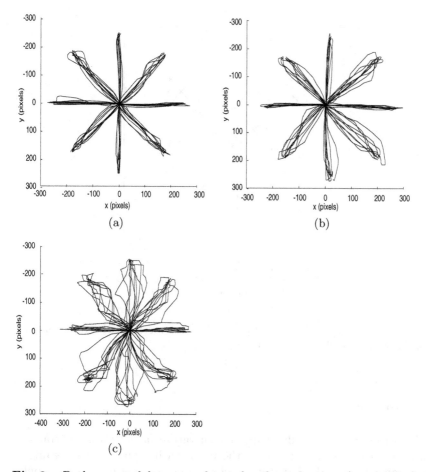

Fig. 2. Paths created by one subject for three devices a)mechanical mouse, b)optical mouse and c)optical trackball in eight directions.

Also, the oblique directions (45, 135, 225 and 315 degrees) show higher standard deviations than the horizontal and vertical paths. This can be seen in figure 3 and 4 as well.

To test for differences in variability between direction and device, a repeated measure ANOVA was performed with 'direction' and 'device' as within subject factors and 'user' as between subjects factor. Two main effects were found: for device ($F_{2,18} = 22.938, p = < .01$), direction ($F_{7,63} = 13.243, p < .01$), as well as an interaction effect between device and direction ($F_{14,126} = 3.918, p < .01$). Also an effect of 'user' ($F_{1,9} = 147.029, p < .01$) was found.

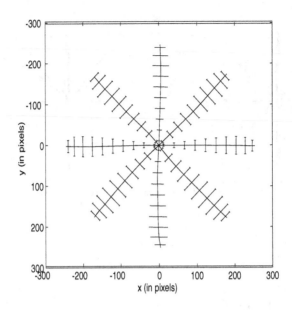

Fig. 3. Mean path and st.dev. for all three devices (mechanical mouse, optical mouse and optical trackball) in eight directions.

3   Conclusions

Although there is a statistically significant curvature (as opposed to straightness) in some of the measured paths, the mean paths appear rather straight in comparison with standard deviations. For target estimation purposes only negligible losses are to be expected if paths are assumed to be straight lines. However, there is some reason for discussing the results on curvature. Curvature in movements to the left and right is imaginable as occurring around the wrist angle. However this angle might (a) be too small to be visible or (b) be easily compensated by the fingers.

Variability around mean paths differs per device and per direction. This means that for a good prediction the target resolution could be higher when the device creates less variable paths (e.g. the optical mouse or the mechanical mouse). Reasons for these differences in variability between devices can be sought in differences in the general friction, direction specific friction (for example, as a result of track wheels) or 'ease-of use'. For example, the optical trackball moves with very low friction. This means that tremors (or noise) in the human motor system will be visible in the observed path. So, it is easier to move smoothly when some friction is present in the device. [4]

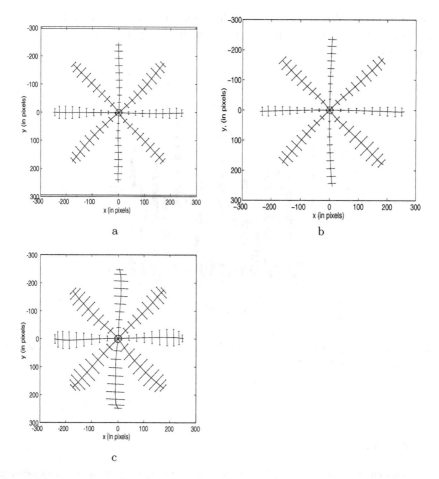

Fig. 4. Mean path and st.dev. for three devices a)mechanical mouse, b)optical mouse and c)optical trackball in eight directions.

Variability also differs per 'user'. This implies that a target estimation algorithm could be further improved by adjusting its parameters beforehand to individual users.

In conclusion it can be said that:
- For prediction purposes, paths can be assumed to be straight lines.
- Variability around the mean path differs per device and per direction. This means that for a good prediction the target resolution could be higher when the device creates less variable paths (e.g. the optical mouse or the mechanical mouse).

- Variability also differs per 'user'. This implies that a target estimation algorithm could be further improved by adjusting its parameters beforehand to individual users.

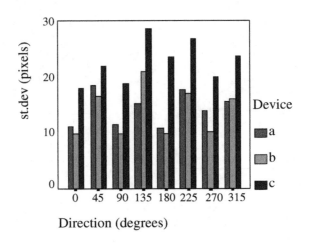

Fig. 5. Mean variability per direction for each device a) mechanical mouse, b) optical mouse, c) optical trackball.

References

1. Akamatsu, M., and Sato, S.: A multi-modal mouse with tactile and force feedback. Int.J. Human-Computer Studies, **40**, 443-453 (1994).
2. Boessekool, J.: Moving two hands. Ph.D thesis, Utrecht University, The Netherlands.(1999)
3. Fitts, P.: The information capacity of the human motor system in controlling the amplitude of movement. Journal of Experimental Psychology 47(6), 381-391.
4. Van Galen, G.P., Van Doorn, R.P., and Schomaker, L.R.B.: Effects of motor programming on the power spectral density function of finger and wrist movements. Journal of Experimental Psychology: Human Perception and Performance,16,(4),755-765.
5. Göbel, M. Luczak, H., Springer, J., Hedicke, V., and Rötting, M.: Tactile feedback applied to computer mice. International Journal of Human-Computer Interaction. 7(1), 1-24.
6. Hollerbach, J.: Planning of arm movements. In: D.N. Osheron,S.M Kosslyn, J.M Hollerbach (Eds.), Visual cognition and action (pp183-211). Cambridge, MA:MIT Press.(1990)
7. Keyson, D.V.: Touch in user interface navigation. Ph.D thesis. Technical university Eindhoven, The Netherlands (1997)

What Impact Does the Haptic-Stereo Integration Have on Depth Perception in Stereographic Virtual Environment? A Preliminary Study

Laroussi Bouguila, Masahiro Ishii, and Makoto Sato

Precision and Intelligence Laboratory, Tokyo Institute of Technology
4259 Nagatsuta cho Midori ku Yokohama shi 226-8503 – Japan
Tel: +81 45 924 5050 Fax: +81 45 924 5016
laroussi@pi.titech.ac.jp

Abstract. The present work aims to study the possibility of displaying force feedback along with stereo graphic in virtual reality interaction. During the different experiments we investigated the effect of providing haptic sensation on Human's instable stereopsis depth perception. From the different result and discussions we find that such haptic-stereo coupling improved the instability of stereopsis depth perception. As well clearly shortened the necessary time for depth judgment. Which are 2 important factors for interactive mixed reality systems. However, current experiments didn't show to which extent the haptic-stereo coupling improved the accuracy of localizing and manipulating objects in virtual environment.

Introduction

Our understanding of the three dimensional environment around us is inferred from a variety of depth cues. The information received from our diverse perceptual modalities is consistently and reliably integrated into a unitary perception of the world. To reach such capability of complete and accurate perception in multi-modal virtual environment. Artificial display systems and feedback cues have to work into concert with each other so as to create the illusion of natural sense of interaction.

While the needs and the roles of multi-modal virtual environment are well documented by a large body of theoretical development, relatively little is known about the perceptual issues resulting from the combination of different artificial display systems. In real world, human's senses such as vision, audition, haptic, etc. are almost always in agreement with each other, so an accurate depth perception is possible. In virtual reality, however, technological limitations are usually such that only a small subset of available cues can be fully implemented. Other cues are either missing or not well displayed. As well, the use of different technology with different bandwidths and mechanisms make the integration between modalities not consistent and in correspondence with human sensitivity. Uncontrolled feedback cues in a virtual scene can end up providing false depth information and may create a sensory conflict, which can lead to distorted perceptions and unskillful interaction. In the current study

S. Brewster, R. Murray-Smith (Eds.): Haptic HCI 2000, LNCS 2058, pp. 135-150, 2001.

we discuss the possibility of integrating artificial haptic feedback with stereographic images and their coupling's effect on depth perception in virtual environment.

Research Background and Motivation

It has been proven in many researches that stereoscopic images are very effective in improving interactions in virtual environment. As well, haptic sensations are known to impart users with realistic feeling about physical interactions, which improve the control over virtual objects. However, in most virtual reality systems, when these two modalities are coupled together, the real world (users) and the virtual world are separated, and do not interact directly with each other. For example, when the task of the user is to grasp a virtual object, usually we provide an imaginary graphic hand to interact directly with the virtual object (small sphere in figure 1-b), whereas the real hand is used to control the interaction without co-existence with the object, see figure 1-b. Such indirect control makes the user think in terms of manipulating objects in remote site, and do not have the conviction that he is within the virtual environment itself. Although, representing body's parts involved in the virtual environment with similar graphics has sufficient accuracy for interactions (Butts and McAllister 1988, Spain 1984, Beaton 1987 and Reinhardt 1990), yet, it keeps the real and the virtual worlds non fused, and felt as being two different environments. What we want to achieve is direct control over the virtual object as seen in figure 1-a.

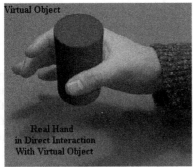

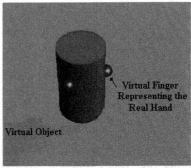

Fig. 1-a. Real hand in direct interaction with Virtual object.

Fig. 1-b. Indirect interaction between real hand and virtual object.

Issues of Direct Coupling of Haptics and Stereopsis

In order to provide an accurate integration between stereopsis and haptics cues, three facts have to be considered.
1. Misperception of the binocular stereopsis cue. This phenomenon is common where the location of the same object can be perceived at different depth each time. The depth instability of stereopsis affects directly the coordination between the visual

and haptic modalities. A simple reaching to grasp task cannot be done appropriately. Drascic and Milgram 1991.
2. Perception of real hand and stereoscopic images differ in a variety of ways. The main difference is that we use accommodation to perceive depth for real objects, whereas we use convergence to perceive depth for virtual objects. Miyashita and Uchida 1990. See figure 2.

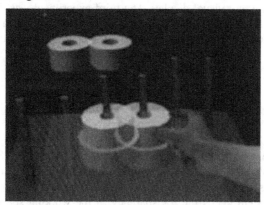

Fig. 2. Difference between stereographic and real object visual display.

3. Occlusion and focus issues between real and virtual objects. Real objects have much stronger visual cues than stereographic virtual objects. For example the hand may occlude the virtual object, but the inverse situation is not possible, which violate interposition cue.

The first issue is of particular interest in the development of mixed and augmented reality systems. The problem of misperceiving the location of objects at different depths is especially important if one of the principal tasks of the user is to reach and grasp an object, or to align objects. The force feedback sensation has to be always displayed in accordance with the virtual environment; any mismatching between the two modalities may cause the failure of the tasks. The present paper presents the results of our investigation about this issue.

Purpose of the Research

In the current research, we are interested in giving the user the ability to reach and touch virtual objects by his hand as in real world, see figure 2. We aim to display haptic sensation at the same position where objects are perceived. This entails establishing whether or not the haptic display can overcome the stereopsis distance-scaling problem, and be consistently and accurately matched with the stereoscopic display.

At our knowledge there has been no work reported in the literature, which is directly relevant to this particular coupling in virtual environment systems. The results of this study can lead to improve the accuracy of perception and coordination between haptic sensation and visual cues in augmented and mixed reality applications.

In the next section, we present the overall condition of the experiments. In the next sections, we describe and discuss about our experiments. There are four experiments. The first one was dedicated to state the variance of stereopsis depth perception without any force feedback. The second experiment was to the frame the haptic depth consistency without any visual display. The third experiment was the combination of the previous experiments and to study the effect of coupling both haptic and stereopsis on depth perception. The last experiment was carried out to study the depth threshold of force feedback within which the two modalities can be fused. In the last section the remaining problems are discussed.

Method

To get the positions of perceived depth we used the SCALEABLE SPIDAR interface, B. Laroussi and M. Sato. 1997, see Appendix. The device can track the real position of subject's hand as well as provides both stereoscopic images and force feedback sensation. The system keeps the transparency of the working space and do not hide any part of the screen, see appendix A for more details. The stereoscopic image was displayed on a 120-inch large screen and observers viewed it by wearing liquid-crystal-shuttered glasses. In order to limit the perceptual capabilities of the observer's eyes to only a single depth cue, all experiments were performed in a completely dark room, and the stereoscopic image was reduced to a basic random dot stereogram, which display a simple positional depth distance. We adopted such approach to isolate the role of other visual cues from the acquisition of depth information.

Experiment I

Subjects

Four males served as observers. One was experienced observer knowledgeable about stereopsis. The others were naïve. All observers have normal or corrected to normal vision. None of them reported any haptic deficiencies. Although it was not necessary for the experiment, all subjects were familiar with haptic devices and virtual environment.

Apparatus

In all experiments we used the human-scale haptic device SCCALEABLE SPIDAR (Figure 4) to get hand positions as well as to display force feedback sensation. The device is coupled with a large screen where computer generated random-dot stereogram is displayed. The observer was seated on a chair inside the device facing the screen. To provide constant viewing distance and avoid cues known to affect depth perception such as perspective and motion parallax, the observer's head was stabilized with a chinrest at predetermined distance of 70 cm from the screen. All experiments were carried out in a completely dark room to discard any aiming point or background information that the observer may use as depth reference. The random-dot stereograms were made up of a square matrix consisting of 230x230 square dots, each of which had an equal probability of being displayed or not. The square has no background, and all dots were displayed in only red color. The square displayed to the left eye had a range of disparities added to it by shifting its horizontal position. Eight crossed disparities were employed in this experiment. The disparity ranges from 20 dots to 160 dots, and each disparity was in integer multiple of 20 dots. When the observer fuse left and right image he always perceive the square being in front of the screen and at hands reach. Figure 3 gives more detail about the apparatus of the system.

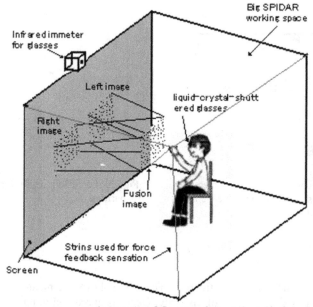

Figure 5: **Apparatus of the experiments installation**

Fig. 3. Apparatus of the experiment installation.

Procedure

Each observer was tested individually. In each session the observer sat on the chair, wear the fingering provided by the haptic device SCALEABLE SPIDAR, the positioned his head on the chinrest and looked straight ahead to the square. The task was to move his right hand forward until it becomes aligned with the right side of the square. Observers were not able to see their hands, because the room was dark and also instructed previously to not occlude the image by heir hands, figure 4. When the observer subjectively believes that his hand is at the same depth as the square he report this judgment vocally by saying "HERE". As the hand position is tracked in real time via the SCALEABLE SPIDAR device, the experimenter on clicking a mouse button recorded it instantly. The same task was repeated randomly at least 4 times for each disparity (8 disparities in all). After each trial the observer was asked to close his eyes while the experimenter change the disparity by clicking another mouse button, this pause is about 2 to 3 seconds.

The procedures were explained beforehand to each observer and given a short time of practice. Each session was preceded by at least 1 minute of dark-adaptation. Observers were allowed free eyes movement and as much time as required to estimate the depth of the square. Observers responded to the all disparities, repeated each 4 times at least (46 trials in all)

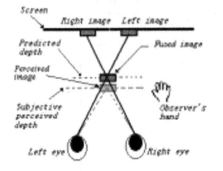

Fig. 4. The observer subjectively positions his hand at the same depth as the perceived square.

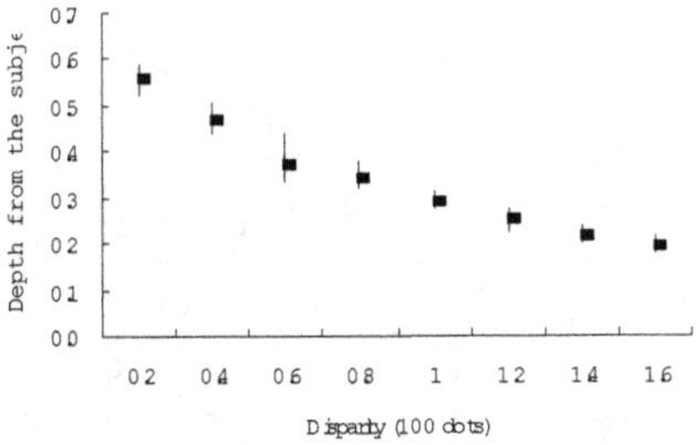

Fig. 5. Perceived depth for the different disparities.

Results

The results are summarized in figure 5. The graph shows the means and deviations of perceived depth as a function of disparity. Depth is expressed in terms of the distance interval between the observer and the perceived square. The small rectangles in the graph represent the mean of depth for each disparity. The vertical line represents the depth variation related to each disparity. The standard errors across disparities ranged from 1.5 cm to 5 cm of the mean depth and averaged 2.3 cm. Nearly all subjects responded quickly and confidently to all trial, usually viewing them for about 2 to 4 seconds before making a response. The results from the naïve observers did not differ in any systematic way from those from the experienced observer.

Discussion

We notice the clear relationship between the perceived depth and the physical disparity for all trials. This clear trend is evident for all subjects, and merely confirms that the magnitude of perceived depth increase with disparity as estimated by the following equation deduced from figure 6.

$$\frac{I}{2d} \forall \frac{R}{2(D ! d)} \tag{1}$$

Where **I** is the interocular distance. **D** is the viewing distance. **R** is the disparity distance and **d** is the depth distance from the observer. Equation (2) gives the depth **d** expressed as function of variable **R**.

$$d \forall \frac{ID}{R \# I} \tag{2}$$

As **D** and **I** are constant values, the depth is affected only by the change of disparity. That is, when disparity becomes smaller the square tends to be farther and inversely. Assuming that the interocular distance is 6 cm, equation (2) was represented by figure 7. Based on this theoretical prediction, the results presented in the graph 1 can be considered as stable and reliable.

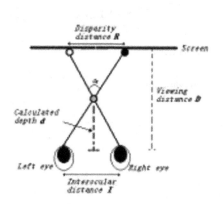

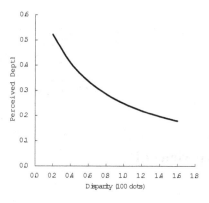

Fig. 6. Simple positional disparity.   **Fig. 7.** Predicted depth.

$$\left| d_R \right| \forall \left| \frac{! ID}{(R \# I)^2} \right| \tag{3}$$

If we look to the accuracy of observers' depth perception in regard to disparities, we find that most of the user showed strong sensitivity to depth variation when the disparity was small. This ability decrease when the disparity become bigger, i.e. the change of disparity from 20 dots to 40 dots generate about 9 cm of depth variation, whereas the same change of 20 dots from 140 to 160 dots gives only 3 cm of depth variation. Ogle [8], Sperling 1983 and others researchers classified this phenomenon into two kinds of stereopsis, "patent" and "qualitative". The first represent accurate stereopsis and occurs when disparity is small. The later represent imprecise stereopsis and occurs when disparity is big. This observation is validated by equation (3), which is the derivative function of equation (2). When the disparity is small the slop is big and gradually flattened while disparity is increasing, see figure 8.

An important question arises immediately in regard to all these data and observations. At which position the force feedback should be displayed in such a way it can be perceived at the same position as the stereoscopic image? The following experiment was conducted to address this issue.

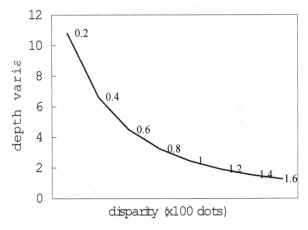

Fig. 8. Sensitivity to depth variation.

Experiment II

Coupling Stereopsis and Haptics

As discussed above, for each disparity, the square can be perceived randomly at different depth positions. It is impossible to predict at which distance the observer will perceive the stereoscopic square. In this experiment we investigate whether coupling force feedback with stereopsis can lead to improve the depth perception. We aim to display both haptic and stereopsis cues approximately at the same depth, in such a way they can be perceived by the subject as the same thing.

Apparatus and Procedure

The same experimental apparatus and procedure as in experiment (I) were used. With the extent of displaying haptic sensation. The observer was asked to move forward his hand until it comes into contact with the virtual wall; the square and the haptic wall were supposed to be at the same depth. The observer then has to judge whether he could perceive either one single fused haptic and stereopsis depth cue or definitely two different depth cues. For each trial the observer was asked to state the haptic depth position in regards to the stereopsis. Subjective feeling about the situation was reported orally by saying "Front", "Same" or "behind". "Front" situation occurs when the haptic wall stops the hand before it reaches the same depth as the visual square. "Same", means both the haptic wall and the viewed square are perceived at the same distance. Observer responds "Behind" when his hand moves forward until it passes behind the square to reach the haptic wall. The position of the haptic wall was within the range of depth deviation determined by the previous experiment. For each disparity we displayed force feedback at eight different depth positions each of which was tried at least twelve times. Both disparity and haptic depth were displayed randomly.

Results and Discussion

The result of this experiment showed that some haptic depth positions are more representative and coincide often with stereoscopic depth than others. These positions are usually located somewhere in between the depth range of each disparity. At the extremities of these ranges simultaneously "Front" or "Behind" situation were dominate, see figure 9. The figure represents the case of disparity equal to 40 dots. As you can see from the figure, the range of positions where both modalities are perceived as one is smaller than the depth variation caused by binocular cue only. We find also that, displaying force feedback at the same position at the mean of visually perceived depths is the most representative position. Usually, there was 70% of chance to reach a complete integration between both modalities. Whereas, displaying the force feedback far from the mean created a conflict situation between the two modalities and usually the user have to ignore one of them depending on the dominance of the cue. As a conclusion, we consider that coupling force feedback with stereopsis increase the stability of depth perception.

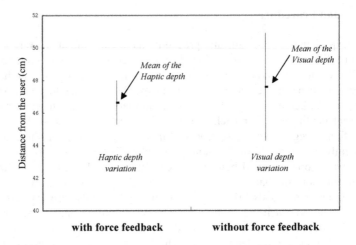

Fig. 9. Threshold of force feedback position.

Experiment III

While the previous experiments most of the subjects reported that they perceived depths faster when they were provided by force feedback sensation. The current experiment was carried to state this fact.

Apparatus and Procedure

The same experimental apparatus and procedure as in experiment (II) were used. The experiment had two sessions, in the first session we don't display force feedback. The observer was asked to move forward his hand until it comes into the same depth position as the stereoscopic square. For each trial the user was asked to close his eyes at first until a beep sound is displayed. Then the subject open his eyes try to fuse both right and left images and position his hand as fast and accurate as possible. The time required for each trial, disparity magnitude and hand position were recorded. Once the subject finished estimating the depth, he was asked to close again his eyes. The experimenter changes meanwhile the disparity magnitude. The second session was identical with the first one except we displayed this time force feedback sensation approximately at the same level of the stereoscopic square. So the subject moves his hand forward until it comes into contact with the haptic wall.

Results and Discussion

The results of this experiment are presented in figure 10. We can observe that the average time required to perceive the depth positions is shorter when the force feedback is provided. When the haptic wall stops the hand, the eyes converge directly at the hand's position, which supposed to be at the same depth as the stereoscopic square.

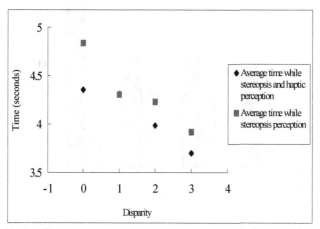

Fig. 10. Small squares represent the average time needed to perceive depth while using only stereopsis. The dark dots represent the perceived depth when both visual and haptic cues are provided.

We think that information of depth preceded the stereopsis; this information is inputted by posture of the subject's arm. When there is no force feedback the subject has to scan the image more times so as to succeed the fusion of both left and right images. Also, we can see that the time needed to decide the position of the stereoscopic square is proportional to the depth. This fact may be caused by the distance that the hand has to move to reach the same depth as the visual or haptic wall. Figure 12 gives more detail about the stability of depth perception in term of time.

If we look to the case of disparity magnitude equal to 80 dots, the variation of perception time is about 3 seconds when no force feedback is displayed. This time delay is dropped to less than one minute when haptic sensations are provided. The same gap can be seen for disparity magnitude equal to 20 dots. This gap is smaller when the disparity is about 40 or 60 dots. These two disparities represents respectively the depth of about 30 to 40 cm, which is considered as the preferred depth of many subjects, may be this can be the raison. We can say that adding force feedback sensation will speed up the depth perception especially when the depth to perceive is too close or too far.

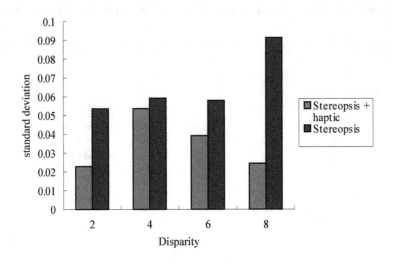

Fig. 11. Standard deviation of perception time.

Conclusion

There are a wide variety of factors that affect the achievement of a complete integration between haptics and stereopsis in virtual environment. However, we proposed a preliminary approach that can fairly improve the perception of a virtual object's location by adjusting the position of the haptic display so as to match the stereoscopic image. Also it was clear that adding force feedback sensation within appropriate threshold distances improve the integration of both haptic and stereopsis modalities. This supports our assumption that haptics may overcome stereopsis scaling distance problem. As well we showed that adding force feedback improved the time needed to perceive depths, this is of special interest in augmenting the reality of virtual environment.

However, there are still many issues to investigate, especially to find a model that can couple haptics and stereopsis with high level of integration when we use real image and not random dot stereograms. Farther studies are necessary about the effect of viewing distance and the effect of occlusion on the depth perception.

References

1. Butts, D.R.W., and McAllister, D.F. "Implementation of true 3D cursors in computer graphics". SPIE Volume 902: 1988. P74-84
2. Spain, E.H., "A psychophysical investigation of the perception of depth with stereoscopic television displays". PhD dissertation, University of Hawaii, May 1984.
3. Beaton, R. J., DeHoff, Weiman, N., and Hildebrandt, W. " An evaluation of input devices for 3D computer display workstations". SPIE vol. 761, p 94-101, 1987.
4. Reinhardt, F.W., "Effect of depth cues on depth juddgements using a field-sequential stereoscopic CRT Display", PhD dissertation, Industrial engineering and operations research dept, Virginia polytechnic institute 1990
5. Drascic, D., and Milgram, P. "Positioning Accuracy of virtual stereographic pointer in a real stereoscopic video world" SPIE vol. 1457, p 58-69, San Jose Sep 1991
6. Miyashita, T., and Uchida, T. "Fatigueless stereoscopic display" 3D □□ Vol. 4 No. 4 April 1990
7. Laroussi, B.Y., Cai and Sato, M. "New haptic device for human-scale virtual environment: Scaleable SPIDAR" ICMR'97 volume IXB, p 67-72, Tampere Finland 1997
8. Ogle, K.N. "The optical space sense". In The Eye vol. 4 ed. Davson, H. New York: Academic
9. Sperling, G. "Binocular vision: A physical and neural theory" Am. f. Psychol. P 462-534, 1983
10. Laroussi, B., and Sato, M. "Object recognition potentiality of haptic virtual environment". Proceeding of ICPA'9, Toronto , July 1997
11. Hirata, Y., Sato, M., and Kawarada H., ``A Measuring Method of Finger Position in Virtual Work Space" Forma, Vol.6, No.2, pp.171-179(1991)

Appendix

Concept OF SCALEABLE-SPIDAR

The device is derived from the original desktop SPIDAR device, which was introduced late in 1990 by Professor Makoto Sato *et al* [11]. As shown in figure 14-a, Scaleable-SPIDAR is delimited by a cubic frame that enclose a cave-like space, where the operator can move around to perform large scale movements. The experimental prototype is $27m^3$ size (3m x 3m x 3m). Within this space, different aspect of force feedback sensations associated mainly with weight, contact and inertia can be displayed to the operator's hands by means of tensioned strings. The front side of the device holds a large screen, where a computer-generated virtual world is projected. Providing such a combination of haptic and visual feedback cues is indispensable to lets the operator's eyes and hands work in concert to explore and manipulate objects populating the virtual environment.

The device uses tensioned string techniques to track hands position as well as to provide haptic feedback sensations. The approach consists mainly on applying appropriate tensions to the four strings supporting each fingering worn by the operator. The force feedback felt on the operator's hand is the same as the resultant force of tension from strings at the center of the fingering; next subsection gives more detail about forces and position computation. In order to control the tension and length of each string, one extremity is connected to the fingering and the other end is wound around a pulley, which is driven by a DC motor. By controlling the power applied to the motor, the system can create appropriate tension all the time. A rotary encoder is attached to the DC motor to detect the string's length variation, Figure 12-b. The set of DC motor, pulley and encoder controlling each string is fixed on the frame.

Force Control
Scaleable-SPIDAR uses the resultant force of tension from strings to provide force display. As the fingering is suspended by four strings, giving certain tensions to each of them by the means of motors, the resultant force occurs at the position of the fingering, where transmitted to and felt by the operator's hand.

Let the resultant force be $\vec{f}$ and unit vector of the tension be $\vec{u}_i$ $(i=0,1,2,3)$, figure 12-a, the resultant force is :

$$\vec{f} = \sum_{i=0}^{3} a_i \vec{u}_i \qquad\qquad (a_i \geq 0)$$

Where a_i represents the tension value of each string. By controlling all of the a_i the resultant force of any magnitude in any direction can be composed [5].

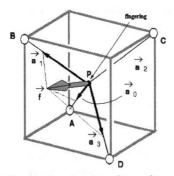

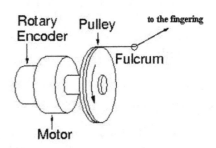

Figure 12-a: Resultant force of tension.   **Figure 12-b**: Motor and rotary encoder.

Position Measurement
Let the coordinates of the fingering position be P (x,y,z), which represent in the same time the hand position, and the length of the ith string be l_i $(i=0, ..., 3)$. To simplify the problem, let the four actuators (motor, pulley, encoder) A_i be on four vertexes of the frame, which are not adjacent to each other, as shown by figure 13. Then P (x,y,z) must satisfy the following equations (Eqs).

$$(x+a)^2 + (y+a)^2 + (z+a)^2 = l_0^2 \qquad\qquad (1)$$

$$(x-a)^2 + (y-a)^2 + (z+a)^2 = l_1^2 \qquad\qquad (2)$$

$$(x-a)^2 + (y+a)^2 + (z-a)^2 = l_2^2 \qquad\qquad (3)$$

$$(x+a)^2 + (y-a)^2 + (z-a)^2 = l_3^2 \qquad\qquad (4)$$

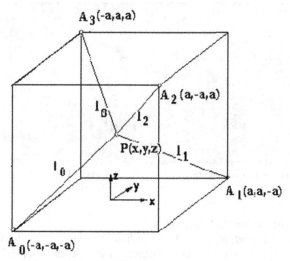

Figure 13: Position measurement.

After differences between the respective adjacent two equations among equation (1)-(4) and solve the simultaneous equations, we can obtain the position of a fingering (hand) as the following equation (5):

$$
\begin{cases}
x = \dfrac{(l_0^2 - l_1^2 - l_2^2 + l_3^2)}{8a} \\[2mm]
y = \dfrac{(l_0^2 - l_1^2 + l_2^2 - l_3^2)}{8a} \\[2mm]
z = \dfrac{(l_0^2 + l_1^2 - l_2^2 - l_3^2)}{8a}
\end{cases}
\tag{5}
$$

Experimental Prototype

The experimental prototype provides two fingerings to be worn by the operator on both hands, Figure 14-a. The fingerings are made of light plastic material and the size can fit to any operator. As well, this small device leaves the hand free and easy to put on and off. Although the operator can wear the fingering on any finger, middle finger is most recommended. The bottom of this finger is close to the center of hand, and the force feedback applied on this position is felt as being applied to the whole palm

To provide the appropriate tensions and lengths of the strings, a personal computer (PC) is used to control an 8-bits D/A, A/D converter and a VME bus, which control respectively the currents entering the motors and detect the changes occurred on each rotary encoder. The PC is connected to a graphics workstation that provides a real-time video image of the virtual world. The apparatus of the prototype is shown by Figure 14-b.

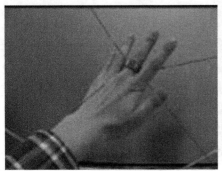

Figure 14-a: The fingering.   **Figure 14-b:** Apparatus of the Scaleable-SPIDAR.

Performance of Scaleable-SPIDAR

Position Measurement Range: the coordinates origin is set to the center of the framework. The position measurement ranges of all x, y and z in[-1.50m, +1.50m].

Static Position Measurement Error: the absolute static position measurement errors are less than 1.5cm inside the position measurement range.

Force Feedback Range: within the force displayable sphere, force sensation range is from $0.005N$ (minimum) to $30N$ (maximum) for all directions.

System Bandwidths:
  ✏✕ Video: 10 ~ 15 Hz
  ✏✕ Audio: 22 kHz (stereo)
Position measurement and force display: > 1200 Hz (depends also on hardware installation)

A Shape Recognition Benchmark for Evaluating Usability of a Haptic Environment

Arthur E. Kirkpatrick and Sarah A. Douglas

Department of Computer and Information Science
University of Oregon
Eugene, OR, 97403 USA
{ted,douglas}@cs.uoregon.edu

Abstract. This paper describes a benchmark task for evaluating the usability of haptic environments for a shape perception task. The task measures the ease with which observers can recognize members of a standard set of five shapes defined by Koenderink. Median time for 12 participants to recognize these shapes with the PHANToM was 23 seconds. This recognition time is within the range for shape recognition of physical objects using one finger but far slower than recognition using the whole hand. The results suggest haptic environments must provide multiple points of contact with an object for rapid performance of shape recognition.

1   Introduction

Haptic interfaces are frequently claimed to permit "more natural" (and hence more usable) interactions than current WIMP interface styles. These claims are based upon analogies with physical environments, where vision and touch have complementary roles and touch is both a familiar and a necessary part of interaction. But do these analogies hold? Existing performance metrics for haptic interfaces summarize the mechanical and electrical characteristics of the interface hardware [1]. These are useful for comparisons of the hardware but provide only a limited indication of the performance of the overall system on actual tasks. We believe that the usability of a haptic interface is best answered by considering all aspects of the interface: the hardware, software interaction techniques, and the task to which they are applied. We call such combinations *haptic environments* and contrast them to our daily interactions with physical objects, which we call *physical environments*.

We have developed a benchmark task for evaluating one aspect of usability of haptic environments. We believe that shape perception is a fundamental component of many haptic perceptual tasks. Consequently, we have designed a task that measures the ease with which observers can recognize members of a standard set of five shapes. In this paper we describe our benchmark and use it to characterize performance of a common haptic environment.

S. Brewster, R. Murray-Smith (Eds.): Haptic HCI 2000, LNCS 2058, pp. 151-156, 2001.

2   The Shape Recognition Task and Stimuli

Many potential applications of haptic environments include haptic shape perception as a component task.   An obvious example is analysis of scientific data, such as a geophysicist searching isosurfaces of a volumetric dataset for the contours of an oil field.   However, there are many other tasks that implicitly require the assessment of shape, even though the primary attribute extracted may not itself be inherently geometric.   In fact, we believe that any task that involves haptic exploration of the properties of an unknown object has an underlying shape component.   To make sense of a stream of haptic sensations, an observer must be able to relate them to some form of spatial representation of the object, both for the haptic description itself and possibly to correlate that description with visual sensations of the object.   Thus even the perception of such non-shape properties as texture or hardness will frequently be described with respect to regions of shape—"it's smooth *on the side*" or "it's hard *at the protrusion*".

Many studies of human haptic performance in physical environments have used either shape recognition or the related task of object recognition.   Shape recognition tasks use stimuli which can only be discriminated based upon the geometric arrangement of their features, whereas object recognition tasks feature stimuli such as familiar household objects for which material properties are also a strongly diagnostic attribute.   Object recognition was used in the classic series of studies by Klatzky and Lederman where observers were asked to haptically identify common objects [3].   In another study, the same authors used a restricted set of objects that could not be readily distinguished by material properties, producing a shape recognition task [4]. Other researchers have used abstract stimuli for shape recognition tasks [2].

The central role of shape perception makes it an excellent benchmark task for evaluating the usability of haptic environments.   The large body of shape recognition results for physical environments provides a base for comparison.   The selection of a set of standard shapes is crucial to the success of such a benchmark.

We began with a class of smooth-flowing three-dimensional shapes defined by Koenderink and van Doorn [5] and used in the shape recognition task of Kappers et al. [2].   These shapes are constructed from two orthogonal parabolas and are a canonical set in the following sense: Any solid shape that is more complex can be constructed from a combination of these shapes.   The shapes are identified by a *shape* scale, computed from the direction of curvature of the two parabolas.   There are five critical points on the scale, named Cup, Rut, Saddle, Ridge, and Cap (see Fig. 1).   The shapes lying at these points are distinguished from one another by the *signs* of the curvatures of their constituent parabolas.   An observer can distinguish them simply by determining whether each parabola is curving up or down or (in the case of Groove and Ridge) is flat.

These five shapes represent an excellent base for a standard set.   They are smoothly curving, can be used to construct larger shapes of arbitrary complexity, and can be readily distinguished by assessing direction of curvature without assessing its degree. Performance of observers recognizing these shapes constitutes a baseline performance for shape recognition in a haptic environment.

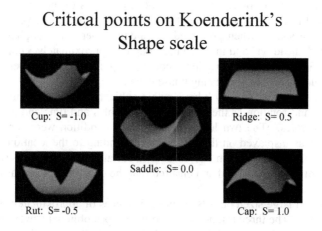

Fig. 1. The Koenderink shape scale.

Shape recognition is potentially based upon both abstract knowledge of the shape (in the case of our shapes, the directions of curvature for the two parabolas) and hand movements specific to an exact configuration. The balance between these two will depend upon the frequency of contact with a specific object. For example, you might identify an arbitrary cup shape using one sequence of hand movements but identify the coffee cup you drink from every day using movements specific to its geometry. This presented us with a dilemma: We needed to teach our participants to haptically recognize the five shapes but did not want them to use recognition methods that relied upon specific geometries of a given stimulus set. We resolved this by training our participants with one set of stimuli and testing them with another. The training phase used medium-sized shapes presented in "head on" configuration whereas the testing phase used small- and large-sized shapes presented in different rotations.

Using these stimuli, we developed a benchmark task, summarized in the next section, for evaluating haptic environments. In addition to evaluating the benchmark, we were interested in the relationship between haptics and vision in shape recognition. The perception of shape using a point force haptic device alone is somewhat difficult. We wondered whether the visual proprioception offered by a screen cursor might improve the time and accuracy of performance by providing a superior representation of the spatial location of the current haptic sensation. To test this, we had our participants perform our benchmark shape recognition task with both a visual cursor display and no visual feedback whatsoever.

3   Method

The benchmark was implemented for SensAble's PHANToM device. The participants never saw a visual representation of the shapes at any time during the protocol—the shapes were only rendered haptically. The protocol had two separate phases, a training phase and a testing phase.

In the training phase, participants were told the names of the five shapes and felt them with the PHANToM. Once they had felt every shape twice, they were asked to identify the five shapes when presented in random order. In this phase, the shapes were presented "head on" and in a size that spanned approximately 3 cm of movement of the PHANToM. When a participant could recognize the shapes perfectly for two consecutive blocks of five, the testing phase began.

The testing phase used a 2 by 2 by 3 within-subjects design, with cursor condition, stimulus size, and rotation as the independent variables and time and accuracy as the dependent variables. The two levels of the cursor condition were cursor present (a visual cursor was displayed on the screen corresponding to the location of the haptic device in the virtual environment) or absent. A curtain prevented the participant from seeing the location of their hand and ensured that the only visual cue was the cursor, if present.

The small and large sized objects spanned distances of approximately 1.5 cm and 7 cm, respectively. The three rotations moved the shapes obliquely away from the head on configuration used in the training phase but were small enough that the front of the shape remained facing the user. The rotations were simply used to provide variety of stimuli and the effects of this factor were not analyzed. Shapes, sizes, and rotations were fully crossed, for a total of 30 combinations in each cursor condition. The complete testing phase consisted of 60 trials.

The haptic environment was a 300-Mhz Pentium II running Windows NT 4.0. The visual display device was a monoscopic color screen and the haptic display device was a PHANToM model 1.5. The haptic rendering loop ran at 1000 Hz and consumed approximately 30% of the processor time. For each trial, the environment recorded the time from first contact with the stimulus until the participant ended the trial by pressing the space bar.

The participants were 12 unpaid graduate students from the computer science department. Nine were male and three female. Their ages ranged from 22 to 42 with a median of 30.6. Ten were right handed and two left-handed. All used the PHANToM with their dominant hand.

4   Results

Participants took quite a while to recognize the shapes. Arithmetic mean, geometric mean, and median time for a trial were 28.6, 22.5, and 23.8 seconds, respectively, with 50% of the values between 13.7 and 37.7 seconds. The distribution of times was clearly lognormal, so the most representative estimate of trial times is the geometric mean. There was also a large range of individual differences: The geometric means of the participant times ranged from 13.7 to 42.7 seconds, a factor of 3.11. The mean score for participant accuracy was 84.5% (s.d. 12.0%).

We computed the mean time and accuracy for each participant under each experimental condition and calculated a two-way within-subjects ANOVA of main effects and interactions for accuracy and log of time. No significant effects were found for accuracy. For time, the effect of cursor condition was both unreliable in direction ($F_{1,11}$ = .098, p = .760) and small (95% confidence interval [-14%, 16%]). No effect was found for order of presentation of cursor condition. Smaller sizes had

12% longer recognition times ($F_{1,11}$ = 6.986, p = .023, 95% c.i. [2%, 22%]). The interaction effect between size and cursor condition was not significant.

5   Discussion

The most striking result of this study is the difficulty of the task. Despite the simplicity of our stimuli and task, participants still had a mean time of 22.5 seconds with a 15% error rate. How does performance in this environment compare with human performance at recognizing physical objects? Using a superset of the five shapes we selected for our benchmark, Kappers et al. [2] found accuracy rates close to 100%. They do not report response times.

Lederman, Klatzky, and Reed [6] devised stimuli simpler than ours, three ellipsoids of revolution that differed only in their height to width ratio. Using both hands, observers could distinguish these objects in 1.0 seconds. For common household objects, whose shapes are more complex than those we used, observers were able to perform haptic object recognition in less than 2 seconds with a 4% error rate [3]. With a set of common objects that did not appreciably differ in material properties (a shape recognition task), the mean time was 6.2 seconds with a 5% error rate [4].

These times are far faster than the performance in our haptic environment, but comparisons must be made cautiously. Participants in all these studies were able to use their full hand. When Klatzky et al. [4] required their participants to wear gloves, the mean response time rose to about 16 seconds. When they further restricted their participants to using a single gloved index finger, mean response time leapt 2.8 times to 45 seconds with an error rate of 25%. Restricting the haptic flow to a single point, requiring the observer to induce object shape over time, dramatically limits performance in physical environments. Note that this last condition corresponds most closely to using a point force device in a haptic environment.

These comparisons suggest that we have a considerable room for improvement of shape display in haptic environments. If we can increase the number of points of contact between the user and a displayed shape, we might get a two- to three-fold improvement in performance—a gain of great practical consequence, given the underlying importance of shape recognition and how long it currently takes.

These comparisons also provide a useful validation of our evaluation benchmark itself. The response times in our task are well within the range that would be predicted from data on a comparable task with physical objects. Our task appears to measure the determining factors in performance of shape recognition.

Finally, we consider the non-significance of the cursor condition. We note that all participants continued to improve performance up until the 60th trial. They do not appear to have reached skilled performance during the course of our benchmark. Some participants reported that they found the visual cursor condition distracting. Many had their hands full merely attending to the haptic sensations. We speculate that the sensory overload may have reduced with practice. The visual cursor might have proved significant when participants had achieved practiced performance.

6   Conclusions and Future Work

Many users clearly have difficulty performing this basic task of shape recognition with a point force device. Given that perceiving shapes is a fundamental component of many tasks for which we might wish to use such devices, this difficulty represents a significant barrier to their usability

Understanding the various factors underlying this low rate of performance is crucial to the usability of environments incorporating point force haptic devices. In the future, we intend to study how long it takes individuals to reach skilled performance, what that level of that performance is, and what factors might facilitate spatial perception with a point force device for different user populations.

We also would like to extend our set of reference shapes with edges, textures, and shapes that are between our five basic shapes. This larger reference set will allow us to explore the effect of multiple factors on shape perception performance.

Acknowledgements

We gratefully acknowledge Intel Corporation for the donation of a Pentium computer and PHANToM. Susan Lederman gave insightful comments on point force haptics and Roberta Klatzky graciously provided the precise numerical values for Fig. 2 of [4]. An anonymous referee of this paper suggested reference [1].

References

1. Hayward, V., and Astley, O.R. Performance measures for haptic interfaces. In *Proceedings of Robotics Research: The 7th International Symposium.* 1996. Springer Verlag, Berlin, pp. 195-207.
2. Kappers, A.M.L., Koenderink, J.J., and Lichtenegger, I. Haptic identification of curved surfaces. *Perception and Psychophysics 56,* (1994), 53-61.
3. Klatzky, R.L., Lederman, S.J., and Metzger, V.A. Identifying objects by touch: An "expert system". *Perception and Psychophysics 37,* (1985), 299-302.
4. Klatzky, R.L., Loomis, J.M., Lederman, S.J., Wake, H., and Fujita, N. Haptic identification of objects and their depictions. *Perception and Psychophysics 54,* (1993), 170-178.
5. Koenderink, J.J., and van Doorn, A.J. Surface shape and curvature scales. *Image and Vision Computing 10,* (1992), 557-565.
6. Lederman, S.J., Klatzky, R.L., and Reed, C.L. Constraints on haptic integration of spatially shared object dimensions. *Perception 22,* (1993), 723-743.

A Horse Ovary Palpation Simulator for Veterinary Training

Andrew Crossan[1], Stephen Brewster[1], Stuart Reid[2], and Dominic Mellor[2]

[1]Glasgow Interactive Systems Group
Department of Computing Science, University of Glasgow
{ac,stephen}@dcs.gla.ac.uk
http://www.dcs.gla.ac.uk/~stephen
[2]Faculty of Veterinary Medicine,
University of Glasgow.
{d.mellor,s.w.j.reid}@vet.gla.ac.uk

Abstract. This paper describes the concept of multimodal cues to aid training in a medical simulator. These cues aim to provide guidance and performance feedback to the user in the form of haptic, graphic and auditory feedback presented during the simulator training. The paper describes current implementations of the cues and their integration into the Horse Ovary Palpation Simulator (HOPS) developed at Glasgow University.

Introduction

Providing training to novices in any safety-critical application can present risks to those involved, but particularly in medicine where a mistake can permanently damage a patient or can even be fatal. The question remains as to the safest method to provide experience to medical personnel without endangering a patient. Traditionally, training in both human and veterinary medicine has taken the form of the apprenticeship model - trainees would perform the procedure under the supervision of an experienced doctor several times before they are considered qualified to perform the operation by themselves. Clearly there are risks to the patient particularly when the trainee may lack the necessary cognitive or psychomotor skills. This system also relies on subjective assessment of the performance level of the trainee by the supervisor. Virtual Reality (VR) simulators are now widely thought to offer the potential of providing a new medical training paradigm. As such, commercial as well as research systems are being developed worldwide. One of the major considerations in building a training simulator is how to provide performance feedback to the user. Higgins *et al.* [12] state:
"it is pointless to build a training simulator that doesn't provide useful feedback on performance to the trainee".
One of the disadvantages of physical simulations is that it can be difficult to extract performance feedback from the model. The majority of the virtual medical training simulations developed do address this issue of feedback by analysing the procedure

S. Brewster, R. Murray-Smith (Eds.): Haptic HCI 2000, LNCS 2058, pp. 157-164, 2001.

data and presenting it to the user after he/she is finished. This paper describes the concept and development of a simulator that guides the user through the environment by providing multimodal cues.

General Overview

Virtual medical simulations are becoming more common, and as the fidelity increases, they are expected to become more widely accepted as a training aid. Flight simulations are often used as an analogy in that they provide training in a multi-dimensional, safety-critical task. Although not widely accepted for many years, improved technology has lead to more realistic simulations that have proved useful in developing, maintaining and assessing pilot skill. They have been successfully used to simulate a wide range of conditions and emergencies, while reducing the learning curve for trainee pilots by providing a safe, controllable learning environment [16].

Simulation training is not a new idea in human and veterinary medicine. Students gain experience in certain techniques through use of plastic or rubber models, but these often lack realism and provide no useful feedback to the trainee. Surgical skills can also be improved in the anatomy labs that are incorporated into the medicine and veterinary medicine courses. Again, there are problems since cadavers are a scarce resource, and are not generally reusable. Living tissue can also have noticeably different haptic properties than cadaver tissue [12]. VR medical simulators have the potential to present anatomical and physiological information to the user simultaneously on reusable models. Simulations currently developed can be divided into those that provide training for minimally invasive surgery (MIS), surgery, or palpation procedures. MIS simulators are by far the most common [4, 13, 15, 17]. In a MIS procedure, surgeons view their interaction with the patient through a monitor, and hence, it lends itself to a virtual simulation. The Preop endoscopic simulator [4] developed by HT Medical Systems is one example of a system combining a force feedback MIS training system with anatomical and physiological models. Other systems exist to simulate other MIS procedures such as arthroscopy or laparoscopy. SKATS [1] and VE-KATS [17] present knee arthroscopy training systems.

Surgery simulations cover a wide range of techniques using different surgical instruments. Cathsim [2] is an example of a commercially available training system for venipuncture. Berkley et al. [3] present a simulation for training in wound suturing. Simulation for cutting procedures in particular present problems as models need to be dynamically adjustable, to allow incisions. Delp et al. [7] have developed tissue cutting and bleeding models for this purpose.

The development of a palpation simulation presents different problems than development of a surgery simulation. During surgery, a medical practitioner interacts with the patient through surgical instruments, so the haptic feedback from the tissue to the surgeon is mediated by the instruments. Palpation, however, involves the medical personnel interacting directly with skin or tissue. The development of palpation simulators tends to be less common, although palpation is an important technique for the diagnosis of many conditions. Two recent examples come from the Human Machine Interface Laboratory at the CAIP Center at Rutgers University. They have developed a simulation using the Rutgers Master II for training in palpation for the detection of sub-surface tumours using experimentally based force-deflection curves [8]. They also present a prostate simulator developed using the PHANToM [5], which can model several different prostate conditions.

One of the most important aspects of a virtual training system is that a user can be given an objective performance rating for the procedure performed. Determining the performance in a medical procedure is difficult however, since it can be a complex, multi-dimensional task with many different outcomes – not just success or failure. Metrics will depend on the training task performed. Gorman *et al.* [11] suggest the following metrics for a task involving driving a simulated needle through a target overlaying a blood vessel: time on task, accuracy, peak force applied, tissue damage, surface damage, and angle error. However, they note the difficulty in calculating tissue or surface damage accurately. For a palpation simulator where the user may wish to examine the whole of an object for specific shape or surface properties, accuracy and angle error may not be so relevant. Particularly in training for diagnosis, metrics can be very high level. For example, in Glasgow University's horse ovary simulator [6], users palpate the ovaries for a follicle to diagnose the stage of ovulation of the horse. The users might be asked "Does a follicle exist on either ovary, and if so, what size is the follicle". Systems exist to allow user performance to be stored over time [4], such that any trends of improvement or otherwise can be noted. This could eventually lead to an objective method of certification of medical trainees [12].

The Glasgow Horse Ovary Palpation Simulator

Using a medical simulator allows trainees to make mistakes while learning, without their mistakes adversely affecting a patient. To provide training however, they must be aware of their mistakes, and learn from them. Providing performance feedback to the user after the simulated procedure is an important step, but this guidance does not affect performance during the procedure. This will allow users to correct their behaviour during the simulation. Feedback cues can also be used to guide users through an unfamiliar procedure, particularly during the initial stages of training where they may not possess the necessary psychomotor skills.

A horse ovary simulation has been developed in collaboration with Glasgow University Veterinary School [12]. It was developed to train veterinary students in equine ovary palpation techniques, and in particular, in diagnosing the stage of ovulation of a horse. This is not only a difficult procedure for students to learn but can be fatal for the horse if performed incorrectly. Veterinarians perform an examination by locating the ovaries, and palpating them. The ovary shape and surface properties indicate the stage of ovulation of the horse.

Users interact with the environment through the PHANToM force feedback device from SensAble Technologies [14], which allows 6DOF input and 3DOF translational output. The model itself consists of two horse ovaries fixed in space (Figure 1), that were developed iteratively with help from experienced horse vets at Glasgow

University Veterinary School. An initial experiment showed no significant difference in performance between students trained by traditional methods and those trained on the simulator. However, the results also showed there was potential for improvement in traditional training methods of ovary palpation [6], as an equally low percentage of ovaries were diagnosed correctly for both training groups.

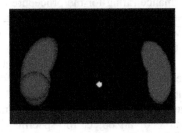

Fig. 1: The Glasgow Horse Ovary Palpation Simulator. The model consists of two ovaries, (on the left and right) with the cursor shown in the centre. A follicle can be seen on front left ovary.

Current work is concentrating on two different areas: Integrating multimodal cues into the environment and improving the fidelity of the models. The feedback suggested can take the form of haptic, audio or graphical cues.

Multimodal Cues

Haptic Cues
Haptic cues provide a method to directly affect the user's path through the environment. We have considered two different forms of guidance that haptic cues could provide:
! ∀ Guidance through pre-recorded movements
! ∀ Interactive guidance.

Guiding a user using pre-recorded movements can be broken down into 2 stages - record and playback. During the record stage, both positional and force information of a user must be stored at specific regular sample intervals. Playback of the procedure would drive the user's interaction point along the path recorded. At each stage, the driving force would equal the force recorded for the current position. By this method, a student could feel the techniques and forces involved in a correct procedure by playing back a recording of an experienced doctor or veterinarian performing the same procedure. Alternatively, a doctor could assess the performance of a student by playing back a recording of their movements.

Interactive guidance can be thought of as a tutor-trainee model. In this situation two interaction points would exist in the same environment. The first is controlled by the trainee, and can be used to explore freely the environment as in a single user simulation. The second is controlled by the tutor, who can influence the student at any time. This could take the form of grabbing the student's interaction point and dragging it through a series of motions. The trainee could then practice the procedure as normal, while the tutor could guide him/her if and only if help is required. This would serve to reinforce the apprenticeship model currently in use, while allowing the tutor to have a more active role in guiding the student.

An initial attempt has been made to integrate pre-recorded haptic guidance into the training environment. During the recording stage, the position of the PHANToM can be sampled at a rate of between 100 and 1000 Hz. The PHANToM's position sensors provide a representation of the current cursor position that can be used to accurately recreate the path recorded. However, recording force information at the sample points presents problems, as the PHANToM device does not have force sensors. The system implemented attempts to estimate the applied force through the reaction force from objects or effects within the scene. By introducing viscosity throughout the scene, a reaction force to any movement can be detected through the device. Playback also presents problems, as even a passive user can affect the path of the cursor, and applying the recorded force vector will not generally move the cursor along the recorded path. The PHANToM drags the user's finger through a series of movements. Resistive forces from the user will combine with the driving force to produce deviations from the path. The current system calculates the magnitude of the recorded force and applies it towards the next sample point on the path. This however can cause instabilities when contacting objects in the scene, demonstrated in Figure 2. When touching an object the user will apply a force to counteract the reaction force from the object. Even if the user is moving perpendicular to the surface of the object, he/she is still applying a force to counter this reaction force. However, the playback force will not take account of this and will drive the user directly towards the next sample point. The reaction force will combine with the playback force to produce a net force vector that is not in the direction of the next sample point. A more complex algorithm must be developed to adapt the playback force direction depending on the reaction force from the contacted object.

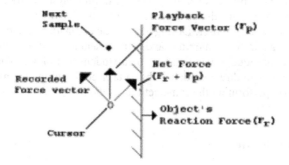

Fig. 2. Demonstration of the problems of playback when the cursor and next sample point lie inside an object. The direction of the playback force will be affected by the object's reaction force and resultant force will push the cursor away from the sample point.

Audio Cues

Audio cues can be used to convey state information about a system to the user. Gaver presents Arkola [10], a system in which continual auditory feedback can be used to monitor the running of a simulated factory, and in particular alert the user when an error occurs. Audio feedback to present state information has also been demonstrated in a medical context to augment a surgical procedure [18]. Surgical instrument position and optimal path information are passed to the surgeon through audio, allowing the surgeons to use the information while keeping their visual focus on the patient. Similar concepts of supplying users with auditory position and path information can also apply to medical simulators. Incorporating audio warnings into a simulation can provide immediate feedback to users that the current action they are performing is incorrect, or dangerous. Unlike haptic cues, audio cues do not directly affect the cursor position, but allow users to correct their actions themselves. In this manner, they can build confidence as they progress through the procedure that their actions are not damaging the patient.

A simple audio warning cue has also been incorporated into the Glasgow ovary simulation. One of the dangers when performing an ovary examination is damage can be caused by palpating an ovary too firmly. An obvious solution is to alert the user when they are applying too much pressure to an ovary. Each of the objects in the environment can be assigned a threshold force value. If more than this threshold force is applied to an ovary during palpation an audio warning is sounded. In the current implementation, the pitch of the audio warning is linked to the force applied above the threshold, so a higher pitch of sound indicates a greater danger.

Graphical Cues

Graphical cues can be most easily used to highlight a specific area of the screen. The user's attention can be drawn to a particular object by colouring it differently from the surroundings. In this way, an area of interest, for example an incision point, can be highlighted. Other possibilities exist however. A training system might include a path following mode where, much in the same way as haptic cues, a pre-recorded procedure is played back the user. During a correct examination, cursor position could be recorded at regular time intervals and a representation of this position can be played back in a subsequent examination for a student to follow. The pre-recorded cursor would provide no direct guidance, but a user could follow the movements with his/her own cursor, performing the same actions as the recording.

Improving the Models

The ovary models are being developed to increase the fidelity of the simulation. This is a particularly important issue for a simulator relying on palpation, where the users are directly interacting with the virtual objects that must feel realistic. Currently, the ovaries are based on the combination of geometric shapes, and while this was judged to be effective by veterinarians, methods to build anatomically accurate models exist.

The "Lucky the Virtual Dog" project generates anatomically accurate models of a dog through the composition of MRI and CT scans [9].

The ovary firmness is modelled with a linear force model. We are trying different non-linear soft tissue models, although their realism will still be decided subjectively by veterinarians.

The next stage in the project will be to integrate two PHANToM devices into the same environment. Users can then use their thumb and forefinger to grasp objects in the scene. This will provide a more realistic simulation in that vets performing an ovary exam will cup the ovary with one or more fingers and palpate it using their thumb. It should also allow the ovaries to become moveable. The ovaries were moveable in our initial simulation, but proved difficult to palpate. With two interaction points, one can provide a reaction force to movement while the other can be used to palpate the ovary. An experiment is currently being developed to test object identification when using two PHANToMs instead of one. This experiment will be performed on the ovary simulator, but will involve a group of novice users with no veterinary knowledge. The users will be trained and then asked to find and identify soft spheres (representing follicles) on the ovary models using touch alone. It is expected that the two-PHANToM simulation will allow users to find and identify the size of follicles with more accuracy than the one-PHANToM simulation. A similar experiment will also be run using experienced horse veterinarians as the user group, to attempt to validate the ovary models.

Conclusion

Presenting performance feedback to users is an essential feature of a simulator, as it will allow them to learn from their simulator experience. Current research has concentrated on providing post procedure performance analysis, but little work has been done on guiding a user during the simulation. Providing users with multimodal cues has the potential to both guide them, and present them with performance feedback during the simulation. However, both the simulator and the cues themselves require further work before a useful system can be developed.

Acknowledgements

This research was funded by the Faculty of Veterinary Medicine at Glasgow University. Thanks must also go to the SHEFC REVELATION Project, SensAble Technologies and Virtual Presence Ltd.

References

1. Arthur, J.G., McCarthy, A.D., Wynn, H.P., Harley, P.J., and Barber, C. Weak at the knees? Arthroscopy Surgery Simulation User Requirements, Capturing the psychological impact of VR Innovation Through risk based design. In *Proceedings of Interact 99* (Edinburgh, UK) IOS Press, 1999, pp. 360-366.
2. Barker, V.L. Cathsim. In *Proceedings of Medicine Meets Virtual Reality* (San Francisco, USA) IOS Press, 1999, pp. 36-37.
3. Berkley, J., Weghorst, S., Gladstone, H., Raugi, G., Berg, D., and Ganter, M. Fast Finite Element Modeling for Surgical Simulation. In *Proceedings of Medicine Meets Virtual Reality* (San Francisco, USA) IOS Press, 1999, pp. 55-61.
4. Bro-Nielsen, M., and Tasto, J.L., Cunningham, R. and Merril, G.L. Preop Endoscopic Simulator: A PC-Based Imersive Training System for Bronchoscopy. In *Proceedings of Medicine Meets Virtual Reality* (San Francisco, USA) IOS Press, 1999, pp. 76-82.
5. Burdea, G., Patounakis, G., Popescu, V., and E., W.R. Virtual Reality-Based Training for the Diagnosis of Prostate Cancer. *IEEE Transactions on Biomedical Engineering* 46, 10 (1999), pp. 1253-1260.
6. Crossan, A., Brewster, S.A., and Glendye, A. A Horse Ovary Palpation Simulator for Veterinary Training. In *Proceedings of PURS 2000* (Zurich) Hartung-Gorre, 2000, pp. 79-86.
7. Delp, S.L., Loan, P., Basdogan, C., and Rosen, J.M. Surgical Simulation: An Emerging Technology for Training in Emergency Medicine. *Presence* 6, 2 (1997), pp.147-159.
8. Dinsmore, M., Langrana, N., Burdea, G., and Ladeji, J. Virtual Reality Training Simulation of Palpation of Subsurface Tumors. In *Proceedings of Virtual Reality Annual International Symposium* (Albuquerque, USA) IEEE, 1997, pp. 54-60.
9. Edinburgh Virtual Environment Centre. *Lucky the Virtual Dog*. http://www.vldtk.ed.ac.uk/projects/lucky/index.html
10. Gaver, W.W., Smith, R.B., and O'Shea, T. Effective Sounds in Complex Systems: The Arkola Simulation. In *Proceedings of CHI 91* ACM Press, 1991, pp. 85-90.
11. Gorman, P.J., Lieser, J.D., Morray, W.B., Haluck, R.S., and Krummel, T.M. Assessment and Validation of a Force Feedback Virtual Reality Based Surgical Simulator. In *Proceedings of Phantom User Group 98* (Dedham, Massachusetts), 1998, pp. 27-29.
12. Higgins, G.A., Merrill, G.L., Hettinger, L.J., Kaufmann, C.R., Champion, H.R., and Satava, R.M. New Simulation Technologies for Surgical Training and Certification: Current Status and Future Projections. *Presence* 6, 2 (1997), pp. 160-172.
13. Kühnapfel, U., Çakmak, H.K., and Maaß, H. 3D Modeling for Endoscopic Surgery. In *Proceedings of the IEEE Symposium on Simulation* (Delft, NL), 1999, pp. 22-32.
14. Massie, T.H., and Salisbury, K. The Phantom Haptic Interface: A Device for Probing Virtual Objects. In *Proceedings of the ASME Winter Annual Meeting, Symposium on Haptic Interface for Virtual Environments and Teleoperator Systems* (Chicago, IL), 1994.
15. McCarthy, A., Harley, P., and Smallwood, R. Virtual Arthroscopy Training Do the virtual skills developed match the real skills required? In *Proceedings of Medicine Meets Virtual Reality* (San Francisco, USA) IOS Press, 1999, pp. 221-227.
16. Rolfe, J.M., and Staples, K.J. The Flight Simulator as a Training Device. In *Flight Simulation* (Ed.), Cambridge Universtiy Press, 1986, pp. 232-249.
17. Sherman, K.P., Ward, J.W., Wills, D.P.M., and Mohsen, A.M.M.A. A Portable Virtual Environment Knee Arthroscopy Training System with Objective Scoring. In *Proceedings of Medicine Meets Virtual Reality* (San Francisco, USA) IOS Press, 1999, pp. 335-336.
18. Wegner, K. Surgical Navigation System and Method Using Audio Feedback. In *Proceedings of ICAD'98* (Glasgow, Scotland), 1998, 6.2

Tactile Navigation Display

Jan B.F. van Erp

TNO Human Factors
Kampweg 5, NL – 3769 DE
Soesterberg, The Netherlands
+31 (0) 346 356458
vanerp@tm.tno.nl

Abstract. The use of the tactile modality is not common in Human Computer Interaction. However, there may be good reasons to do so. For example in situations in which the visual sense is restricted (e.g., in virtual environments lacking a wide field of view, or for the visually handicapped persons), or overloaded (e.g., flying an airplane or driving in an unknown city). The lack of a wide visual field of view excludes the use of peripheral vision and may therefore degrade navigation, orientation, motion perception, and object detection. Tactile actuators applied to the torso, however, have a 360° horizontal 'field of touch', and may therefore be suited to compensate for the degraded visual information.

Keywords: Virtual Environment, tactile, cutaneous, haptic, navigation, orientation.

1 Introduction

This paper will specifically discuss the use of the tactile sense to supplement visual information in relation to navigating and orientating in a Virtual Environment (VE). Attention is paid to the potential advantages, the possible pitfalls, and the missing knowledge.

Virtual Reality (VR) technology allows the user to perceive and experience sensory contact with a non–physical world. A complete VE will provide this contact in all sensory modalities. However, developments in VR technology have mainly focussed on the visual sense. In the last decade, enormous improvements have been made regarding the speed and resolution of the image generators. However, the human senses are not restricted to the visual modality. Using the tactile modality as well in a VE might have several advantages; e.g., tactile information can enhance the immersion of the observer, guide movements, be a substitute for force feedback, and serve as a general information channel.

Rationale. Despite the current power of image generators, the field of view of VE visuals is still reduced compared to real life. This may degrade orientation and navigation performance in a VE. Because the tactile channel has a 360° field of touch, a tactile display may compensate for the lack of peripheral viewing. However,

S. Brewster, R. Murray-Smith (Eds.): Haptic HCI 2000, LNCS 2058, pp. 165-173, 2001.
© Springer-Verlag Berlin Heidelberg 2001

fundamental and applied knowledge is required for successful use of tactile displays for this specific
 application, and moreover, for successful development of devices. At this moment, not all this knowledge is available or applicable. Areas that deserve attention include:

! ∀body loci other than hand and fingers,
! ∀sensory congruency (see next paragraph),
! ∀cross–modal interaction,
! ∀perceptual illusions,
! ∀attention.

Multi-modal Man Machine Interaction (M₄I) and Sensory Congruency. Effective behavior requires that stimulation from several sensory channels be coordinated and made congruent informationally as well as temporally [8]; knowledge of this congruency (or incongruency) is a prerequisite for the success of M₄I. Numerous examples show that information is not always perceived congruently by the different senses. For example, in the spatial domain, vision dominates touch (sometimes called visual capture [6], and found in e.g. estimating length and in perceived size [14], [17]), and touch dominates hearing ([9], [10], [19]). In the temporal domain, the perceived duration of a sound is longer than that of a light of equal length ([1], [4]), and intervals bounded by light flashes appear shorter than those bounded by brief auditory stimuli ([5], [18]). A similar incongruency is found in a simple experiment [21] on the perception of visual and tactile time intervals. The perception of open time intervals, either marked by visual stimuli (blinking squares on a monitor), or tactile stimuli (bursts of vibration on the fingertip with the same duration as the visual stimulus) was studied in uni– and cross–modal conditions. The results of the experiment showed a large bias in the cross–modal condition: tactile time intervals are overestimated by 30% compared to visual intervals (see Figure 1). This indicates that sensory congruency is a non–trivial aspect of integrating sensory modalities.

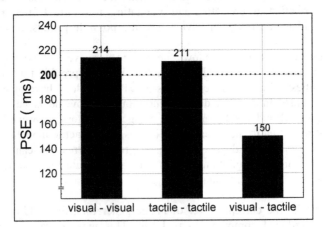

Fig. 1. Point of Subjective Equality (PSE) for a 200 ms standard open time interval. The visual – tactile condition shows that a 150 ms tactile interval is judged to be equal in length to a 200 ms visual interval.

2   Tactile Orientation and Navigation Display

The restricted field of view available for, amongst others, VE users, closed cockpit pilots, or the visually impaired, may degrade spatial orientation and navigation performance. In these situations presenting information via the tactile channel can support the observer. In the early nineties, two tactile naviagation displays for pilots were developed. Gilliland and Schlegel [3] conducted a serie of studies to explore the use of vibrotactile stimulation of the human head to inform a pilot of possible threats or other situations in the flight environment. The tactile display uses the pilot's head as display surface to provide an egocentric view of the environment, that pilots can rapidly relate to their cognitive maps and their orientations within them. The relative accuracy, which represents how close the subject came to designating the correct site, did deteriorate with increased numbers of stimulation sites. However, relative accuracy was reasonably good even with 12 stimulation sites (87%). In operational environments, a functional tactile information system may not require absolute accuracy if it supplies redundant information to enhance situation awareness, or merely alerts the operator to targets or threats. Rupert, Guedry and Rescke [12] developed a matrix of vibro–tactors that covers the torso of the pilot's body. This prototype may offer a means to continuously maintain spatial orientation by providing information about aircraft acceleration and direction of motion to the pilot. Rupert and associates studied the transmission of roll and pitch information by means of the tactile array. Within the pitch and roll limits of their torso display (15 and 45 deg, respectively), the subjects could position the simulated attitude of the aircraft by the tactile cues alone. The accuracy of pitch and roll was within 5 deg, after a learning period of 30 min.

A potential interesting body locus for a tactile navigation display is the torso because of its large surface, its 3D form, and its possible ego-centric 'view'. Furthermore, information presented to the torso is not likely to interfere with tactile information presentation to, for example, the hands. A simple tactile display could consist of a number of actuators located in a horizontal plane. By stimulating a certain area, the display could indicate a direction, e.g., to a point or object of interest.

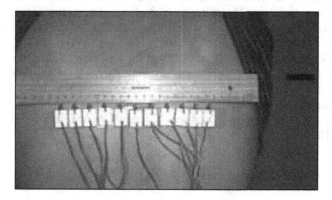

Fig. 1. Placement of the tactile actuators on the back for the spatial sensitivity experiments (scale is cm).

The first step in the development of the proposed application is cataloguing the relevant perceptual characteristics, i.e., the spatial and temporal information processing capacity of the torso. After this initial phase, the next step is to understand the perceptual biasses and use of navigation information presented on the torso, i.e. the usability aspects of the proposed display.

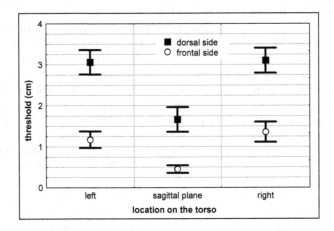

Fig. 2. Spatial accuracy of the torso for vibro–tactile stimuli. The threshold is the minimum (centre-to-centre) distance between two actuators needed to reach a 75% correct localisation performance.

2.1   Determining the Spatial Sensitivity of the Torso

Since only indirect data are available regarding the spatial resolution of the torso for vibro–tactile stimuli, basic research was needed to formulate the requirements for an optimal display configuration. On the one hand, one wants to use the full information processing capacity that is available; on the other hand, one wants to keep the number of actuators to a minimum. Therefore, a series of experiments was conducted in which the spatial resolution of the torso was determined (for the apparatus, see Figure 2, for details of the experiment, see [16]).

The results of the experiments showed that the sensitivity for vibro–tactile stimuli presented to the ventral part of the torso was larger than for stimuli presented to the dorsal part (see Figure 3). Furthermore, the sensitivity near the sagittal plane of the torso is larger than to the sides. Moreover, the sensitivity is larger than was expected on the basis of the existing psychophysical literature on two—point thresholds (e.g., see [7], [20]).

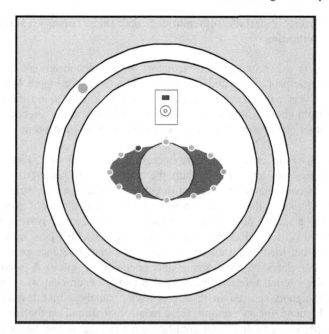

Fig. 3. Top view of the set-up for the direction discrimination task. With a dial, the observer can position a cursor (a spot of light projected from above) along a white circle drawn on the table. The cursor should be positioned such that it indicates the direction associated with the tactile stimulus.

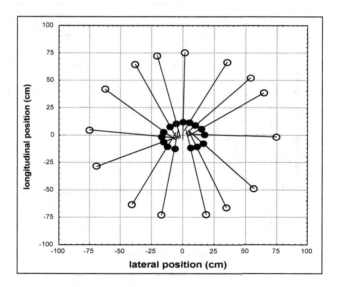

Fig. 4. Example of the mean responses (open circles) of one observer associated with the tactile stimulus on the torso (filled circles). The intersections of the lines connecting those points hint at the existence of two internal reference points.

2.2   Presenting Spatial Information on the Torso: Tactile Direction Discrimination

In a follow–up experiment, tactile actuators were attached around the participant's torso. The participant was seated in the centre of a table (see Figure 4) On this table, a white circle was painted, and the participant's task was to position a spot light (projected from above) on this circle such that it indicated the direction of the tactile stimulus (either one or two adjacent actuators were activated at a time).

The results of this experiment were interesting in several ways. First of all, none of the participants had any trouble with the task. This is noteworthy since a point stimulus does not contain any explicit direction information. The strategy people use is probably similar to the one known in visual perception, namely using a perceptual ego–centre as a second point. Several authors determined the visual ego–centre (e.g., [11]), that can be defined as the position in space at which a person experiences him or herself to be. Identifying an ego–centre or internal reference point is important, because it correlates physical space and phenomenal space. A second reason to determine the internal reference point in this tactile experiment was the striking bias that all participants showed in their responses, namely a bias towards the sagittal plane, see Figure 5 for an example. This means that stimuli on the frontal side of the torso were perceived as directions coming from a point closer to the navel, and stimuli on the dorsal side of the torso were perceived as coming from a point closer to the spine. Further research [15] showed that this bias was not caused by the experimental set–up, the visual system, the subjective location of the stimuli, or other anomalies.

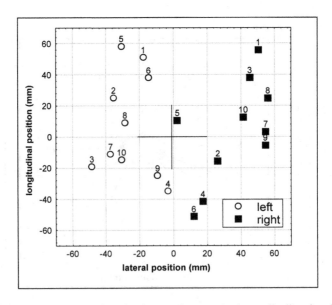

Fig. 5. The Internal Reference Points for the ten observers in the tactile direction determination task. The numbers indicate the individual observers.

The most probable explanation is the existence of two internal reference points: one for the left side of the torso, and one for the right side. When these internal reference points are determined as a function of the body side stimulated, the left and right points are 6.2cm apart on average across the participants (see Figure 6). The third noteworthy observation is related to the variance of the responses as a function of the presented direction: performance in the front–sagittal region is very good with standard deviations between 4° and 8° (see Figure 7), and somewhat lower towards the sides.

More details on the experiments can be found in [15]. The most relevant implications for the application of tactile displays for spatial information are the following:

! ∀observers can perceive a single tactile point stimulus as an indication of external direction,

! ∀the consistency in the perceived direction varies with body location. Performance near the sagittal plane (SD of 4°) is almost as good as with a comparable visual display, but lowers toward the sides,

! ∀direction indication presented by the illusion of apparent location (the percept of one point stimuli located in between two simultaneously presented stimuli) is as good as that of real points,

! ∀small changes in the perceived direction can be evoked by presenting one point stimulus to the frontal side, and one to the dorsal side of the observer.

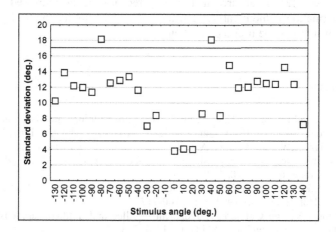

Fig. 6. Standard Deviation of the tactile responses as function of the stimulus angle (0° is the mid—sagittal plane with negative angles to the left). The horizontal lines summarize the results of a post hoc test; pairs of data points differ significantly when separated by the two lines.

3   Discussion

Some potentially beneficial applications of tactile displays in VE or HCI are presented in the Introduction. The present paper focussed on tactile information as supplement to degraded visual information, more specifically for navigation. After choosing what information the tactile display must be designed for to present, the relevant perceptual characteristics of the users must be determined. Although there is substantial literature on tactile perception, the available knowledge isn't by far as complete as on visual and auditive perception. Gaps in the required knowledge, e.g., on tactile perception of body loci other than the arms, hands, and fingers, must be filled before applications can be successful. Besides data on fundamental issues such as spatial and temporal resolution, perceptual illusions might be an interesting area in relation to display design. Illusions such as apparent position (which may double the spatial resolution of a display), and apparent motion (which allows to present the percept of a moving stimulus without moving the actuators) offer great opportunities to present information efficiently. Still more illusions are discovered (e.g., see [2]).

After cataloguing all relevant basic knowledge, specific applications must be studied to further optimise information presentation and display use. Another important point, which is not fully addressed in this paper, is the interaction between the sensory modalities.

As shown in this paper, sensory congruency and response biasses are of major interest in this respect. An enhanced Human Computer Interface will be multi–modal, but the interaction between the tactile and the other senses (e.g., regarding attention switching, see [13]) is an area that is only recently being addressed. Just adding tactile information without careful considerations does not automatically enhance the interface or improve the user's performance.

References

1. Behar, I., and Bevan, W. The perceived duration of auditiory and visual intervals: Cross–modal comparison and interaction. American Journal of Psychology, 1961, 74, 17 - 26.
2. Cholewiak, R.W., and Collins, A.A. The Generation of Vibrotactile Patterns on a Linear Array: Influences of Body Site, Time, and Presentation Mode. *Perception and Psychophysics*, 62(6), 2000, 1220-1235.
3. Gilliland, K., and Schlegel, R.E. Tactile Stimulation of the Human Head for Information Display. Human Factors; 1994, 36; 4; 700-717.
4. Goldstone, S., and Goldfarb, J. Judgment of filled and unfilled durations: Intersensory effects. Perceptual and Motor Skills, 17, 1963, 763 - 774.
5. Goldstone, S., and Lhamon, W.T. Auditory–visual differences in human judgment. Perceptual and Motor skills, 34, 1972, 623 - 633.
6. Hay, J.C., Pick, H.L. Jr., and Ikeda, K. Visual capture produced by prism spectacles. Psychonomic Science, 1965, 2, 215-216.
7. Johnson, K.O., and Phillips, J.R. Tactile spatial resolution. I. Two point discrimination, gap detection, grating resolution, and letter recognition. *Journal of Neurophysiology*, 1981, 6 (6), 1177-1191.
8. Kolers, P.A., and Brewster, J.M. Rythems and Responses. Journal of Experimental Psychology: Human Perception and Performance, 1985, 11, 150-167.

9. Lederman, S.J. Auditory texture perception. Perception, 1979, 8, 93-103.
10. Pick, H.L.Jr., Warren, D.H., and Hay, J.C. Sensory conflicts in judgments of spatial direction. Perception and Psychophysics, 1969, 6, 203-205.
11. Roelofs, C.O. Considerations on the visual egocentre. *Acta Psychologica,* 1959, 16, 226-234.
12. Rupert, A.H., Guedry, F.E., and Reschke, M.F. The use of a tactile interface to convey position and motion perceptions. AGARD meeting on Virtual interfaces: reserach and applications, october 1993.
13. Spence, C., and Driver, J. Cross—Modal Links in Attention Between audition, Vision, and Touch: Implications for Interface Design. *Int. J. of Cognitive Ergonomics,* 1979, 1 (4), 351-373.
14. Teghtsoonian, R., and Teghtsoonian, M. Two varieties of perceived length. Perception and Psychophysics, 1970, 8, 389-392.
15. Van Erp, J.B.F. Direction estimation with vibro-tactile stimuli presented to the torso: a search for the tactile ego-centre. Report TM-00-B012. Soesterberg, The Netherlands: TNO Human Factors, 2000.
16. Van Erp, J.B.F., and Werkhoven, P.J. *Spatial characteristics of vibro–tactile perception on the torso.* Report TM-99-B007. Soesterberg, The Netherlands: TNO Human Factors, 1999.
17. Walker, J.T. Natural visual capture in bilateral length comparisons. Perception and Psychophysics, 1972, 11, 247-251.
18. Walker, J.T., and Scott, K.J. Auditory-visual conflicts in the perceived duration of lights, tones, and gaps. Journal of Experimental Psychology: Human Perception and Performance, 1981, 7, 1327-1339.
19. Warren, D.H. Spatial localization under conflict conditions: Is there a single explanation? Perception, 1979, 8, 323-337.
20. Weinstein, S. *Intensive and extensive aspects of tactile sensitivity as a function of body-part, sex and laterality.* In: The Skin Senses, edited by D.R. Kenshalo. Springfield, C.C. Thomas, 1968, pp 195-218.
21. Werkhoven, P.J., and Van Erp, J.B.F. *Perception of vibro–tactile asynchronies.* Report TM-1998-B013. Soesterberg, The Netherlands: TNO Human Factors, 1998.

Tactile Information Presentation in the Cockpit

Henricus A.H.C. van Veen and Jan B. F. van Erp

TNO Human Factors, P.O. Box 23
3769 ZG Soesterberg, The Netherlands
Tel.: +31 346 356449
vanVeen@tm.tno.nl

Abstract. This paper describes two aspects of the application of tactile information presentation in the cockpit. The first half of the paper discusses why the tactile channel might be used instead of, or in addition to, the more common visual and auditory channels. It lists several categories of information used in cockpits and explores their appropriateness for tactile stimulation. The second half of the paper briefly describes an experiment on the perception of vibro-tactile stimuli under high G-load conditions (in a centrifuge). It is concluded that the perception of vibro-tactile stimulation on the torso is not substantially impaired during high G-load conditions, at least up to 6G.

1 Why We Should Use Tactile Information Presentation in Cockpits

The tactile channel is a relatively neglected information channel in display research, also in cockpit displays. Worldwide only a few groups have current research programmes in this area (e.g., see [2], [3], [4]). Visual displays dominate the design of cockpits, and auditory displays are increasingly being used as well. Tactile displays, however, are virtually absent in cockpits. Nevertheless, there are many situations in which the tactile channel can become an important or even vital alternative, because the visual (and/or auditory) channel is not available, not adequate, or overloaded (e.g., see [2]). Some relevant considerations (some more speculative than others) are:

! ∀The enormous amount of information that is available to the pilot is offered primarily in a visual format. The limits of the visual processing capabilities of pilots constitute a real design constraint in the development of new cockpits.
! ∀The view on the outside world in a cockpit (field-of-regard) is generally and obviously limited, because only a part of the cockpit is transparent. Systems that use forms of indirect sight (such as camera-monitor systems) can be used to overcome this limitation, but always have a restricted instantaneous field-of-regard.
! ∀High G-loads, such as experienced in fighter jets, can severely degrade visual perception. Maybe tactile perception does not suffer from this problem.

S. Brewster, R. Murray-Smith (Eds.): Haptic HCI 2000, LNCS 2058, pp. 174-181, 2001.
© Springer-Verlag Berlin Heidelberg 2001

! ∀Visual information can be hard to interpret, e.g., when representing 3D spatial information on 2D visual displays. Presenting such information to the skin might reduce those interpretation problems. The surface of the skin is a 2D surface like a visual display, but unlike such a display it is also a closed manifold embedded in a 3D space (sphere topology), and can therefore be used to represent part of the 3D spatial relations directly, namely, directions in 3D space.

! ∀Pilots commonly experience visual and visual-vestibular illusions, some of them resulting in disorientation. It is conceivable that tactile stimulation could support the pilot in recognising the occurrence of such illusions and in avoiding their negative effects on performance.

! ∀Visual attention is usually restricted to a single entity (with the exception of moving objects). Thus, tracking multiple visual information sources in parallel is probably limited. How this translates to the tactile modality (and multi-modality) is not exactly known, but there are some indications that tactile attention may be directed to more than one location concurrently.

The above considerations are really examples of the earlier mentioned arguments for using tactile instead of, or in addition to, visual/auditory stimulation: non-availability, inadequacy, and processing overload. Another dimension along which this problem needs to be studied is the type of information that is suitable for presentation via the tactile channel. At least four relevant categories of information present in cockpits can be identified:

1. Geometric information: the projection of spatially organised information on a spatially organised medium. Major examples are:

! ∀Directions in 3D space. Waypoints, other aircraft, targets, etc., can all be characterised by a direction in 3D space. These directions change rapidly when the pilot moves through the environment. Information of this type could be presented continuously, when the pilot asks for it, or could be used as a cueing/warning system (e.g., see [1]). See figure 1.

! ∀Reference frames. An artificial horizon can be represented in the tactile modality by stimulating those parts of the torso that form the intersection of the torso with the actual horizon. See figure 2.

! ∀Borders in the sky. Borders in the sky can originate from airspace rules (restricted areas, minimum height, etc.), from course restrictions (tunnel-in-the-sky) or course planning, from missions (e.g., dropzones), and probably from many other causes. When such borders are interpreted as surfaces in 3D space, pilots can be made aware of them by appropriate tactile stimulation during approach (e.g., tactile stimulation of the relevant side of the body with increasing intensity or frequency upon approach) and passing (e.g., similar to the type of stimulation suggested for indicating reference frames) of such surfaces.

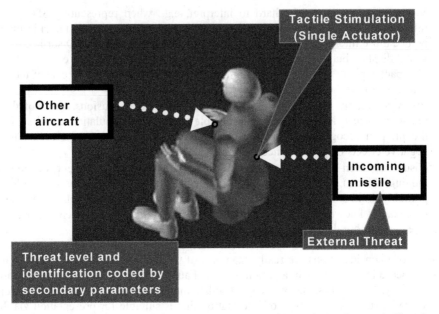

Fig. 1. <u>Geometric information: Directions in 3D space</u>. It has been shown that a pointlike vibro-tactile stimulation on the torso is easily understood by people as an external direction in space. This can be used to effectively indicate directions in 3D space to pilots, such as those associated with other aircraft. It is hypothesized that several of such directions can be distinguished simultaneously.

2. Warning signals: the principles for warning hierarchies in use for controlling visual and auditory warnings can also be developed for the tactile domain. However, a multi-modal approach - which modality should be used with which strength and form - would probably be even more powerful.
3. Coded information: all other types of information not included in the first two categories can of course be projected to the tactile domain in a coded form. Examples are flight manoeuvre related data, such as altitude, speed, attitude, and feedback signals in hovering manoeuvres, but also information like fuel supply, identification of radar signals, time-to-contact, payload information, etc. Optimal ways of coding need to be developed.
4. Communication: The tactile modality might also be used for simple but effective forms of communication between crew members or between members of a formation. Such a communication channel might be useful for covert operations, for communicating simultaneity between individuals, for indicating directions of danger by remote tactile stimulation on another persons body, etc.

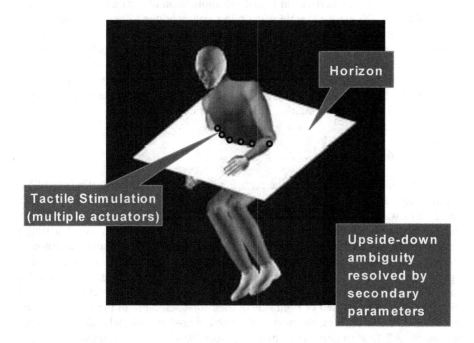

Fig. 2. <u>Geometric information: Reference frames.</u> It is hypothesized that a tactile sensation of the horizontal plane can be elicited by activating the appropriate vibro-tactile actuators on the torso. Upon rotations of the body in space, other actuators should be activated. In the figure above, the person is tilted to the right.

These contemplations can be used to derive a human factors research agenda for investigating the advantages and disadvantages of using tactile versus visual and auditory information presentation in the cockpit. For instance, additional studies on multi-modal attention and processing capacity need be performed before it can be confirmed that tactile stimulation can be used to overcome current processing overload problems. The second half of this paper discusses an experiment along one of the other lines, namely vibro-tactile perception under high G-load.

2   Vibro-Tactile Perception under G-Load

Earlier work at TNO Human Factors has shown that tactile displays can be used effectively for presenting spatial information, such as the direction of waypoints. For these studies, a tactile display was designed that allows for an intuitive way of presenting external directions by means of vibro-tactile stimulation. This display is worn on the torso and can be extended to a maximum of 128 actuators distributed over the body.

The current pilot study aims to probe the perception of vibro-tactile stimulation under high G-load. The motivation is that the application of tactile displays in fighter jets would be much more valuable when pilots can continue to perceive and process tactile stimulation under high G-load conditions where the visual channel degrades strongly or becomes completely unusable. The main factors that potentially hinder tactile perception during high G-load are: mechanical aspects of human skin receptors, pressure suits and straining procedures, reduced attention for tactile stimulation caused by the high stress and workload levels, and mechanical aspects of the actuators used for the stimulation (our tactile display was not designed for high-G applications).

2.1   Methods

The experiment was conducted in the centrifuge of the Aeromedical Institute (AMI) in Soesterberg, The Netherlands, under supervision of a medical doctor. Each of the four participants was subjected to a number of G-profiles (see Table 1), starting with a so-called relaxed G-tolerance test. During all profiles, subjects were wearing a simple version of the tactile display, consisting of three or four tactile actuators mounted on the left and right side of the torso. The actuators were activated as a group (left or right) in a 100ms on - 200 ms off rhythm, during 6 seconds maximum. Subjects had to press one of two buttons (left or right), immediately upon detection of tactile stimulation at either the left or right side of their torso. Because of the obviously short durations of the G-profiles, the next trial started almost immediately after the subject responded. All four subjects were male, between 30-40 years old, member of either two institutes, and participated voluntarily. When considered necessary, a medical examination was conducted before the experiment. During the experiment, a medical doctor continuously monitored the subjects by means of verbal communication, video monitoring, and ECG (electrocardiogram) monitoring. Subjects either had previous experience with G-loads (1, 4) or vibro-tactile stimulations (2, 3).

Table 1. Five different G-profiles used during the experiment.

Profile	Description	Subjects
Tolerance	0.33 G/sec increase of G-load, aborted when subject experiences troubles with vision.	All
4G steady	0.33 G/sec increase of G-load up to 4G, then steady for 30sec. Subject strains leg muscles.	1, 2 (twice), 3
4G fast	Similar to 4G steady, but with 1G/sec.	4
6G fast	1 G/sec increase of G-load up to 6G. Subject wears pressure suit (legs only) and performs straining.	4
6G steady	Similar to 6G fast, but with additional 15 sec steady at 6G.	4

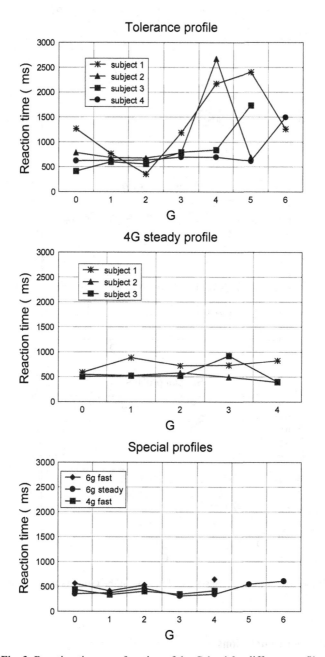

Fig. 3. Reaction time as a function of the G-load for different profiles.

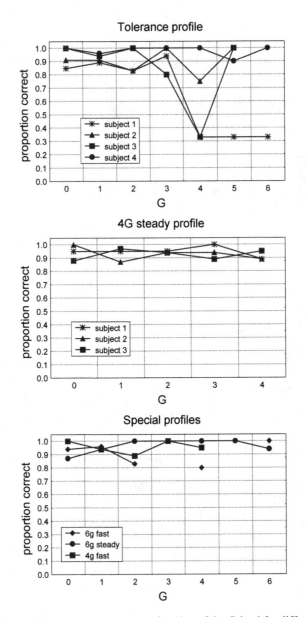

Fig. 4. Proportion correct responses as a function of the G-load for different G-profiles.

2.2   Results and Conclusions

Figures 3 and 4 summarise the results. The results obtained with the G-tolerance profiles show stable response levels (reaction time and percentage correct) up till about 3G, but decreased performance close to the individual G-tolerance levels. This initial performance reduction at higher G-levels disappeared completely in subsequent G-profiles, possibly due to the familiarisation with the task and physiological condition. Note that this is even true for those G-levels that are close to the individual relaxed G-tolerance levels. Reaction times stabilise at around 500 msec (subject dependent) and percentages correct responses are invariably high (between 85 and 100%).

Apparently, the perception of vibro-tactile stimulation on the torso is not substantially impaired during high G-load conditions, at least up to 6G. Note that the torso is certainly not the most sensitive part of the body with respect to vibro-tactile stimulation, in terms of detection thresholds and spatial resolution for instance. Furthermore, it seems that there are no differences between the conditions with and without a pressure suit and extended straining (subject 4 in the 4G fast versus 6G fast and 6G steady conditions).

Acknowledgements

TNO Human Factors kindly acknowledges the support from our colleagues at the Aeromedical Institute in Soesterberg, The Netherlands, in conducting the G-load experiments in their centrifuge.

References

1. Erp, J. B. F. van. Direction determination with vibro-tactile stimuli presented to the torso: a search for the tactile ego-centre. Report TM-00-B012. Soesterberg, The Netherlands: TNO Human Factors
2. Rupert, A. H. Haptic solution to directed energy threats. NATO RTO HFM Symposium on "Countering the directed energy threat: Are closed cockpits the ultimate answer?", Antalya, Turley, 26-28 April 1999. RTO-MP-30, AC/323(HFM)TP/10 (1999)
3. Raj, A. K., McGrath, B. J., Rochlis, J., Newman, D. J., and Rupert, A. H. The application of tactile cues to enhance situation displays. 3rd Annual Symposium and Exhibition on Situational Awareness in the Tactical Air Environment, Patuxent River, MD, 77-84 (1998)
4. Raj, A. K., Suri, N., Braithwaite, M. G., and Rupert, A. The tactile situation awareness system in rotary wing aircraft: Flight test results. NATO RTO HFM Symposium on "Current aeromedical issues in rotary wing operations", San Diego, USA, 19-21 October 1998. RTO-MP-19 (1998)

Scaleable SPIDAR: A Haptic Interface For Human-Scale Virtual Environments

Laroussi Buoguila, Masahiro Ishii, and Makoto Sato

P&I, Tokyo Institute of Technology
4259 Nagatsuta, Midori ku, 226-8503 Yokohama - Japan
laroussi@pi.titech.ac.jp

Abstract. The paper aims to present a new human-scale haptic device for virtual environment named Scaleable-SPIDAR (Space Interface Device for Artificial Reality), which can provides different aspects of force feedback sensations, associated mainly with weight, contact and inertia, to both hands within a cave-like space. Tensioned string techniques are used to generate such haptic sensations, while keeping the space transparent and unbulky. The device is scaleable so as to enclose different cave-like working space. Scaleable-SPIDAR is coupled with a large screen where a computer generated virtual world is displayed. The used approach is shown to be simple, safe and sufficiently accurate for human-scale virtual environment.

1   Introduction

The uses of high quality computer-generated imagery, auditory and interactive scenes have recently been applied to many cave-like virtual environments. Accurate simulations and graphical display of these virtual environments are being used to impart users with realistic experiences. As well as, to provide a more comprehensive understanding of specific problems. However, visual and auditory cues alone do not allow the user to clearly perceive and understand physical interactions such as contact, pressure and weight. The importance of such sensory modality in virtual workspace had already been showed in many researches. To create an immersible human-scale virtual environment, the ability to interact physically with virtual environment, as well as the full and direct use of both hands are indispensable to control over objects and to develop a physical skill. However, to provide such capability of perception and action in a human-scale virtual environment, usually some mechanical equipment attached to a stationary ground as well as to the operator's body are required (Salisbury 1992). This direct contact between hard equipment and operator limits the range of movement and may occlude the graphical display. As well, the weight and the bulk of the mechanical attachments are clearly perceived by the operator, figure 1. Although GROPE-project (Brooks, 1990) may be the most famous human-scale virtual environment systems with force display. Yet, most of the current haptic devices are designed for desktop usage and display force feedback to only one hand. Unlike video

S. Brewster, R. Murray-Smith (Eds.): Haptic HCI 2000, LNCS 2058, pp. 182-193, 2001.

and audio, force information is very difficult to send through air. To form a 3D force at a certain point, say point A, lead a "hard" mechanical device from a "force source" to point A may be the only "simple" and precise way. If A is moveable, then the force display device will become much more complicated in structure compared with video and audio display. Particularly, when the virtual environment workspace becomes larger, that is the point A may go far away from the force source, the haptic device structural strength needs to be enhanced to keep the precision.

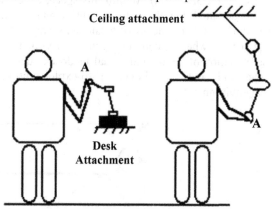

Fig. 1. Typical mechanical attachment.

This enhancement usually makes the whole system bulky, heavy and expensive, as well limits the user's moving freedom. On the other hand, the machinery based forces displays are usually low dynamic performance. In a mechanical system, the dynamic performance is mainly decided by system's weight and moment of inertia. As the haptic devices in human-scale virtual environment are heavy, they would have lower dynamic performance than the ones in a relatively small system, desktop devices. Unfortunately, the task in large working space tends to need higher moving speed and bigger acceleration. How to balance precision and dynamic performance? While improving both of them are the key points to realize usable and accurate force display in human-scale virtual environment.

We propose a new approach, based on tensioned string techniques, to display force feedback sensation on both operator's hands in a large space. While allowing smooth movement and keeping the space transparent.

In the next sections, we explain the features of Scaleable-SPIDAR. A trial system was developed and tested through experiments. Additionally, an application was developed to evaluate the profitability of our device. In the last section, the remaining problems are discussed.

2   Concept of Scaleable-SPIDAR

The device is derived from the original desktop SPIDAR device, which was introduced late in 1990 by Makoto Sato *et al* (Ishii 1994). As shown in figure 2, Scaleable-SPIDAR is delimited by a cubic frame that enclose a cave-like space, where the operator can move around to perform large scale movements. The experimental prototype is $27m^3$ size (3m x 3m x 3m). Within this space, different aspect of force feedback sensations associated mainly with weight, contact and inertia can be displayed to the operator's hands by means of tensioned strings. The front side of the device holds a large screen, where a computer-generated virtual world is projected. Providing such a combination of haptic and visual feedback cues is indispensable to lets the operator's eyes and hands work in concert to explore and manipulate objects populating the virtual environment.

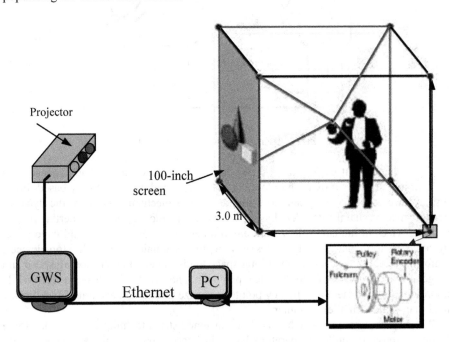

Fig. 2. Overview of Scaleable-SPIDAR.

The device uses tensioned string techniques to track hands position as well as to provide haptic feedback sensations. The approach consists mainly on applying appropriate tensions to the four strings supporting each fingering worn by the operator. The force feedback felt on the operator's hand is the same as the resultant force of tension from strings at the center of the fingering; next subsection gives more detail about forces and position computation. In order to control the tension and length of each string, one extremity is connected to the fingering and the other end is wounded around a pulley, which is driven by a DC motor. By controlling the power applied to the motor, the system can create appropriate tension all the time. A rotary encoder is attached to the DC motor to detect the string's length variation, Figure 4. The set of DC motor, pulley and encoder controlling each string is fixed on the frame.

2.1   Force Control

Scaleable-SPIDAR uses the resultant force of tension from strings to provide force display. As the fingering is suspended by four strings, giving certain tensions to each of them by the means of motors, the resultant force occurs at the position of the fingering, where transmitted to and felt by the operator's hand.

Let the resultant force be $\vec{f}$ and unit vector of the tension be $\vec{u}_i$ $(i=0,1,2,3)$, figure 3, the resultant force is:

$$\vec{f} = \sum_{i=0}^{3} a_i \vec{u}_i \qquad (a_i \forall 0)$$

Where a_i represents the tension value of each string. By controlling all of the a_i the resultant force of any magnitude in any direction can be composed.

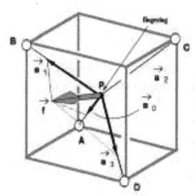
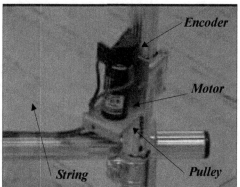

Fig. 3. Resultant force of tension.   **Fig. 4.** Motor and rotary encoder.

2.2   Position Measurement

Let the coordinates of the fingering position be $P(x,y,z)$, which represent in the same time the hand position, and the length of the ith string be l_i $(i=0, ..., 3)$. To simplify the problem, let the four actuators (motor, pulley, encoder) A_i be on four vertexes of the frame, which are not adjacent to each other, as shown by figure 4. Then $P(x,y,z)$ must satisfy the following equations (Eqs).

$$(x \ni a)^2 \ni (y \ni a)^2 \ni (z \ni a)^2 = l_0^2 \qquad (1)$$

$$(x \% a)^2 \ni (y \% a)^2 \ni (z \ni a)^2 = l_1^2 \qquad (2)$$

$$(x\,\%a)^2 \ni (y \ni a)^2 \ni (z\,\%a)^2 \,!\, l_2^2 \tag{3}$$

$$(x \ni a)^2 \ni (y\,\%a)^2 \ni (z\,\%a)^2 \,!\, l_3^2 \tag{4}$$

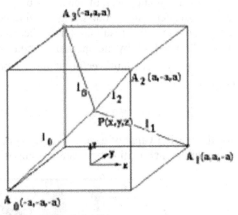

Fig. 5. Position measurement.

After differences between the respective adjacent two equations among equation (1)-(4) and solve the simultaneous equations, we can obtain the position of a fingering (hand) as the following equation (5):

$$\begin{cases} x\,! & \dfrac{(l_0^2 - l_1^2 - l_2^2 + l_3^2)}{8a} \\[2mm] y\,! & \dfrac{(l_0^2 - l_1^2 + l_2^2 - l_3^2)}{8a} \\[2mm] z\,! & \dfrac{(l_0^2 + l_1^2 - l_2^2 - l_3^2)}{8a} \end{cases} \tag{5}$$

3   Experimental Prototype

The experimental prototype provides two fingerings to be worn by the operator on both hands, Figure 6. The fingerings are made of light plastic material and the size can fit to any operator. As well, this small device leaves the hand free and easy to put on and off. Although the operator can wear the fingering on any finger, middle finger is most recommended. The bottom of this finger is close to the center of hand, and the force feedback applied on this position is felt as being applied to the whole palm. To provide the appropriate tensions and lengths of the strings, a personal computer (PC) is used to control an 8-bits D/A, A/D converter and a VME bus, which control respectively the currents entering the motors and detect the changes occurred on each rotary encoder. The PC is connected to a graphics workstation that provides a real-time video image of the virtual world. Figure 7 shows the apparatus of the prototype.

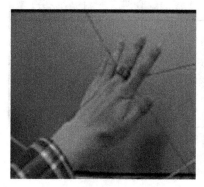

Fig. 6. The fingering pointer.   **Fig. 7.** Apparatus of Scaleable-SPIDAR.

Performance of Scaleable-SPIDAR

Position Measurement Range: the coordinates origin are set to the center of the framework. The position measurement ranges of all x, y and z in [-1.50m, +1.50m].

Static Position Measurement Error: the absolute static position measurement errors are less than 1.5cm inside the position measurement range.

Force Feedback Range: within the force displayable sphere (Cai 1996), force sensation range is from $0.005N$ (minimum) to $30N$ (maximum) for all directions.

System Bandwidths:

Video: 10 ~ 15 Hz

Audio: 22 kHz (stereo)

Position measurement and force display: > 1200 Hz (depends also on hardware installation)

Comparison With Other Haptic Devices: the next tabular shows the performance of Scaleable-SPIDAR compared with two other well-known force display devices, PHANToM (Sensable.com) and Haptic-Master (Iwata 1990).

Table 1. Comparision with other haptic devices.

Haptic device	Work space (cm)	Position resolution (mm)	Peak force (kgf)	Inertia (gf)
Haptic Master	40x40x40	0.4	2.1	220
PHANToM	20x27x38	0.03	0.87	75
Scaleable-SPIDAR	300x300x300	15	3.0	50

4   Experiments and Application

In this section, the implementation of a haptic feedback experience with Scaleable-SPIDAR and an evaluation application are described.

4.1   Experiments

An investigation is carried to state the feasibility and the effect of the Scaleable-SPIDAR's force feedback on an interactive task. As "Space-Pointing" movements are considered as basic operations in any virtual reality applications and they are expected to be performed accurately within the minimum of time, a pushing button task was simulated to study how perfectly the operator can perform this task with and without force feedback. The operator is provided with a virtual flat wall, where five hemisphere shaped buttons are fixed on it; one of them is lighted red and the others are green. A graphical representation of the hand is displayed to give visual feedback cues. The apparatus of the setting is presented in figure 8. The operator is asked to move his hand on the top of the red button and push it to a certain deep. If he succeeds, an audible bell is displayed and the red button changes to green while the next green button is lighted up to red. The order is the same as writing the letter "Z". The times spent from a button was lighted up to red until it is successfully pushed are recorded as "Task Times" (TTs) under the following conditions:

Condition 1: Visual Cues Only: in this condition, the operator is only able to get visual feedback cues, force feedback information is not available; hence, operator's hand can pass through the buttons and the wall.

Condition 2: Visual and Force Feedback Cues: in this case the operator can feel force feedback when his hand comes into contact with the wall or any of the button. The spherical shape of the buttons and the flatness of the wall are haptically perceived.

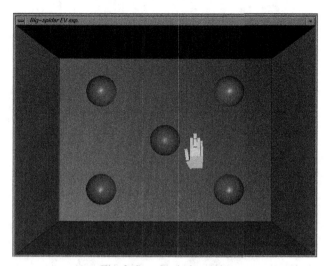

Fig. 8. Space pointing task.

Condition 3: Force Feedback Cues Only: after the operator has remembered the buttons' positions in his mind, the hand's visual feedback cues are disabled; thus the operator can not "see" the position of his hand in the simulated scene. That is he do not know whether his hand is moving close to the button or not, but only "feel" force feedback reactions when the hand runs over the virtual wall or the buttons.

Four right-handed subjects participated in the experiment, including two of the authors. None of them reported any haptic deficiencies. Although it was not necessary for the experiment, all subjects were familiar with haptic devices and virtual environment. Each subject was told about the three different conditions and the task to be performed. There was three different sessions of trials for all subjects. In each session the red button should be pushed successfully 40 times. Before any session a short time of practice was given.

4.2   Results

TTs' means and variances are presented in figure 9 under the different conditions. When force feedback is available together with visual information. The "push button" task can be performed faster and only cost about 65% of the time needed for the "visual feedback only" condition. At the mean while, after plenty of practice even with the "force feedback only" condition, the user can still finish the "push button" task faster than the "visual feedback only" condition. This is because after practices, and by trials the operator has remembered the space positions of the buttons and can quickly move his hand toward the red button since the order is fixed and previously known.

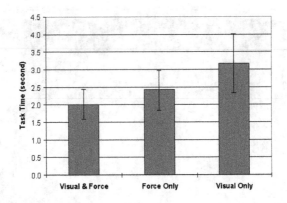

Fig. 9. Mean task time of the different conditions.

It was found also, that in condition 1 80% of the TTs is devoted exclusively to push the button, whereas only 20% of the TTs is needed for positioning the hand in front of the red button. Nearly the opposite situation is present for trials done under condition 3, where 30% of the TTs is devoted exclusively for the pushing task and the other 70% of times are used to localize the targeted button. Also, as it can be seen from figure 9 that, the TTs variance are smaller when force feedback is available.

The difference of time spending in both condition 1 and 3 is significant. In the former one subjects have mainly a lack of depth perception, but good navigational performance. The later condition shows better capability of manipulation and interaction with objects, although the navigation is slow. The combined influence of visual and haptic modalities has a clear effect on the subject's performance in the second condition.

As conclusion, Scaleable-SPIDAR's force feedback system is shown to be able to improve the interaction with objects. Such haptic capability and enhancement is not only desirable but could be indispensable for dexterous manipulation.

4.3   Experimental Application

Scaleable-SPIDAR is used to simulate the experience of the basketball's free throw shot, which is considered a skillful action that requires large space to play and where the haptic sensation of the ball is crucial to shoot a hoop. Being inside the playing space, the operator face a large screen where a 3D basketball's playground, backboard and a ball are displayed. As well, a graphic representation of the player's hands to give a visual feedback cues, figure 10.

Fig. 10. Virtual BasketBall game.

In order to control the ball and perceive haptically its weight and shape, the player has to wear the two fingering on both hands. As the player start moving inside the frame the system tracks the hands' position, and when they come into contact with the virtual ball appropriate forces are displayed, such as its weight. If the player doesn't held tight enough or open her/his hands, the ball will fall down and bounds on the floor. After making a shot, the ball begins a free falling movement determined by the hand's velocity and orientation while freeing the ball. If the ball doesn't go through the hoop, it may rebound from the backboard, basket's ring or objects surrounding the playground. The virtual ball is designed 40*cm* in diameter and weights 300*g*.

To show the force feedback effectiveness in such skillful operation, we asked two users to play this game, while recording the distance between their hands. Two sessions was organized, one with force feedback, that is the user felt haptically the spherical shape of the ball as well as its weight. And a second session, where only visual feedback cue is provided. The results of this experiment is shown by figures 11and 12. The horizontal axes show the time and the vertical show the distances between the two hands. Time spent for each trial is devised into three parts. Part A where the user is trying to catch the ball. Part B is when the ball is hold by the user. During this part the user start first by ensuring the fact of holding a ball (B1), this part is still characterized by some vibrations due to user's behavior as well as software optimization. Then the user brings his attention to the backboard and aims the hoop (B2) and finishes this part by throwing the ball toward the basket (B3). At last in part C the hands become free again.

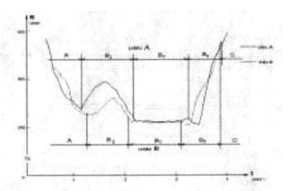

Fig. 11. Distance between the two hands with force feedback.

The part to which we are interested is B2, where there is a direct and full contact between the virtual ball and user's hands. As the figures 9a-b show, the distance between the two hands is more stable when force feedback is displayed. In this case the user unintentionally does not think about the ball, instead he is concerned about the game and his skills to shoot a hoop. Without force feedback, the user cannot easily keep his hands in right distance to hold the ball. The only thing he can do while holding a ball, is to keep looking whether or not his hands are deep inside the ball.

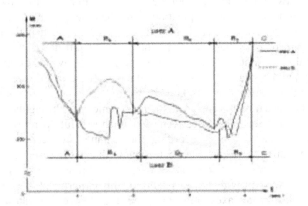

Fig. 12. Distance between the two hands without force feedback.

Other results of this interactive experience showed that, with force feedback sensation the player improve considerably his performance of scoring up to 60% better than throwing the ball without force feedback. Haptic sensation is revealed to be indispensable to show the real skills while manipulating virtual object.

5   Discussion and Conclusion

Tensioned strings techniques are used to realize force feedback on both hands in a large space. Although the approach makes the human scale device very light and easy to use as well as safe, it also has some problems. Mainly, the strings may interfere with each other if the operator tries to turn around her/himself or cross deeply his hands. Actually, this backdrop is inevitable for any system using direct contact attachment with the operator to generate force feedback. Another problem, that was partially improved by (Cai 1996) but still remain, occurs when the operator moves her/his hands with a very high speed. This kind of movement makes the string no longer straight and causes a length miscalculation, which affects the precision of hands' position.

The concept of the Scaleable-SPIDAR is new and unique and it offers possible application in a wide variety of fields. Its main features, are the ability to display different aspects of force feedback within different size cave-like space without visual disturbance; As well, the device is not bulky, and easy to use; Another distinguishing characteristic of Scaleable-SPIDAR, is that the operator does not think in terms of manipulating an input device, instead he has a full and direct use of his hands.

Recently we are investigating the use of scaleable-SPIDAR in a visual-less virtual environment, that is to explore what can be accomplished within an "invisible" but audible and tangible virtual environment. Such system has a great deal of interest in building new computer interfaces for blind persons.

References

Brooks, F.P., Young, M.O., Batter, J.J., and Kilpatrick, P.J. (1990)" Project GROPE- Haptic Display for Scientific Visualization" Computer Graphics, Proc. ACM SIGGRAPH'90, Vol.24, No4, pp. 177-185.

Cai Y., Ishii, M., and Sato, M. "Position Measurement Improvement on a force Display Device Using Tensioned Strings". IEICE TRANS. INF. &SYST. Vol. E77-D, N°6 June 1996.

Hirata Y., Sato, M., and Kawarada, H.``A Measuring Method of Finger Position in Virtual Work Space" Forma, Vol.6, No.2, pp.171-179(1991) http://www.sensable.com/product.htm

Ishii, M., and Sato, M. 1994a, "A 3D Spacial Interface Device Using Tensioned Strings," Presence-Teleoperators and Virtual environments, Vol. 3. No 1, MIT Press, Cambridge, Ma, pp. 81-86

Iwata, H.: ``Artificial Reality with Force-Feedback: Development of Desktop Virtual Space with Compact Master Manipulator," (Computer Graphics), 24(4), 165-170(1990)

Salisbury, J., and Srinivasan, M. 1992, "Virtual Environment Technology for Training (VETT)" BBN Report No 7661, VETREC, MIT, Cambridge, MA

The Sense of Object-Presence with Projection-Augmented Models

Brett Stevens and Jennifer Jerrams-Smith

Department of Information Systems, University of Portsmouth
1-8 Burnaby Road, Portsmouth, Hampshire, UK, PO1 3AE
{brett.stevens,jenny.jerrams-smith}@port.ac.uk
http://www.tech.port.ac.uk/~stevensb/

Abstract. Projection-augmented models are a type of non-immersive, coincident haptic and visual display that uses a physical model as a three dimensional screen for projected visual information. Supporting two sensory modalities consistently should create a strong sense of the object's existence. However, conventional measures of presence have only been defined for displays that surround and isolate a user from the real world. The idea of object-presence is suggested to measure 'the subjective experience that a particular object exists in a user's environment, even when that object does not'. This definition is more appropriate for assessing non-immersive displays such as projection-augmented models.

1 Introduction

Virtual reality was originally conceived as an advanced human-computer interface that immersed a user within a realistic three-dimensional environment [12]. However, this form of immersive virtual reality requires expensive equipment and can have negative side effects for a user [2]. Therefore, it has been suggested that virtual reality should be redefined as any *"advanced human-computer interface that simulates a realistic environment and allows participants to interact with it."* [8].

This definition includes non-immersive displays such as conventional computer monitors as well as projection-augmented models. This prototype display uses a physical model to act as a three-dimensional screen for projected visual information.

One of immersive virtual reality's key benefits is its ability to induce a sense of *presence*, defined by Witmer & Singer [14] as the *"subjective experience of being in one place or environment, even when one is physically situated in another"*. However, this paper suggests an alternative definition for presence that is more appropriate for non-immersive displays.

2 Object-Presence

Witmer and Singer [14] state that presence in a virtual environment is dependent on immersion and involvement. Whilst Slater and Wilbur [11] suggest that one of the

S. Brewster, R. Murray-Smith (Eds.): Haptic HCI 2000, LNCS 2058, pp. 194-198, 2001.

key components of immersion is the extent to which a virtual environment surrounds the user. However, a virtual environment is constructed from objects, which permits the definition of presence to be re-written as "the subjective experience of being *co-located with a set of objects*, even when one is physically *not in such a situation*". If this definition is used, the implication that the user should be surrounded, inherent in the concept of environment, is replaced with the idea that a user should have a feeling of being 'with' an object.

Considering the other components of immersion as suggested by Slater and Wilbur [11]. The quality of a display (*vivid*), the range of sensory modalities (*extensive*) and the correspondence between the user's actions and displayed information (*matching*) are all aspects of how naturally a display supports a user. These components are not unique requirements for immersive displays. Indeed the only other factor unique to immersion apart from the ability to surround a user, is the extent to which a user is removed from reality (*inclusion*). Thus the difference in presence between immersive and non-immersive displays results from a display surrounding and isolating a user. However, some tasks do not require the user to be surrounded or isolated.

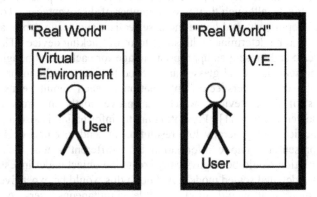

Fig. 1. Presence and Object-Presence.

Presence forms an important subjective measure of a user's virtual experience, although it is only useful in relation to performance [3]. It is assumed that the more natural the display feels, the greater its usefulness [9]. This naturalness may better enable a user to utilize 'real-world' skills in a virtual environment although it may also help to transfer learning from the virtual environment back into the real-world [9]. The conventional definition of presence suggests that non-immersive displays are inadequate, even for tasks that do not require the user to be surrounded and isolated. Therefore, a new measure is needed to assess presence for non-immersive displays that will more closely consider task requirements and how naturally a display supports a user. "*It is here*" is the idea that a display medium brings an object or person to the user [9]. This idea has only been investigated for conventional television programmes, where it assesses the belief that the actual object being displayed exists within the television set. However, this concept can be extended to provide a measure for non-immersive displays where the object appears to be in the user's physical environment, instead of inside the display.

Following the style used by Witmer and Singer [10], "the subjective experience that a particular object exists in a user's environment, even when that object does not" will be termed '*object-presence*'. This definition does not distinguish between real or virtual environments although in the context of immersive virtual reality, object-presence and presence would be interdependent. More interestingly though, is the subjective experience that an object exists in the real world. This can be thought of as a special case of virtual reality, where the user is co-located with a virtual environment (Fig 1). Presence and object-presence have a close relationship. Both have been conceptualised as types of transportation [9] where the user is either transported to the virtual environment or the virtual environment is transported to the user. This sense of object-presence is an important element for projection-augmented models.

3   Projection-Augmented Models

Conventional virtual reality displays have the potential to present dynamic three-dimensional objects, although they have a number of disadvantages. To support most physiological depth cues, and hence increase realism and scene depth, a user's "point of view" needs to be determined with some form of tracking device. This information is used to create and present an appropriate image for each eye although, because two images are presented, special glasses are needed to filter out the incorrect image [7]. To present the correct perspective information to each simultaneous user requires multiple sets of these devices, which can prove costly in terms of equipment, processing power and time [1]. Presenting haptic information is also a problem as the facilitating devices are generally low resolution or tend to either occlude the visual display or present the haptic information in a different spatial location [4]. An alternative solution would be to physically create the object under investigation, or for large objects a detailed scaled model. Although this would be expensive to create and difficult to modify, it would allow multiple simultaneous users to receive high-resolution visual and haptic information from any perspective [10].

Projection-augmented models are a hybrid of these techniques where a simplified physical object acts as a three dimensional screen for a matching graphical model projected onto its surface [10]. The visual image can be altered easily like a conventional display but, because it is presented on the surface of a physical object, all physiological depth cues are supported for multiple users. The physical object can also be touched, which should provide coincident haptic and visual information, a sense that "what you see is what you feel". Supporting two sensory modalities consistently should create a strong sense of palpability, or awareness that the object exists [5], and hence a strong sense of object-presence. However, if the visual and haptic information is not consistent, for example if the visual information does not relate to the object's surface but to its inner workings or surrounding atmosphere, it will cause an intersensory discrepancy. This may result in either the visual, or haptic, information being ignored or in some cases, the incongruous information may be combined to create an inaccurate representation of the object [13].

Fig. 2. "Table-top Spatially Augmented Reality" [10] and "The HapticScreen" [6].

The physical model could either be a static surrogate object [10] or a dynamically deforming physical simulation [6]. Both of these examples use relatively low-resolution objects although the projected image provides a more realistic visual representation of the object's surface (Fig 2). In this context, object-presence is a measure of how much the presented object seems to exist, i.e. the combination of physical and visual information, not the existence of the physical object alone.

4 Summary

Projection-augmented models offer a unique method for presenting visual and haptic information in the same spatial location. The visual information is projected onto a physical model which supports the ability to touch the object under investigation [10] and allows multiple simultaneous users to view it stereoscopically, without the need for head-tracking or stereoscopic glasses. Although only at the prototype stage, both static [10] and dynamic [6] models should allow a user to naturally access information.

One of the measures applied to a virtual reality display is the extent to which a user feels present. Linked to the idea of a display supporting the user in a "natural" way, it is assumed that the more natural the display feels the greater its usefulness [9]. This naturalness may enhance a user ability to utilize 'real-world' skills in a virtual environment although it may also help to transfer learning from the virtual environment back into the real world. The conventional definition of presence requires a user to be isolated from the real world and surrounded with a virtual environment. Although this definition is appropriate for some tasks, others do not require the creation of an entire environment.

Non-immersive displays can provide a realistic natural stimulus to a user even though they have a limited field of view. The idea of object-presence is suggested to measure the extent to which information presented with a non-immersive display seems natural to a user. This concept replaces the feeling of being surrounded by an environment with the sense of being co-located with a collection of objects. This is more applicable to non-immersive displays and should provide an interesting measure for use with projection-augmented models.

Projection-augmented models support nature interaction modes and should create a strong sense of object-presence. Future work includes the need to identify a measure of object-presence that is applicable to projection-augmented models and to determine if a link between task performance and object-presence exists.

Acknowledgments

We thank Miss Amanda Brightman, Dr David Callear, Dr Steve Hand and Dr David Heathcote for their comments and suggestions.

References

1. Agrawala, M. et al.: The two user responsive workbench: Support for collaboration through individual views of a shared space. In: Proceedings of SIGGRAPH'97: Computer Graphics Proceedings, Annual Conference Series. Los Angeles, California: USA. ACM Press, (1997) 327-332.
2. Cobb, S.V.G., Nichols, S., Ramsey, A., and Wilson, J.R.: Virtual Reality-Induced Symptoms and Effects (VRISE). Presence Teleoperators and Virtual Environments, (1999) 8(2), 169-186.
3. Ellis, S.R.: Presence of mind: A reaction to Thomas Sheridan's "Further musings on the psychophysics of presence". Presence Teleoperators and Virtual Environments, (1996) 5(2), 247-259.
4. Henderson, A.: The nanoManipulator. (1999). Available from http://www.cs.unc.edu/Research/nano (Accessed: 30 November 1999).
5. Hinckley, K.: Haptic issues for virtual manipulation. Unpublished doctoral dissertation, University of Virginia (1996).
6. Iwata, H.: HapticScreen. In: Proceedings of SIGGRAPH'98: Conference Abstracts and Applications. Boston, Massachusetts. ACM Press, (1998) 117.
7. Krueger, W., and Froelich, B.: The responsive workbench. IEEE Computer Graphics and Applications, (1994) 14(3), 12-15.
8. Latta, J.N., and Oberg, D.J.: A conceptual virtual reality model. IEEE Computer Graphics and Applications, (1994) 23-29.
9. Lombard, M., and Ditton, T.: At the heart of it all: The concept of presence. Journal of Computer-Mediated Communication, (1997) 3(2), Available from http://www.ascusc.org/jcmc/vol3/issue2/lombard.html (Accessed 17 May 2000).
10. Raskar, R., Welch, G., and Chen, W.-C.: Table-top spatially-augmented reality: Bringing physical models to life with projected imagery. In: Proceedings of International Workshop on Augmented Reality IWAR'99. (1999)
11. Slater, M., and Wilbur, S.: A framework for immersive virtual environments (FIVE): Speculations on the role of presence in virtual environments. Presence Teleoperators and Virtual Environments, (1997) 6(6), 603-616.
12. Sutherland, I.E.: A head mounted three dimensional display. In: Proceedings of the fall joint computer conference (AFIPS). (1968) 33(1), 757-764.
13. Welch, R.B., Warren, D.H.: Immediate perceptual response to intersensory discrepancy. Psychological Bulletin, (1980) 88(3), 638-667.
14. Witmer, B.G., and Singer, M.J.: Measuring presence in virtual environments: A presence questionnaire. Presence Teleoperators and Virtual Environments, (1998) 7(3), 225-240.

Virtual Space Computer Games with a Floor Sensor Control – Human Centred Approach in the Design Process

Jaana Leikas, Antti Väätänen, and Veli-Pekka Räty

VTT Information Technology, P.O.Box 1206
FIN-33101 Tampere, Finland
Tel. +358 3 316 3111
jaana.leikas@vtt.fi, antti.vaatanen@vtt.fi, veli-pekka.raty@vtt.fi

Abstract. Traditionally computer games are played with a keyboard and a mouse or a joystick. The playing relies mainly on visual and auditory senses. Tactile or haptic user interfaces and natural movements of the human being, e.g. running, are seldom utilised in computer games. The Lumetila project (Virtual Space – User Interfaces of the Future) aims at developing a 'natural' user interface in a computer game where the user uses his body movements to control the game. To create an immersive, captivating and highly usable game, the development will be carried out in the context and practice of Human-Centred Design approach, where the computer game is designed and evaluated with end-users in every step of the iterative design process.

Keywords: Computer games, floor sensors, virtual space, user interfaces, human-centred design, usability.

Introduction

Traditionally, computer games are played alone, the player against the computer, or in a two player game mode. The narration and the plot of the computer games have changed only little during the last decades, although effective computers and high-resolution displays have added entertainment value to the games. Generally, the game user interface still contains a computer with a display and a keyboard, as well as a mouse or a joystick as a game controller. At the moment, the development of computer game controllers is rapid producing advanced ways for controlling computer games on the market. Force feedback joysticks and steering wheels are becoming controllers in computer games. However, these solutions still rely on the old way of controlling the game by using mainly one's hands and fingers.

Although technology enables already more accurate and more versatile sensors for recognising body movements of the players, only few computer games to make use of this technology have been developed.

The Lumetila project aims at exploring how people can, and how willing they are, to use their own body to control a computer game, and how they can interact with the

S. Brewster, R. Murray-Smith (Eds.): Haptic HCI 2000, LNCS 2058, pp. 199-204, 2001.
© Springer-Verlag Berlin Heidelberg 2001

computer game and with other players by moving around in a room. Our approach is to weaken the boundaries between the room surrounding the players and the interactive virtual space. With effects equipment and computer software we will create new immersive virtual spaces (Fig. 1).

Fig. 1. Visualisation of the Lumetila – Virtual Space
(image by Tiina Kymäläinen, VTT Information Technology).

The Design Process

There are several methodologies and different methods to carry out the design work. We chose the Human-Centred Design (HCD) approach to the Lumetila design. This approach aims at utilising the opinions of the end-users of the product as efficiently as possible in different stages of the development process. According to the approach, people who develop new applications have continuing co-operation with potential users of the new solution. Thus, the application is designed and tested with users in every step of the iterative design process in order to enable a highly functional and usable outcome of the system.

In line with the ISO 13407 standard (Human-Centred Design Processes for Interactive Systems) the key aspects in our design process have been: 1) appropriate allocation of function between the user and the system, 2) active involvement of users, 3) iteration of design solutions, and 4) multi-disciplinary design team.

There is a range of different methods and techniques that can be used to achieve the goals of human-centred software development. The tools that have been applied within industry are e.g., planning, ISO standards, expert-based evaluation and inspection, early prototyping, usability performance evaluation, and subjective assessment. These techniques were, however, not seen suitable as such for the Lumetila design. As in every software solution, also in the Lumetila solution the user interface is the most critical part: it is the part of the system, which gives feedback and creates experiences to the user. Furthermore, in the Lumetila project the main aim is to create a totally new type of a user interface and to study its applicability in a game solution. Thus, to create our own method to user interface design when adapting the HCD approach was seen the most profitable way to come up with new, innovative ideas and to design an immersive, captivating and highly usable game (Fig. 2).

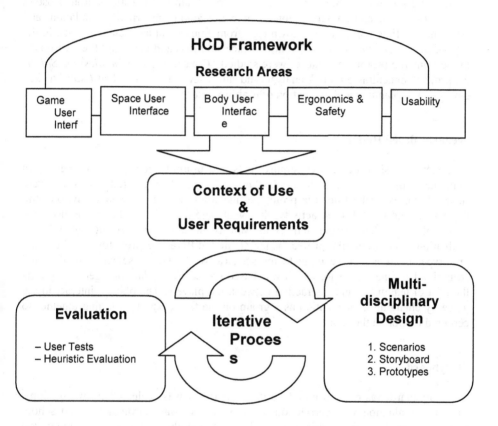

Fig. 2. The Human-Centred Design Process and Approach of the Lumetila project.

In the Lumetila project the HCD process has been twofold:
1. State-of-the art survey on experiences of computer game user interfaces as well as experiences on using the space or one's own body as a user interface in a game or an artwork.
2. Participatory evaluation; The potential end-users participate in the development process by carrying out scenario-based design together with the developers of the solution, evaluating the scenario-based storyboard, and testing the Lumetila prototype in Lumetila environment.

Focus Areas

During the state-of-the art survey, the project concentrated on 5 focus areas that gave input to the design work. These focus areas, tightly connected to each other, were Game User Interface, Space User Interface, Body User Interface, Ergonomics and Safety, and Usability. In the area of *Game User Interface*, different games were used as a point of view when studying new ways for human-computer interactions. Concerning the *Space User Interface*, the project examined questions around user's possibilities to interaction, navigation and experience in many artistic installations and different free time applications known e.g., from amusement and science parks. In the area of *Body User Interface,* different interface solutions and ideas and their adequacy to the Lumetila prototype contexts were studied. Concerning *Ergonomics and Safety,* the project concentrated on risk analysis and safety level definition. The *Usability* area gave input to planning and evaluation of usability issues.

Scenario-Based Design

To generate design ideas, user requirements and usability goals, a basic method in Lumetila project has been *Scenario-Based Design*. The created scenarios were fictional stories of the Lumetila prototype, including the Virtual Space environment, the players and their desired activity, the events and the effects. They were also used as a tool for modelling user activity as well as planning and carrying out usability evaluation. The Lumetila project team created different genres for the Lumetila prototype in order to give input to the scenario work and the selection of the final scenario. The final scenario, which was based on the *Group Balance* genre, supports the idea of teamwork and interaction between the players. The players interact in the game by changing their position as a group on the floor, e.g., by running together to certain direction in the room.

Storyboard

The storyboard was created based on the scenario. It was evaluated in two sessions: The first evaluation was carried out as a pluralistic walk through with 20 school children who gave their opinions on the plot and the characters. Secondly, the storyboard was given to 19 families via Internet. After familiarising themselves with the storyboard they answered questions concerning the plot, the characters, and their interests in computer games in general. The storyboard was amended according the feedback from the user tests.

LumePong as a Test Game

The LumePong game (Fig. 3) was created in order to test the functionality and relevance of the planned user interface of the Lumetila prototype. The technical environment to be used in the Lumetila prototype, especially the floor sensors and the player recognition, was tested with the users. The Virtual Space for the game was created at the Usability Laboratory of VTT Information Technology.

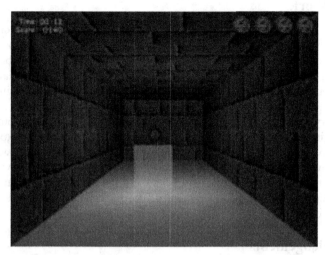

Fig. 3. A screen shot of the LumePong game. The player controls the grey 'racquet' and tries to hit the ball by moving his body.

The LumePong game is based on the well-known Pong game. In our virtual space version there is a real time 3D graphics environment where the player controls a 'racquet' by moving around on the floor. The floor has pressure sensors for recognising the player's movements: when a player goes forward, the 'racquet' goes up, when he moves backwards the 'racquet' goes down, and so on.

Findings

The HCD process and the chosen design methodology proved to be a practicable way to design the Virtual Space Game. Our approach focuses on a multi-disciplinary working method, which actively keeps in view the valuable opinions of the different members in the design group. It also efficiently allows the voices of the end-users to be heard in the very beginning and throughout the design process.

The project group found scenario-based design an appropriate and motivating method for the game design. The storyboard of the Lumetila prototype was created through many vibrant phases in the scenario building process.

To compare the differences and the similarities of the Lumetila idea to other virtual reality systems as well as to computer games' narrative, proved to be a good working method. Through this we could envisage the possible problems when designing Lumetila on the basis of earlier virtual reality systems or computer games' narrative and style. All the foundings were consoling.

As well as the floor sensor system, a real-time 3D graphics engine and special effects devices are essential factors in creating the immersion and experience in the Virtual Space. The room for the Virtual Space is equipped with a 3D sound system and light effect devices. The fact that the players need not wear any virtual reality devices, e.g., data glasses or gloves, helps creating a total immersion, as well as starting the game and acting as a group.

Future Work

Based on the positive findings of the scenario work and the LumePong evaluation, VTT Information Technology will continue to develop the Lumetila prototype together with its partners. The Lumetila prototype will be a location-based entertainment game suitable for people of all ages. It will not require any special skills to play it: using one's own body as a controller of the game will be the main factor in the game.

To carry on the iterative HCD process, also the Lumetila prototype will be evaluated in the Virtual Space room, described earlier, by usability experts (heuristic usability evaluation) and potential end-users. The evaluation results will be brought into the development work. One of the most interesting factors to be evaluated will be how well the Lumetila prototype will meet the original challenge of our design work: do we succeed in creating an interactive natural environment with a shared experience between the players.

Acknowledgements

In the Lumetila project VTT Information Technology works in collaboration with Cube Ltd., Nokia Research Center, Tampereen Särkänniemi Ltd., and the University of Lapland. Tekes, the National Technology Agency, co-funds the project. We like to thank all the project participants.

References

1. Bevan and Macleod: Usability measurement in context. Behaviour & Information Technology, 1994, VOL. 13, NOS.1 and 2 (1994) 132-145
2. Bias, R.G.: The Pluralistic Usability Walkthrough Coordinated Emphathies. In: Nielsen, J., and Mack, R. (eds.): Usability Inspection Methods. John Wiley and Sons, New York, NY (1994)
3. Daly-Jones, O., Bevan, N., and Thomas, C.: Handbook of User-Centred Design. Telematics Applications Project IE 2016. European Usability Support Centres. Information Engineering Usability Support Centres (1997)
4. ISO 13407. Human-centred design processes for interactive systems. International Organization for Standardization (1999)
5. Johnson, P.J.: Human Computer Interaction: psychology, task analysis and software engineering. McGraw Hill, London (1992)
6. Maguire, M.: RESPECT User Requirements Framework Handbook. European Usability Support Centres. Requirements Engineering and Specification in Telematics (1997)
7. Nielsen, Jakob.: Usability Engineering. Academic Press, New York, NY (1993)
8. Nielsen, J., and Mack Robert, L.: Usability Inspection Methods, John Wiley & Sons (1994)
9. Norman, D. A: Things that make us smart. Addison-Wesley, Reading, MA (1993)
10. Preece, J.: Human-Computer Interaction. Addison-Wesley (1994)
11. Rubin, J.: Handbook of usability testing. How to plan, design, and conduct effective tests. John Wiley & Sons (1994)
12. Räty, Veli-Pekka.: Virtual Space – User Interfaces of the Future. VTT Information

Sensing the Fabric: To Simulate Sensation through Sensory Evaluation and in Response to Standard Acceptable Properties of Specific Materials when Viewed as a Digital Image

Patricia Dillon[1], Wendy Moody[1], Rebecca Bartlett[2], Patricia Scully[2],
Roger Morgan[2], and Christopher James[2]

[1]Fashion & Textiles, School of Art
Liverpool John Moores University
68 Hope Street, Liverpool, L1 9EB
laswmood@livjm.ac.uk; dvapdill@livjm.ac.uk
[2] School of Engineering, Byrom Street, Liverpool, L3 3AF
r.morgan@livjm.ac.uk

Abstract. This paper describes initial investigations, primarily from a textile and the related industries perspective, in developing and refining current fabric/texture simulation and interface design. We have considered the interactive possibilities of fabrics within a virtual environment using a simple haptic device, a commercially viable computer peripheral - Logitech's Wingman Mouse, which was developed by the Immersion Corporation for two dimensional (2D) exploration for the Games industry and desktop web navigation. Also, however because a majority of computer users are accustomed to using a mouse. The Wingman already has the facility to set up some simple mechanical variables to represent some of the more obvious tactile impressions in fabrics, e.g. denim for its overall roughness, and corduroy for its repetitive bumps.
The results and issues involved are discussed in this paper.

Keywords. Textiles and related industries, haptic, fabric, touch evaluation.

1   Introduction

The Textiles industry has become increasingly aware of the need to enhance the sensory experience when viewing highly tactile images, particularly fabrics, via the Internet or using other virtual systems. [1], [2], [3] In order to engage this creative sector in fully utilising such a system for observing and working with textiles, for example, to communicate, trade, develop ideas across both the clothing and interiors sectors within the industry, we need to improve on the present sensory experience. Our initial research is focussed on the introduction of the sense of touch to the overall experience. [1], [2]

Haptic technology has presented an opportunity for the textiles and related industries to work within a virtual environment, i.e. using haptic interfaces as an aid

S. Brewster, R. Murray-Smith (Eds.): Haptic HCI, LNCS 2058, pp. 205-217, 2001.

for viewing, selling, marketing, global communication, manufacturing, education, and even the design of textiles and its related products. It also has further favourable implications for the consumer, i.e. online shopping. [1], [2], [3]

Benefits related to a highly visual and tactile industry will include, helping to reduce visual and information overload [4], [5], improving performance, time and choice, i.e. speedier and improved selection processes in selling fabrics and its related products online, within industry or for the consumer. It will allow the industry to continue to work effectively as possible within a virtual environment, avoiding sensory de-sensitivity in working with their natural instinct to touch. It will therefore in theory eventually add value in as much as improving and nurturing the sensory system. It may be an auspicious and gratifying concept, but one however that will never supersede current activity, especially in its present form.

The creative, unpredictable, seductive working methods, and minds of textile professionals along with their knowledge and experience of fabrics and tactile products, offer a challenge to engineering and programming expertise. In particular, it is necessary to put quantitative evaluations on various parameters which are widely understood in the textile industries, but which are at present mainly qualitative. The development of a textiles industry led virtual multi-modal system presents a stimulating problem. It demands refinement of texture simulations, which at present are often too crude to be convincing.

1.1   Aims

The aim of the project is to develop an intuitive multi-modal system for sensing fabric through evaluating the criteria involved that will satisfy industry standards and expectations.

What this project hopes to achieve is a definition of what is really essential to convey the 'feel' of a fabric, together with a set of quantitative or semi-quantitative values which can be used as descriptors. Some of these will then be implemented to control a haptic interface device.

2   Methods

2.1   Touch Evaluation Study

Sensory evaluation studies of products are often used within various industries to gain an understanding of consumer products, and find new ways to improve or market them [6], [7], [8], [9]. In the present work a small-scale Touch Evaluation Study of five different fabrics has been designed for the Wingman Mouse. Initial considerations for the criteria were developed based on existing sensory testing definitions set for evaluating handfeel/touch properties, plus some additional properties relating to fabrics selected [8]. Numerical values have been assessed for tactile parameters according to a new set of semi-quantitative descriptors. In the future this information may in principal be used to refine and regulate the level of feel of a virtual fabric in existing haptic interfaces, and in the development of a tailored haptic interface and multi-modal system.

The following qualities were selected for their challenging attributes:

Narrow Barrel Corduroy:- variable texture, stiffness, repetition of surface, friction
Jumbo Corduroy:- hairy texture, softness, repetition of surface
Velvet:- directional pile, softness, silkiness, smoothness
Random Velvet:- random pattern, variation in depth, distinct surface/colour difference
Stretch:- multiple-stretch capabilities

The procedure was developed to allow a restricted form of tactile evaluation which would simulate as closely as possible the conditions under which the Wingman mouse would be used, i.e. measurements were primarily based on how the mouse is used for touching - a two dimensional touch-stroke technique. This procedure is summarised below. It is important to note that the evaluator has previous experience with fabrics, that she is female, and that the evaluation was carried out in a natural setting, as these issues may have affected judgement and results:

1. Swatch samples laid out flat on a table and taped down.
2. Evaluated using clean washed hands.
3. Evaluation consisted of: visual and touch; touch without sight (blindfolded); visual only.
4. Contact with fabric: up, down; left and right; and diagonal.
5. An evaluation period of 3 seconds.
6. Contact was made using all five fingers of right hand, but essentially the three middle fingers due to their longer length, and therefore longer contact time with the fabric, contact being made primarily at the distal to the finger tip region of the fingers.

Parameters to be addressed are summarised in Table 1. It should be noted that the numerical value, though intended to be systematic and quantitative, is on an arbitrary scale of value from 1 to 15, e.g. for Roughness, 1 = smoothest and 15 = roughest. Results are shown in Fig's 1, 2, 3, 4, and 5.

Definitions and Scales for Handfeel Properties

Property	Key	Reference			Physical Parameters
Stiffness *³	ST	Pliable	↗✗	stiff	Shear Modulus
Depression Depth	DD	high	↗✗	low	Bulk Modulus
Depression Resilience/Springiness	DR	slow	↗✗	fast/springy	Young's Modulus, Damping
Tensile Stretch *¹*³	TS	no stretch	↗✗	high stretch	Shear Modulus
Tensile Extension speed recovery *¹*³	ESR	slow	↗✗	quick	Damping
Hand Friction/Slipperiness	HF	no drag	↗✗	drag/slippy	Coefficient of Friction
Roughness (overall surface)	RG	smooth	↗✗	rough	Small-scale Surface Texture
Gritty	GT	smooth	↗✗	gritty	Medium-scale Surface Texture
Lumpy [, i.e. Overall: bumpy, embossed, fiber bundles]	LM	smooth/ not lumpy	↗✗	lumpy	Large-scale Surface Texture
Grainy	GR	smooth	↗✗	fuzzy/nappy	Medium-scale Surface Texture
Softness of surface	SFT	soft	↗✗	hard	Reciprocal of Modulus
Ribbed/Ridges (length	RB	small	↗✗	large	Dimensions
Fuzziness	FZ	bald	↗✗	fuzzy/nappy	Force Displacement Graph
Furriness	FR	light	↗✗	heavy	Force Displacement Graph
Temperature *³	TP	cold	↗✗	warm	Thermal Diffusivity
Thickness *³	TH	thin	↗✗	thick	Dimension
Moistness *³	MO	dry	↗✗	wet	Water Absorption, Thermal Diffusivity
Weight *³	WT	light	↗✗	heavy	Mass Per Unit Area
Noise Intensity *³	NI	soft	↗✗	loud	Sound Frequency/Intensity when Touched
Noise Pitch *³	NP	low/bass	↗✗	high/sharp	Sound Frequency/Intensity when Touched
Shearness *³	SH	transparent	↗✗	non-transparent	Optical Properties
Drape *²*³	DP	high	↗✗	Low	Modulus

*¹ Measurements based on two-handed evaluation

*² Measurements based on two-handed evaluation of holding fabric up to a light source where considerations for use would then be made

*³ Properties that will require visual/other support to Wingman.

Figure 1. Corduroy - Small Barrel (100% cotton), Colour: Brown
End use: Clothing, Furniture Covering

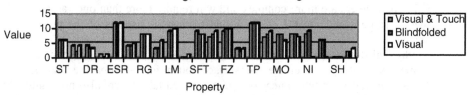

Figure 2. Corduroy - Large Barrel (100% Cotton), Colour: Silver grey and cream
End use: Furniture covering, Clothing

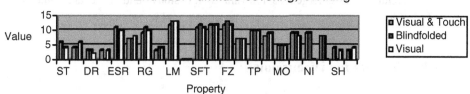

Figure 3. Velvet (100% Viscose), Colour: Bottle Green
End use: Clothing, Interiors

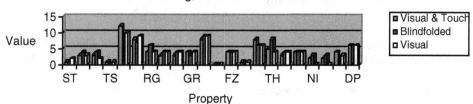

Figure 4. Random Patterned Velvet (37% Viscose, 63% Acetate), Colour:
Silver grey and golden brown
End use: Interior, Furniture covering

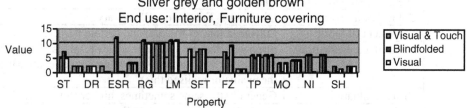

Figure 5. Stretch Fabric (57% Tactel, 31% Polyester, 12% Lycra)
End use: Clothing

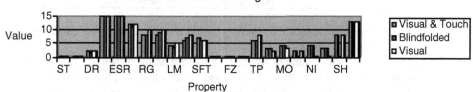

2.2   Programming

Some touch parameters of fabrics can be identified with simple physical variables. Other parameters are more complex and will require more than one variable to define them. Table 1 and Fig's 1, 2, 3, 4, and 5 illustrate aspects of the problems to be solved.

Physical dimensions of the fabrics were measured and then programmed into the Immersion software to create the surface touch force-feedback simulation of the fabrics. Physical stretch dimensions of the stretch fabric were also programmed in to the Immersion software, mimicking the stretch qualities of the fabric. Colour mappings a technique used to key textures for the random velvet quality.

Several issues emerged as relevant to the study, and these are summarised as follows.

3   Results for Discussion

3.1   Touch Evaluation Study

During the evaluation process, certain issues arose which affected the measurement/judgement of the five fabrics. These are outlined below in Table 2.

Table 2. Issues affecting measurement/judgement.

Subject	Outcomes
Light reflection (visual)	Enhanced surface qualities
Shearness/stretch eval.	Clarified structure
Colour/print/textures	Distracting, Enhancing, Illusionary
Movement of fabric	Enhanced fabric structure and certain properties
Blindfolded evaluation	Stronger tactile awareness (Visual and touch evaluation was enhanced through experience when the evaluator realised this)
Visual evaluation	Generally the same sometimes, higher (trans-modal)
Variable pressure	Dependent on property, handle
Reaction/judgement	Extended evaluation period led to extended natural exploration of the fabric and enhanced feelings or related emotions and memories

1. A time lapse between each category of evaluation needs to be employed to avoid any confusion or repetition of results.
2. The natural environment – lighting, surrounding textures, sound, smell and temperature, that can offer different moods and feelings, has an affect on creative judgements, and could affect multi-modal focus considerations within a system. A

controlled clinical setting may be more appropriate for evaluating tactile qualities for translating handfeel properties into haptic parameters, however comparisons with natural settings would be relevant, especially for natural exploration in a natural/normal environment.

3. Visual perception can distort a subjective property i.e. softness, especially if an individual has no previous experience with fabric.

4. In the fabric structure of the velvet for example, the feel of the pile changes when direction of touch changes. In effect the pile has memory.

5. 'Touch-stroke' was a limiting method of handle due to the different properties requiring evaluation, e.g. shearness and stretch.

Fig's 1, 2, 3, 4, and 5 indicate, primarily due to the evaluator's experience with fabrics, that pure visual evaluation is close to visual and touch evaluation. The natural instinct/reflex to touch however provides a sense of reassurance and verifies any initial visual or perceptual presumptions. Haptic interfaces will therefore prove to be of great importance for handling, viewing and consequently responding to a digital fabric or texture in a virtual environment. In the selection or the experience of interaction with fabric and textures, various feelings can be prompted, for example through touching a wool based fabric, the sense of warmth and comfort it provides related maybe to a childs' 'security blanket', toys and teddybears, the mother and father figure, a favourite 'woolly' jumper, or regional associations e.g. Scotland. The emotions and memories that can be stirred, combined with colour and decisions regarding its end use, could make the virtual interactive experience further enhanced through developing existing multi-modal technologies.

Those trained in textiles and its related industries, whether male or female, have an appreciation and understanding of fabric, its application attributes and market needs. Previous tactile evaluation studies have been created by comparing the tactile properties with the physical properties in the hope that the tactile/perceptive results given by test subjects would correspond with the physical characteristics. It has been shown that *'those who had the relevant experience gave results, which were very close'*. [6] This was indeed found also in the above evaluation.

3.2   Wingman Evaluation

The analysis concluded that the mouse in its present form does not sufficiently represent acceptable tactile responses and handle considerations for the textiles industry needs. However it has to be remembered that the Wingman has been tailored for the games industry. There are for example irrelevant vibrations travelling through the mouse that do not relate to natural touch. Targeted then matched simulation of sensations to the essential areas in the hand and fingers would be more suitable for feeling textures.

One of the benefits to the force-feedback facilities within the Wingman device and another haptic device, i.e. the PHANTOM, developed by SensAble Technologies, allows you to feel stretch fabrics, and weight properties.

The velvet, stretch and corduroy were relatively successful considering the constraints of the software and hardware available. However furry or hairy attributes cannot yet be successfully simulated, the dragging and friction facility within the

Wingman was used which created an illusionary effect. Overall, the fabric impressions developed however remain relatively crude. Positive feedback from a visually impaired tester however proved that there are great possibilities for the visually impaired in the future, i.e. online shopping. The low sensitivity control levels within the Immersion software, limited progress. It would be possible however to refine fabric simulation further through the availability to translate precise or more detailed physical measurements of a fabric's structure, into haptic software. This would in theory improve and add to the overall physical feel of the fabric. However problems related to file sizes, especially for the Internet may present problems.

A virtual multi-modal support network for certain properties, (perceptual cues), will add to the sensing of the fabric, i.e. the sound of a fabric being touched, with accurate display of properties targeted requiring visual, touch and sound parameters. Using a system of control mechanisms and fabric memory/behavioural attributes, e.g. developing effects like those available in the Wingman: targeting, manipulation, dragging, stretching, sliding, pressure-clinging and pressure-scrolling.

Accurate colour representation, as well as touch, within a virtual environment is another integral factor for the textiles industry [1]. The colour palette of a PC or Mac is not always the same from one machine to another. In industry there are fixed Pantone colours for each season so there is a reference system in place. For the consumer and those within industry who rely on pure colour representation, and have little time to waste cross-referencing, it remains a major problem. Sensing the 'feel' of colour may enhance the experience and provide a new approach to colour in a virtual environment.

3.3   Effective Evaluation of Properties

Through the evaluation, four fundamental natural handle techniques have been observed in evaluating properties.[1] Provisional suitable devices are outlined below in Table 3.

Table 3. Handle Techniques.

Handle Technique	Properties Evaluated	Device
Touch-stroke	Surface quality (texture)	Sliding Mat/Mouse
Rotating Cupped Action	Stiffness, weight, temperature, comfort, overall texture, creasing	Glove
Rotating between the Fingers action one hand *(thumb and 2/3 fingers)* –	Texture, stiffness, temperature, fabric structure, both sides of a fabric, friction, stretch (force-feedback)	Multiple finger probe/ Glove
Two-hands rotating action	Stretch, shearness	Glove

---

[1] *They are also are simplified and natural, compared to current sensory testing centre methods.* [8]

The last three would indicate the need for three-dimensional evaluation within a virtual environment, compared to using a mouse (2D). A combination-device may be required, however this will need to be clarified through prototyping and controlled testing.

3.4   Design Issues

! ∀ Handle Techniques
! ∀ Pressure variables (whether in a 2D or 3D viewing/working environment)
! ∀ Simultaneous simulation of fabric/texture sensations with digital image
! ∀ The fabric of the device. Conventional devices, including the Wingman and the PHANToM, are made of a thermoplastic material, which is cold and hard, and although appropriate from an engineering viewpoint and for feeling some materials, may not be the best material to present fabric based information to the user. Materials with different properties could enhance or decrease the value of tactile sensation. A material that is spongier or softer, flexible/pliable would be suitable, e.g. a rubber. Alternatively a weightless haptically enhanced woven fabric e.g. the weightless qualities of fine silk, i.e. ideally, texture simulations would be programmed into the weave of a fabric, producing sensation transmissions, and/or small miniature surface transformations.
! ∀ Workspace issues – remote contact with the fabric image, illusions created through working within a virtual environment (re-educational issues).

3.5   Other Issues

A device that mimics the touch-stroke handle technique could be a good communicator for marketing, selling and communication of furnishing fabrics, due to the manner in which some of these fabrics are touched. The touch-stroke manner of handling a fabric is however limiting for fashion professionals and consumers buying clothing. Fashion fabrics are primarily evaluated to acknowledge their properties and realise the potential of their use using the action of rubbing the fabric between the fingers on both sides of the fabric. For the consumer with regard to clothing, there are also issues related to trying the garment on that may also need to be considered i.e. body-scanning technology [3]. There are also obviously some fashions fabrics, when touched by hand that will not feel the same as when they are on the body. This could confuse and distort a buyer's judgement if they have no experience of the fabric, which is rare, or especially with a consumer if they have no knowledge at all. However visual explanatory support or even a full body haptic body attachment to the fundamental touch-sensory areas of the body could rectify this!

The Internet is potentially a powerful marketing tool for the textiles industry. Textile resource websites tend to list fabric company details on their webpages. Alternatively there are textile companies who have on-line multiple search databases full of fabric swatches, (some allowing the buyer to order swatch samples at no extra cost). A major retailer is still sending out furnishing/interior swatches, on request, to its customers without charge, even though they ceased production of their directory catalogue with swatch samples some years ago (clothing and interiors), due to cost implications [1]. We could also argue that one of the reasons why a dynamic two year old global trend forecasting and resource website for the textiles and related industries is losing some of its clients to traditional trend forecasting companies, who provide trend books and tailored packages to their clients (i.e. traditional methods of working), and are subsequently cutting staff, is due to the fact that clients cannot touch and feel fabrics or textures. It may also be due to the lack of accessible global communication of correct colour and texture representation, as mentioned earlier, available on screen and consequently, printing quality/effects. It may also involve general information overload, rather than visual overload, and lack of tailored information to the various industries that it serves that could save time and on-line costs.

Gender could also be seen to have an impact on expectations, and be dependent upon their previous experience with fabrics. Women tend to be more tactually aware compared to some men (traditional expectations would apply here). An impression of a type of fabric may therefore be 'enough' information for a man but inadequate for a woman. This difference has actually been found by comparing the impressions of the authors of this paper. As well as gender issues, social and cultural conditioning, (different foods, weather conditions, religions and beliefs), past experiences, memories and experience with fabrics have bearing on the responses given by the participants in previous evaluation studies, *'The differences show that women have applied their knowledge and previous experiences in the handling of textiles. However, the differences could also be explained by "heavy handedness", which would account for the higher values assigned by the men to weight, roughness, and softness. In other words, the men found fabrics to be heavy, rough and soft, which the women found to be light, smooth, and hard.'* [6] *(Nordic culture)* **[sic]**

In an attempt to understand the subjective responses of touch and categorisation, deliberations and evaluations could also involve an affinity with the activity of touch or relevant expertise, i.e. textile professionals. This is especially true of the sensory observations made by consumers where they demonstrated preconceived notions, without any solid experience in the subject they were actually dealing with, i.e. fabric. [6] There are also subjectivity issues relating to our identities or personalities, hormones, genetics, and evidently indistinguishable memories that exist and are different from one person to the other that need careful consideration (psychological and neurological).

4   Further Work

The development of sensory testing techniques in evaluation studies (example discussed earlier) and an investigation into other textile related industry requirements will focus the debate for the development of a haptic interface and multi-modal system.

To develop this research, a testing and advisory panel will be established to achieve an Industry Standard Tactile Evaluation Study in association with a major manufacturer of fabric and care products. The panel will be made up from:

! ∀ Textile and Fashion Industry experts
! ∀ The Visually Impaired
! ∀ Ordinary consumers

On an individual basis the panel's acute sensory, neural, psychophysical and physiological response to fabrics through handle will be evaluated and recorded, and a definitive Universal Fabric Language produced. This will be recorded as a database, defining touch variables based on the identification and evaluation of the physical parameters and perceptive responses associated to first response touch of fabric or texture and natural exploration. Experienced handle evaluation and other industry expectations will be further considered within the research. The related psychological, cognitive and behavioural relationship implications will also be recorded.

Controlled modality analysis of the essential conditions of fabric interaction in a real environment that can be applied to working in a virtual environment, will determine the limitations and implications involved with behaviour, movement, reaction, visual display, and viewing. Texture perception analysis will determine the initial or most essential and intuitive sensation property/ies. It will involve measuring the time spent measuring the period in contact with fabric relative to specific, and essential, properties felt during that time and dependant upon the variable interactive and specific touch directions involved, decision or reaction, process and adaptation, touch-pressure, colour implications, modal-focus, and cross-modal analysis, e.g. sound and texture, i.e roughness.

Texture perception involves issues relating to social and cultural semiotics of texture and fabrics (a conscious and sub-conscious language) i.e. the sensual seduction of silk, plus memories and other cognitive influences (personal) that may create sensory cues to enhance the overall sensory experience of 'feeling' a fabric. For the textiles industry they could be translated into textile and fashion trends – inspirational and/or memory cues.

The above indicates the criteria to be followed for developing the fabric language. This information can be translated into multi-modal programming and engineering parameters for a fabric database and related trend system. Of the physical parameters suggested, the mechanical variables, (with necessary refinement), (elastic moduli, stress-strain curves, friction coefficients, surface profiles and mass), can be simulated by a suitable haptic interface device. Properties related to sound are relatively easy to add. Thermal properties and those related to air and water vapour, are outside the capacity of a haptic device, and will require the addition of a controllable thermal element such as a Peltier refrigeration module. [10].

There are other essential fabric performance characteristics, which are not included in Figure 1 due to Immersion's Wingman's hardware and software limitations, that currently rely on a mixture of visual, touch, sound and various rigorous testing methods, i.e. aesthetic, physical properties relating to comfort and wearability or usability, mechanical, manufacturing, sound and other end-use/product issues. Some of these will become part of our study. [2]

This paper illustrates just some of the problems to be solved and issues involved in developing a satisfactory virtual multi-modal system, which will no doubt involve more than one system due to specialist areas, e.g. manufacturing.

It may never be possible to simulate the tactile impression of a fabric entirely, but it may be possible, by concentrating on the more important elements, to convey an adequately accurate impression, at least for professionals and those who are familiar with fabric technology, but also possibly by some consumers, dependant on product and market expectations. It should be noted that everyone can recognise their friends' voices on the telephone, despite the poor bandwidth of a conventional phone line, and that everyone can recognise a familiar face, even in a black-and-white photograph, so some degree of approximation is obviously acceptable. The question is how much?

The above will form the basis of developing the criteria involved with developing a satisfactory multi-modal system and effective ergonomic design principles for an appropriate haptic interface.

An appropriate multi-modal system will need to create an experience for the virtual user that is intuitive, reassuring and inspired.

5   Conclusion

This research we believe will add to the necessary refinement in fabric and texture simulation of sensation in response to a fabric, when viewed as a digital image. Such evaluation and refinement is imperative if the industry is to be convinced. Also, *'We might even end up with haptically-enhanced interfaces that are in fact harder to use than standard ones and haptics may become just a gimmick rather than the key improvement in interaction technology that we believe it to be.'* [11]

It is intended that the research will add a unique contribution to existing haptic technologies, and eventually provide a workable solution to the successful marketing, promotion, sales, and working methods of the textiles and related industries (including education), its consumer and for the visually impaired.

5.1   Possible Outcomes

! ∀ **Aesthetic Response:-** Virtual Trend and Trade Resource, Virtual Magazines
! ∀ **E-Commerce – Trade/Consumer:-** Textiles & related industries, Retail
! ∀ **Textiles and Textiles Science:-** Testing, Manufacturing and Design, Education and Training
! ∀ **Other** *(including other media)*:- Museums, Exhibitions, Trade Fairs, Therapy, Film/TV, Games

Acknowledgements

We thank our respective departments for all their support and encouragement

References

[1]   Dillon, P., and Moody, W.: Liverpool John Moores University, 'FabricFinder' Project: Market Research and interviews in association with fashion and textiles trade organisations, trade show organisers, and industry, (1999/2000)
[2]   Comments from the above
[3]   Maitland, J.: Fashion on the Web – can you feel it. Drapers Record, 3rd June, (2000)
[4]   Colwell, C., Petrie, H., and Kornbrot, D.: Department of Psychology, University of Hertfordshire, Hardwick, A. and Furner, S., British Telecommunications plc (research Laboratories): Use of haptic device by blind and sighted people: perception of virtual textures and objects. www.bt.com/innovation/exhibition/haptic/preprint/device.htm (1998)
[5]   Sorid, D.: Giving Computers a Sense of Touch, NY Times, 7th March, (2000)
[6]   Anttila, P. The Kuopio Academy of Crafts and Design, Helsinki: The Tactile Evaluation of Textiles on the basis of the cognitive Psychology, compared with the physical analysis, Symposium on Experience, Impressiveness and Research, 18th-19th February, (1999)
[7]   Aldrich, W.: Fabric, Form and Flat Pattern Cutting, Blackwell Science Ltd, (1996)
[8]   Civille, G.V., and Dus, C.A.: Sensory Spectrum Inc., Chatham, New Jersey (US): Development of Terminology to Describe the Handfeel Properties of Paper and Fabrics, Journal of Sensory Studies, 5., Food and Nutrition Press, Trumbull, Connecticut, (1990), pp. 19-32
[9]   Robinson, K.J., and Chambers, E.: the Sensory Analysis Centre, Dept. of Food and Nutrition, Kansas State University, Manhattan, B.M. Gatewood, Department of Clothing, Textiles and Interior Design, Kansas State University, Manhattan, 'Influence of Pattern Design and Fabric Type on the Hand Characteristics of Pigment Prints', Textile Research Journal, Volume 67, 11th November (1997), USA
[10]   Caldwell, D.G., Tsagarakis, N., and Wardle, A.: University of Salford: Mechano Thermo and Proprioceptor Feedback for Integrated Haptic Feedback, IEEE Robotics and Automation Conference, Albuquerque, New Mexico, April (1997)
[11]   Oakley, M.R. McGee, Brewster, S., and Gray, P.: Putting the Feel in 'Look and Feel', Glasgow Interactive Systems Group, Glasgow Interactive Systems Group, Glasgow University. In ACM CHI 2000 (The Hague, NL), ACM Press Addison-Wesley, pp. 415-422, (2000).